THE ELECTIONS
OF 2000

THE ELECTIONS OF 2000

Edited by
Michael Nelson
Rhodes College

A Division of Congressional Quarterly Inc.
Washington, D.C.

CQ Press
A Division of Congressional Quarterly Inc.
1414 22nd Street, N.W.
Washington, D.C. 20037

202-822-1475; 800-638-1710

www.cqpress.com

Printed and bound in the United States of America

05 04 03 02 01   5 4 3 2 1

LIBRARY OF CONGRESS CATALOGING-IN-PUBLICATION DATA

The elections of 2000 / edited by Michael Nelson.
    p. cm.
  Includes bibliographical references and index.
  ISBN 1-56802-531-9
  1. Presidents—United States—Election—2000. 2. United States.
Congress—Elections, 2000.   I. Nelson, Michael, date.
  JK526 2000e
  324.973'0929—dc21
                                                    2001000969

For J. L. M., my great friend

Faithful friends are a sturdy shelter:
whoever finds one has found a treasure.

Faithful friends are beyond prize;
No amount can balance their worth.

—ECCLESIASTICUS 6:14–15

Contents

Preface

The elections of 2000 ended essentially in a tie. Only five popular votes of every thousand that were cast separated Al Gore, the Democratic candidate for president, from George W. Bush, the Republican nominee. The electoral vote remained in suspense for more than a month after the election. As recount after recount proceeded in Florida, Bush's lead sometimes dropped as low as 154 votes. Toward the end of that process, a 4–3 Florida Supreme Court decision seemed likely to tip the state and the presidency to Gore. But to the Democrats' dismay, the Florida ruling was overturned by a 5–4 U.S. Supreme Court decision in Bush's favor. The final electoral vote tally was 271 for Bush and 266 for Gore, the closest result that any living American has ever witnessed.

The congressional elections were, if anything, even closer. The Democrats gained two seats in elections for the House of Representatives; if they had won just six additional seats, they would have become the majority party. The national popular vote in House elections was 49 percent Republican and 48 percent Democratic. The Senate ended in a literal tie as a result of the 2000 elections: fifty Republicans and fifty Democrats. In response, Senate leaders broke precedent by deciding to place an equal number of Republicans and Democrats on each of the standing committees.

The Elections of 2000 goes a long way toward explaining what happened in 2000 and why. Like its four predecessor volumes, beginning with *The Elections of 1984,* it also does much in addition. Even more than most elections, the elections of 2000 cannot be understood apart from all that political scientists know about the presidency, Congress, the courts, the parties, the electoral process, the media, the voters, state politics, and the Constitution. The book's nine chapters were written with care by outstanding political scientists and closely edited for clarity of meaning and felicity of expression. Each of them looks back in time to place the events of 2000 in historical, institutional, and theoretical context, then looks forward to assess the elections' implications for the future of American politics:

- Stephen Skowronek analyzes the elections of 2000 in the context both of deeply rooted historical patterns concerning the "recurring establishment and disintegration of relatively durable political regimes" and of new, "postmodern" aspects of American politics (Chapter 1).

- Harold W. Stanley explains how the presidential nominating process worked in 2000, arguing that the front-loading of primaries and caucuses toward the start of the election year has restored the influence of party leaders in choosing the Republican and Democratic candidates for president (Chapter 2).

- Michael Nelson places the general election campaign of 2000 within the context of well-established features of the contemporary political era, such as the rising political status of the vice presidency, the institutionalization of presidential debates, and declining voter turnout (Chapter 3).

- Daniel Wirls analyzes voting behavior in the 2000 presidential election and finds an aging, shrinking electorate that is sharply divided between the parties along regional, racial, and cultural lines (Chapter 4).

- Matthew Robert Kerbel, although he is optimistic about what the growing use of the Internet in politics may portend for the future, documents and laments the tendency of the news media to trivialize the 2000 presidential election by framing it almost entirely in terms of strategy and tactics rather than leadership and purpose (Chapter 5).

- Richard J. Ellis finds the state initiative campaigns of 2000 to be the latest and most extreme example of how a process designed to be democratic has mutated into a tool of special interest groups and wealthy individuals (Chapter 6).

- Paul J. Quirk and Sean C. Matheson weigh the presidential election of 2000 against three criteria that are important for successful presidential governance: the candidates' qualifications, commitments, and support (Chapter 7).

- Gary C. Jacobson explains the essentially even outcome of the 2000 congressional elections and speculates both about their short-term consequences for governing and about the prospects for the midterm elections of 2002 (Chapter 8).

- Michael Nelson treats the postelection election of 2000 as an example of "politics by other means," in which institutional combat between the parties supersedes electoral competition (Chapter 9).

My thanks go to these contributors—who include both familiar names from earlier books in this series, such as Jacobson, Quirk and Matheson, Stanley, and Kerbel, and new members of the team, especially Skowronek, Wirls, and Ellis. Thanks, too, to the outstanding editorial and production team at CQ Press for the assurance, skill, and helpfulness with which they have treated this book: managing editor Ann Davies; chapter editors Richard Chapman, Carolyn Goldinger, Kathryn Krug, and especially Sabra Bissette Ledent; production editor Tom Roche; and CQ Press director of college publishing Brenda Carter. Aware of the quadrennial burdens that the writing and editing of these books impose on family life, I thank Linda Nelson, my wife, and Michael and Sam, our sons, for being patient, loving, and supportive. Jay Mason, to whom this book is dedicated, continues to enrich my life as my most valued colleague, collaborator, and critic, and above all as my great friend.

Contributors

Michael Nelson is professor of political science at Rhodes College. He is the author or coauthor of several books on the presidency and presidential elections, including *The Presidency and the Political System* (6th ed., 2000), *The American Presidency: Origins and Development, 1776–1998* (1999), *A Heartbeat Away* (1988), *Presidents, Politics, and Policy* (1984), and four earlier books on presidential elections from 1984 to 1996. He edits the Interpreting American Politics series for Johns Hopkins University Press and has published books on humanities education, including *Alive at the Core: Exemplary Approaches to General Education in the Humanities* (2000). He has won national awards for his articles on music and baseball, and more than forty of his articles have been reprinted in works of history, political science, and English composition. His most recent book, cowritten with John Lyman Mason, is *Governing Gambling: Politics and Policy in State, Tribe, and Nation*.

Richard J. Ellis is Mark O. Hatfield Professor of Politics and chair of the politics department at Willamette University. Among the books he has written or edited are *Founding the American Presidency* (1999), *The Dark Side of the Left: Illiberal Egalitarianism in America* (1998), and *Speaking to the People: The Rhetorical Presidency in Historical Perspective* (1998). His newest book, *Democratic Delusions: The Initiative Process in America,* will be published in 2001 by the University Press of Kansas.

Gary C. Jacobson is professor of political science at the University of California, San Diego. He specializes in the study of U.S. elections, parties, interest groups, and Congress. Jacobson is the author of *The Politics of Congressional Elections* (5th ed., 2001), *The Electoral Origins of Divided Government* (1990), and *Money in Congressional Elections* (1980), and he is coauthor, with Samuel Kernell, of *The Logic of American Politics* (2000) and *Strategy and Choice in Congressional Elections* (2d ed., 1983).

Matthew Robert Kerbel is professor of political science at Villanova University, where he specializes in media politics. He is the author of four books and numerous articles about the media, campaigns, and the presidency, including *If It Bleeds, It Leads: An Anatomy of Television News* (2000), *Remote and Controlled: Media Politics in a Cynical Age* (2d ed., 1999), and *Edited for Television: CNN, ABC, and American Presidential Elections* (2d ed., 1998). His interest in media politics derives from his previous work as a television newswriter for public broadcasting in New York and as a radio news reporter.

Sean C. Matheson is instructor of political science and international relations at Knox College and a doctoral candidate in political science at the University of Illinois at Urbana–Champaign. He has published or presented work on electoral politics, and American foreign policy. His dissertation examines congressional rhetoric and the politics of presidential impeachment.

Paul J. Quirk is professor of political science at the University of Illinois at Urbana–Champaign. He is the author of *Industry Influence in Federal Regulatory Agencies* (1981) and coauthor of *The Politics of Deregulation* (1985), along with numerous articles and essays on the presidency, presidential elections, public opinion, and public policymaking. He has served on the editorial boards of several leading journals, including the *American Political Science Review.* His current research concerns the processes and quality of deliberation in American politics.

Stephen Skowronek is the Pelatiah Perit Professor of Political Science at Yale University. He is the author of *The Politics Presidents Make: Leadership from John Adams to Bill Clinton* (1997) and *Building a New American State: The Expansion of National Administrative Capacities, 1877–1920* (1982). He is managing editor of *Studies in American Political Development.*

Harold W. Stanley is professor of political science at the University of Rochester. He is the author of articles and books on voting, political parties, and elections, and he is coeditor of *Vital Statistics on American Politics, 1999–2000.* He is president of the Southern Political Science Association, and he is currently visiting research professor in political science at Southern Methodist University.

Daniel Wirls is associate professor of politics at the University of California, Santa Cruz. He is the author of *Buildup: The Politics of Defense in the Reagan Era,* as well as articles and chapters on political behavior, Congress, and American political history. He was a 1993–1994 American Political Science Association congressional fellow. Currently, he is completing a cowritten manuscript on the origins of the U.S. Senate.

THE ELECTIONS OF 2000

1

The Setting: Change and Continuity in the Politics of Leadership

Stephen Skowronek

The political convulsions of Bill Clinton's tenure in office were extraordinary. Indictments of historic proportion were followed by even more stunning rebounds. More than one observer likened the reversals and counterpunches to a national spectacle in which larger-than-life antagonists entertained a bemused but largely passive citizen audience.[1] Safe to say, Clinton will stand out historically as the champion prizefighter of American politics. He proved himself a wily combatant who could weather near-constant assaults on his legitimacy, a master strategist who could confound his opponents' best efforts to isolate and stigmatize him, and a nimble tactician who could float free of firm commitments, political anchors, and fixed identities to stay abreast of the concerns of the moment. Future scholars may be hard-pressed to describe Clinton as either a resolute leader or an especially productive one, but those standards miss the most striking feature of his presidency: his survival under siege and his perseverance as a political force to be reckoned with.

The presidential election of 2000 extended the chain of extraordinary contests that marked Clinton's tenure. In this one, however, commentators invoked a different image to capture the president's abiding political significance. No longer the prizefighter at center ring, he became "the elephant in the living room," a pervasive presence that no one wanted to discuss. This was curious. Clinton had done more than persevere; he had delivered handsomely on the theme of his initial run for the presidency in 1992—"It's the economy, stupid." The reluctance of the major candidates to grapple with his achievements or claim his legacy suggests that the eight-year assault on his political legitimacy had not been entirely for naught. The wearisome trench warfare and the stigma of disgrace hovering over the highest office in the land provided Republican candidate George W. Bush with a mission he could call his own: the restoration of national honor and political comity. At the same time, Clinton's travails made it difficult for his heir apparent, Al Gore, to capitalize on the strong, seemingly decisive case he was given for his succession: the promise of continuity. The euphoria of good times—of unprecedented prosperity, of peace and unrivaled global power—were met and neutralized during the campaign by lingering concerns about the degradation of presidential authority under Clinton's watch and by the promise of severing connections with those who had caused so much trouble. The upshot was a stunningly inconclusive election that left American politics even more unsettled than it had been before.

If these muddied events demonstrate anything at all, it is that good times are not sufficient to secure a course of leadership. Contests over leadership authority are always more broad-ranging and more specifically political than the state of the economy alone will convey. Presidential leadership is a bid to redefine, or at least to rearticulate, the terms and conditions of legitimate national government, and the political struggles that mark a president's tenure in office are all, in one way or another, tests of his authority to sustain his bid. George W. Bush promised relief from the long string of political confrontations that had stretched over the Clinton years, but these confrontations were themselves suggestive of the high political stakes at issue in Clinton's leadership effort, and the clouded circumstances of Bush's own ascension to power do not bode well for a quick resolution. The central problem confronting the new president is, as it was for all of his predecessors, to come up with a premise for national political action compelling enough to withstand the assaults of interested parties on all sides, no matter what they throw at him.

Historic patterns in the politics of presidential leadership testify to the priority of these questions of authority. This chapter situates recent American presidents within these larger patterns in order to identify continuities and changes in the politics of leadership. It considers the political claims that recent American presidents have set forth in their own behalf, the political contests that those claims have constituted, and the ability of contemporary presidents to sustain leadership authority.[2]

Two Paths to the Present

For anyone thinking about how authority claims and leadership politics have evolved over the years, two different histories of the presidency command attention. One of these is well documented in the contemporary presidential scholarship.[3] It tells of all that changed in American government during the last quarter of the twentieth century and about how those changes have altered presidential politics. These changes have been gradual and cumulative, but the post-Watergate era appears in retrospect to frame a distinctive universe of political and institutional action for American presidents. Within this contemporary frame, Jimmy Carter, Ronald Reagan, George Bush, and Bill Clinton emerge as a group of leaders who shared a similar leadership environment, a set of circumstances that set them apart from the presidents of earlier eras. These circumstances include a host of interrelated developments: a proliferation within government of independent political entrepreneurs, an internal and collective disaggregation of governing institutions, a breakdown of elite consensus on social and cultural values, a demobilization of the electorate and the political detachment of the citizenry, an augmentation of the political value of interest-based organizations and their financial resources, and a growing dependence of leaders on the mass media and polling to negotiate the problems of governance.

Clinton's leadership was in many important respects but a fuller elaboration of the well-documented implications of these developments. His empathetic television persona, his "continual campaign," his preoccupation with managing public opinion, his protean political vision, his controversial fund-raising activities, even his investigation-wracked administration—all fit recent scholarly conceptions of an office now operating at a new stage in its political evolution.[4] Set within this frame, Clinton's was the most perfect expression to date of what scholars have dubbed the "postmodern" presidency, and Clinton himself was the epitome of what they have called the "personal" president.[5]

Concepts like these capture basic, system-level dynamics at work in reshaping the politics of leadership, and yet they also present continuity and change in presidential leadership in a particular and partial way. They locate continuities within the confines of the last quarter-century—in the resources and constraints shared by incumbents of this period and in the corresponding strategies and styles these incumbents have adopted. They locate changes across historical eras in contrasts between contemporary politics and the politics of earlier periods. In fact, a "postmodern" reading of recent presidential history goes far toward detaching the past from the present. While highlighting the uniqueness of the office occupied by recent incumbents, it renders earlier historical experience largely irrelevant to an understanding of how things work today. What this approach reveals about the more distant past is that it produced presidents who had different resources at their disposal, adopted different strategies, developed different styles, and wielded a different sort of influence.

There are, however, other system-level factors at work today shaping the politics of leadership, and the effects of contemporary conditions may themselves be better appreciated when these other factors are brought into view. Carter, Reagan, Bush, and Clinton shared certain distinctive resources and strategies for leadership, but they did not come into office with the same political purposes. Nor did any of them pass to his successor the same leadership challenge with which he himself had begun. In fact, these presidents ventured very different claims on their own behalf; they offered to bring about very different kinds of changes in American politics; and their efforts to make good on those claims significantly altered the political environment in which their successors took office. If these different individual efforts were wholly idiosyncratic, then scholars would really be quite limited in what they could say about how much postmodern institutional conditions are affecting the ability of presidents to lead. If, on the other hand, these different individual efforts themselves fit larger patterns—if there are in fact historical regularities to be found in the political claims that successive incumbents assert and in the political contests they set up—then scholars may be in a position

to say a lot more about the consequences of the postmodern institutional
environment than they have so far. Reference to an alternative presidential
history, one that brings leadership claims asserted in the past more closely to
bear on the different political ambitions by recent presidents, would be especially useful in this regard.

The alternative history that I have in mind for this purpose charts
change in American politics through the recurring establishment and disintegration of relatively durable political regimes. This regime-based structure of
American political history has been widely observed by political scientists
and historians alike. It demarcates the rise and decline of Federalist Nationalism between 1789 and 1800, of Jeffersonian Democracy between 1800 and
1828, of Jacksonian Democracy between 1828 and 1860, of Republican
Nationalism between 1860 and 1932, and of New Deal Liberalism between
1932 and 1980. Each of these regimes can be identified with the empower-
ment of an insurgent political coalition whose reconstruction of basic governing arrangements endured through various subsequent configurations of
party power. Just as America's fragmented constitutional system has made
sweeping political change rare and difficult to achieve, it has worked similarly to perpetuate the ideological and programmatic commitments of the
few insurgencies that have succeeded. To this extent at least, the regime structure of American political history may be considered a byproduct of the constitutional structure of American government.

Attention to this history reveals the different challenges that presidents
face at different moments in a political sequence, and in so doing, it points to
an alternative way of assessing the presidents of the last quarter of the twentieth century.[6] Carter, Reagan, Bush, and Clinton can each be compared with
presidents of earlier eras who acted at roughly parallel moments in other
sequences. Doing so will serve to identify both the characteristic warrants
claimed for national political leadership at these different junctures and the
typical political contests these claims engendered. Beyond that, it will facilitate an inquiry into just how much today's "postmodern" institutional environment is changing things—that is, how these typical leadership ambitions
and their characteristic political effects are being altered by the new strategic
setting in which contemporary presidents act. After examining recent presidents in this way, the analysis will return to the contest for the presidency in
2000 and the prospects for the new president.

Jimmy Carter and Other Late-Regime Affiliates

In 1976, it was still possible to think of a Democratic presidential victory as a restoration of the normal state of affairs that had been ushered in by
Franklin D. Roosevelt, the New Deal, and the establishment of a liberal political regime. Richard Nixon's 43 percent victory in 1968, George McGovern's
anomalous candidacy in 1972, the strengthening in 1974 of the Democratic
Party's long unbroken control of Congress—all suggested that the recent

Republican interregnum of Nixon and Gerald Ford might be, like Dwight D. Eisenhower's in the 1950s, a pause in preparation for the next leap forward on the liberal agenda. But as Jimmy Carter reassembled the national political alliance that had defined the government's basic commitments of ideology and interest since the New Deal, confidence in liberal solutions to the nation's problems was fast fading. Already torn by the political turmoil of the civil rights movement and the Vietnam War, the governing establishment of the liberal regime returned to power in 1977 with its basic assumptions exposed and vulnerable. The once solidly Democratic South was up for grabs, the cold war foreign policy consensus was a shambles, and changes in the international economic environment had begun to raise questions about the basic governing formulas on which the expansion of liberal programs had been premised. Fiscal Keynesianism—the management of taxes and government expenditures to balance stable economic growth with maximum employment—strained under the multiple burdens of an energy crisis, "stagflation," aggressive foreign economic competition, and defensive blue-collar unions. Radical conservatism, which had been but a minor annoyance when Barry Goldwater ran for president in 1964, was resurgent in 1976 and better positioned than ever to peg liberal government itself as the source of the nation's burgeoning problems.

Carter was elected, at least in part, because he understood exactly what was at stake for liberal government in the 1970s. He had tempered his promise of another round of reforms on the order of Lyndon B. Johnson's Great Society with concerns about cost and efficiency, and he had made the repair and rehabilitation of the beleaguered apparatus of liberal government his priority. Against the increasingly strident attacks of Republicans, Carter insisted that "the problem is not that our program goals are unworthy or that our bureaucrats are unfit." Rather, the problems stemmed from "the inefficient operations of the federal government."[7] Carter argued that the processes of government had, over the years, gotten so bogged down in red tape that they blocked the effectiveness with which liberal programs were being implemented. The president maintained that these problems were technical, not fundamental; that liberal government could be made to work again by reforming its methods of operation. His knowledge of the latest management and budgeting techniques would, he promised, breathe new life into the substantive commitments of the liberal order.[8]

Several things can be said about Carter's hapless struggle to make good on this promise. First, his was a subtle and complicated message. A candidate who recognizes serious problems in the governing establishment while promising continuity in basic governing commitments sets up a delicate balancing act. Throughout his campaign for the White House, Carter was hounded by the press to explain how he could solve the governmental problems he recognized without threatening basic liberal commitments. His standard reply was enigmatic: there were "no easy answers."

The second thing to be said is that no American president has been able to bring about a change of this sort. The historical record is full of examples of presidents who have offered, and conscientiously tried, to rehabilitate old and battered political establishments. Carter's failure is of a piece with those of John Adams, John Quincy Adams, Franklin Pierce, James Buchanan, and Herbert Hoover. All were nominal affiliates of long-established political regimes, regimes that had, in the course of events, come to appear less as legitimate guides to new governing solutions than as central parts of the governing problem. In each case, the basic commitments of ideology and interest with which the president was affiliated had become vulnerable to direct attack from the most radical segments of his opposition, and the president responded by promising to fix things up.

These presidents employed very different leadership resources and acted in accordance with very different norms and techniques of governing. They brought to office quite assorted attributes of character and skill, and they pursued a variety of strategies in their relationships with Congress, their party, and the public. But none was able to make good on their shared purpose of orchestrating the repair and rehabilitation of a political establishment in trouble. Although the promise has been made repeatedly, and the American electorate has repeatedly responded to it, the task of breathing new life into an old order seems to be beyond the political capacities of the presidential office.

It is instructive that each of these presidents was singled out in his time, and is often treated today, as a political incompetent, plain and simple. The problem, Americans like to tell themselves, is that they lacked the political skills needed to make the presidency work. Carter was accused of being too technocratic in his approach to policy and politics, of leading like an engineer, of having too narrow an interest in the details of government, of letting himself get consumed by the nation's problems and never getting on top of them. Some observers called him "Jimmy Hoover" to dramatize his incompetence and drive home his resemblance to the last engineer to make it to the White House.[9]

The Carter-Hoover comparison was used at the time to prove that engineers make bad politicians and to suggest that someone with more political savvy might have done a better job. But once it is recognized that technocratic appeals to repair and rehabilitate government tend to appear at similar junctures in a regime's development, the charges of personal incompetence lose much of their bite, and the political appeal of such leaders comes more clearly into focus. The technocratic approach to leadership—the tendency to submerge problems of substance in the mechanics and processes of government—is especially well suited to the election of a leader affiliated with a vulnerable regime. When Carter told the American people that there were "no easy answers" to the problems of the day and that they needed a leader who was smart enough to tackle these problems in all their complexity, he was offering the liberal establishment its best hope for survival and offering the rest of the nation an alternative to the more radical solution being promulgated by the regime's opponents. As a political appeal, Carter's "no easy answers" smoothed over long-simmering tensions within the ranks of the Democratic Party and held off, at least momentarily, the Republicans' broadside assault on the substantive commitments of the liberal regime. Presidents who are late-regime affiliates rest their authority to lead on their technical competence precisely because the more basic commitments of ideology and interest with which their regimes are associated have already been thrown into question. Appeals of this sort seem destined to recur in American politics so long as political regimes linger beyond their ability to generate substantive responses to the governing challenges of the day.

The problem is not that these presidents offered the wrong message for their times. The problem is that the best case for leadership in these circumstances is a weak one, the most tenuous of all for sustaining political initiative in the American presidency. The pattern of failure has been remarkably similar for late-regime affiliates. Almost immediately, these presidents have found themselves caught between the stark demands of their supporters for regime maintenance and the blunt charges of regime bankruptcy coming from their opponents. The subtleties that made their promise of repair and rehabilitation attractive during the campaign appear quite different under the political pressures of governing. Hard choices need to be made, and fundamental questions about the legitimacy of the establishment press in on each. Holding the most equivocal of warrants for changing things, these presidents quickly lose control over the meaning of their own actions.

All told, history suggests that presidents affiliated with a vulnerable regime are in an impossible leadership situation. Their open recognition of serious problems within the establishment coupled with their promise of continuity leaves them little authority to support the inherently disruptive and highly politicizing effects of presidential action. Initiatives that reach out to allies, or that appear to extend established commitments, are portrayed by opponents as symptoms of the nation's problems. Actions that confront allies, or that appear to alter substantive commitments, alienate the president's natural base of support and leave him politically isolated. The efforts of these presidents to control the terms of national political debate have, for these reasons, tended to collapse almost immediately and never recover.

In its basic outlines, Carter's hapless struggle for credibility was both typical of late-regime affiliates and unique among recent presidents. The postmodern aspects of his presidency did not alter the basic dynamics of leadership in this situation in any categorical sense. Still, the effects of this new environment may be discerned in certain details, and, though not decisive, their significance for the future is worth pondering. Most notable in this regard is that Carter was, in comparison with other late-regime affiliates, far more the independent political entrepreneur. He had built his own political organization to contest and win the Democratic nomination in 1976. In weathering the crises of his White House years, he was able to draw on extensive staff resources for governing and technical resources for communication that were directly under his control in the White House.

President Carter was, in short, far less constrained in action by the political baggage of the past than the late-regime affiliates who preceded him, and in circumstances like these, any additional capacities for independent entrepreneurship must be counted a clear plus. A century and a half earlier, John Quincy Adams found himself immobilized by the crisis of legitimacy that gripped his administration during its first year. Franklin Pierce quickly lost control of his party and found himself subordinated to its most controversial elements. Herbert Hoover felt compelled to wrap himself in Republican orthodoxy even when his own actions began to depart from it. Carter, however, responded to his increasingly precarious political position with ever-more-vigorous assertions of his political autonomy. Symbolic assaults on the congressional pork barrel during his first year in office were followed by a stunning midterm indictment of the entire governing establishment.[10] Late in his term, Carter reversed liberal priorities in fiscal and monetary policy and then went on to beat Massachusetts senator Edward M. Kennedy, the liberal standard bearer, in a bruising battle for the Democratic nomination in 1980. By continually defying the constraints imposed by his party's liberalism, Carter vastly expanded the range of independent action by a late-regime affiliate. By the time he accepted the Democratic nomination in 1980, he had put considerable distance between himself and the party establishment. Even in the final moments of his campaign, Carter was showing how the resources of the postmodern presidency might alter leadership prospects. His ability to focus all eyes on his efforts to engineer the release of the American hostages held by Iran nearly succeeded in changing the subject entirely and, with that, the political standard by which he might be judged. If, in the end, there was still no escaping responsibility for the dismal state of liberal government in 1980, there was, in Carter's effort, a newfound sense of the possibility of going it alone.

Ronald Reagan and Other Reconstructive Leaders

Although the leadership position of late-regime affiliates has repeatedly proven untenable, the political effect of these presidents has nonetheless been profound. Time and again, presidents who have offered personal competence and technocratic repair as premises for action have, in effect, called attention to the government's paralysis and become the leading symbols of political collapse. In their fitful struggles for credibility, late-regime affiliates unwittingly deepen the sense of systemic political failure and confirm the insurgents' message that the old order is beyond all hope. From such presidents, opposition movements gain not only unparalleled control over the political definition of the moment at hand but also a warrant for a wholesale reconstruction of American government.

Notwithstanding his vigorous assertions of independence, Carter had just such an effect. His vulnerabilities placed his successor, Ronald Reagan, in the situation that has traditionally proven the most favorable to political mastery in the American presidency. As the leader of an insurgency that was targeting the liberal regime's most basic commitments, candidate Reagan had little patience with Carter's efforts to distance himself from its failures. He deftly turned the president's difficulties into proof that something fundamental was wrong with liberal government. Reagan forthrightly declared the old order bankrupt and held its defenders directly responsible for a national crisis. As he put it to the Republican national convention in 1980, "The major issue in this campaign is the direct, political, personal, and moral responsibility of the Democratic party leadership—in the White House and in the Congress—for this unprecedented calamity which has befallen us." [11] Or as he declared in his first inaugural address, "In the present crisis, government is not the solution to our problems; government is the problem." [12] Taking direct aim at the governing regime liberalism had created, Reagan proposed to regenerate the polity by reconstructing basic commitments of ideology and interest.

At the time, Reagan was called "The Great Communicator," and his irresistible political appeal was attributed to his training as a movie actor. His distinctive talents were described as perfectly suited to the distinctive demands and leadership opportunities of the postmodern presidency. But a striking fact of American history is that nearly all presidents who have come to power in situations like this have proven to be great communicators. The presidents who traditionally make the list of America's most effective political leaders—Thomas Jefferson, Andrew Jackson, Abraham Lincoln, and FDR—were, like Reagan, opposition leaders standing steadfast against already discredited political regimes. These were men of very different character and political skill. They employed very different resources and acted in accordance with very different norms and techniques of governing. What they shared was a moment in a political sequence in which presidential authority is at its most compelling and least vulnerable to challenge, a moment when opponents stand indicted in the court of public opinion and allies are not yet secure enough in their new positions of power to compete for authority. It is in such rare circumstances that the bluntly disruptive political effects of presidential action are most easily justified and sustained.

Consideration of these presidents as a group suggests several things about the political capacities of the American presidency. First, it suggests that presidential mastery of American politics depends above all on the widespread perception of a systemic political collapse. Presidents have been able to fend off detractors and establish a new course only when they have been perceived as the only alternative to national ruin. The masters of presidential politics were all immediately preceded by a president like Carter—that is, by a late-regime affiliate who struggled fitfully with a complicated message of support for a faltering regime. John Adams and Thomas Jefferson, John Quincy Adams and Andrew Jackson, James Buchanan and Abraham Lincoln, Herbert Hoover and Franklin Roosevelt, Jimmy Carter and Ronald Reagan—these repeated historical pairings of apparent political paralysis in the presidency followed by the sudden appearance of a masterful politician suggest nothing less than an intimate connection between prior incapacity and towering success in presidential leadership.

Note further that the presidents who have most fully mastered the problems of sustaining leadership authority and orchestrating political change have been not only great communicators, but also great repudiators. They have come to office promising to root out the entrenched remnants of the discredited past and to recapture some essential American values lost in the indulgences of the old order. Determined ideologues, they have successfully employed this repudiative leadership stance to identify their political ideas with the basic task of restoring the moral integrity of the nation. In this vein, Lincoln told the people that their "republican robes" had been "soiled and trailed in the dust" by a conspiracy of entrenched elites and that the people needed to "wash them white in the spirit if not the blood of the Revolution."[13] FDR spoke of chasing the "money changers" from their high seats of power and of restoring the "ancient truths" of American civilization.[14] Reagan posed a choice not between "left or right" but between "up or down"—"down through the welfare state to statism" or "up to the ultimate in individual freedom, the dream conceived by our Founding Fathers."[15] This historically contingent authority to repudiate forthrightly the legacy of the immediate past in the name of recovering lost values said to be emblematic of the body politic must be counted the most precious leadership resource an American president can have in orchestrating change. Armed with the authority to repudiate, presidents have managed to keep their detractors at bay and to sustain the most profound disruptions and transformations of the American polity. Without it, they have gotten caught up in the many checkpoints of the American constitutional system and found themselves more or less besieged.

The singular success of this leadership stance indicates once again that the presidency is not a place for complicated messages. The presidency's political interventions are too blunt and disruptive for a subtle and nuanced claim of legitimacy; the only irresistible appeal has been the blunt, repudiative one. For anyone who believes that the problems facing American government are subtle and complicated—that there are, in fact, no easy answers—this will be one of the more sobering observations to be drawn from America's political history.

Repeatedly, however, reconstructive leaders like Reagan have demonstrated the potency of the repudiative posture in redefining the terms and conditions of legitimate national government and of doing so in ways that endure long after they leave office. Whatever else the Reagan reconstruction achieved, it recast basic political definitions. After Reagan, liberalism would be saddled with the stigma of "tax and spend"; indeed, "liberal" became "the L word," its full expression banished from legitimate political discourse. In its place, a new conservative agenda was associated with fundamental American values, and even future Democratic presidents were compelled to invoke those values as the source of new solutions to governing problems.

Reagan rode to reelection in 1984 saying that he had reset the clock, making it "morning again in America." By recasting the federal government around a new constellation of ideological and programmatic commitments, reconstructive leaders do just that; they install new regimes. But there is more involved in resetting the political clock in America than simply declaring it so. Traditionally, reconstructive presidents have used their repudiative authority to dislodge the residual institutional supports of the old order. Jackson's repudiation of entrenched elites took institutional form in the destruction of the Second National Bank; Lincoln's repudiation of the "slave-power conspiracy" took institutional form in the destruction of slavery itself; and FDR's repudiation of "economic royalists" took institutional form as a frontal assault on the independence of the Supreme Court. Bank War, Civil War, Court Battle—these blunt confrontations with the institutional infrastructure of the old order have been the reconstructive presidents' special province in regenerating and redirecting American politics. For the most part, the positive and constructive task of fleshing out the new regime has fallen to Congress. The American presidency has proven most effective politically as a battering ram, a negative instrument for displacing entrenched governing elites, destroying the institutional arrangements that support them, and clearing the ground for something new.

It is on this count that Reagan's reconstruction takes on a decidedly postmodern character. Just as surely as his distinctive ambitions and achievements set Reagan apart from other recent incumbents, a comparison with earlier reconstructive presidencies highlights the limits of his success in forcibly dislodging the residual institutional infrastructure of the old order and clearing new ground on which his alternative might take hold. After an aggressive first-year jolt to established priorities in taxation and spending, the Reagan administration found itself mired in an institutional standoff with a divided Congress. Most striking in this regard was the early rejection by the newly empowered Republican Senate of administration hints of an assault on the cornerstone of liberal government, Social Security. Unable to press the case against liberalism's programmatic commitments to a decisive institutional breakthrough, the Reagan reconstruction was thrown back on more indirect means. In place of the frontal attack, the president opted for a slow strangulation of activist government.

An exploding budget deficit became the chief transformative instrument. The deficit promised to reconstruct the regime by restricting new federal initiatives, retrenching existing commitments, and propelling a search for alternative solutions to governing problems in the states and private sector. By saddling later presidents with a monumental governing problem, the deficit promised to fix attention on Reagan's priorities long after he left office. And yet by projecting reconstruction over a longer term and by not decisively eliminating any of liberalism's governmental services or institutional supports, Reagan left the shape of his new order radically open-ended.

Ironically, Reagan's reconstructive achievement was limited by the very same features of contemporary American government that had bolstered Carter's more independent stance. In a governmental system in which both Congress and the presidency have come under the control of relatively autonomous political entrepreneurs, it is more difficult for a reconstructive leader to mobilize the requisite number of supporters behind a systemic polit-ical transformation. Insurgents quickly find themselves less dependent on one another than on the governmental services they provide individually to their various constituencies. The greater autonomy of all political institutions and actors, the tighter integration of administrative services and supports into interest networks of social and economic power, and the consequent weak-ening of collective, cross-institutional resolve at the political center all con-stitute new constraints on presidentially led political reconstructions of American government. The result in Reagan's case was a reconstruction that, by historical standards, played out as more rhetorical than institutional, its comparatively shallow foundations laid on an ideological aversion to red ink.[16]

George Bush and Other Orthodox Innovators

The American presidency has been least effective as an instrument for political leadership when the president is, like Jimmy Carter, saddled by a set of politically vulnerable governing commitments and compelled to try to rehabilitate the faltering regime that supports them. The American presiden-cy has been most effective as an instrument for political leadership when the incumbent is, like Ronald Reagan, opposed to a set of politically vulnerable governing commitments and free to hammer away at the interests, institu-tions, and ideas that gave them vitality. Between these extremes lie two other leadership postures that, although they are subject to a bit more historical variation, have nonetheless framed distinctive political contests.

One is well represented by George Bush, a president who came to power affiliated with a set of governing commitments that he affirmed forthrightly as providing a clear and compelling guide to future action. "There's a gener-al thrust and President Reagan set that," Bush said. "We're not coming in to correct the ills of the past. We're coming in to build on a proud record that has already been established." [17] Bush presented himself to the nation in 1988 as a faithful son of the Reagan Revolution, an orthodox innovator pledged to continue an agenda that was his rightful inheritance. The Republican con-vention that nominated Bush responded to the Democrats' call for a change with the refrain "we are the change," meaning that the Reagan Revolution was ongoing, that the Democrats' "change" was really a retreat back to the discredited past, and that the task at hand was to complete the transforma-tion Reagan had set in motion.

On the face of it, the leadership claims of orthodox innovators seem as clear, simple, and compelling as those of the reconstructive leaders whose handiwork they vow to elaborate. Unlike late-regime affiliates, the orthodox innovator's warrants for action are not complicated or strained by questions about the adequacy of the governing formulas with which they are associated. Instead, these presidents present themselves as stalwart regime boosters, preachers to the choir. They stand foursquare on their robust inheritance with straightforward pledges to deliver on the regime's most basic commitments of ideology and interest.

Some notable variation exists in what actually gets done in this regard. Orthodox innovators who have come to office directly on the heels of a reconstructive leader have had a hard time building on their inheritance. Like Bush, James Madison, Martin Van Buren, and Harry S. Truman each stood directly in the shadow of a reconstructive leader and was plagued by the comparison. Although each was expected to act as a mere stand-in for the reconstructive leader, they actually grappled with a very different leadership problem.[18] Practically speaking, they had to turn their predecessor's legacy into a workable system of government, a sober business that had little of their predecessor's blunt appeal.

By contrast, orthodox innovators who have entered office with a bit more distance from the reconstructive leader have been able to erect grand superstructures on the regime's foundations. James Monroe, James K. Polk, Theodore Roosevelt, and Lyndon Johnson all spurred great bursts of orthodox innovation. All were stalwart regime boosters, but each drew on a more fully developed sense of what a second round of orthodox innovations should look like. These presidents came closest to realizing the orthodox innovator's conception of political leadership as a culmination of the work of the past and a demonstration of the enduring vitality of established commitments. This prospect will figure prominently in the presidency of George W. Bush, a Republican who brings to power a clear agenda for a second round of conservative innovation and whose party has at least nominal control of both houses of Congress. But more on that later.

Notwithstanding these variations, orthodox innovators share a common set of problems in sustaining leadership authority and effectively orchestrating political change, and the distinctive political contest they set up deepens insight into the political capacities of the office they inhabit. The difficulties they face are inherent in the idea of orthodox innovation itself, of negotiating changes that will stand as faithful representations of prior governing commitments. Exactly what these commitments entail, how they are to be adapted to new conditions, and what more they can accommodate is never entirely clear. Different factions of the faithful will understand these matters differently. With every action the president takes, however, his particular view of the matter becomes more distinct. Orthodox innovators cannot escape the dilemma that their version of the established faith is going to foment doubts and qualms among their own followers. Try as they might to

explain themselves to the faithful—to convince them that they are fair managers of their interests and consistent ministers of their creed—the orthodox
innovators have no good defense against charges from within that they mis-
interpreted or mishandled their charge. These presidents remain but one of
several leaders of the regime, each of whom can speak with some authority
about what its real commitments are. Ultimately, it is these "followers" who
set the boundaries of appropriate regime policy, and typically they do so at
their president's expense. Characteristically, orthodox innovators are discredited not by their partisan opponents but by their ostensible allies.

George Bush's experience was classic in this regard. He launched his
1988 presidential campaign with an iron-clad profession of his orthodoxy in
representing the faith: "Read my lips: No New Taxes." [19] But after a year and
a half of trying to work within that constraint, Bush felt compelled to chart
his own course toward fulfilling the conservative agenda. He broke his pledge
in order to gain from the Democratic Congress another objective of the Reagan Revolution, a strong deficit-reduction plan. Instantly, he was denounced
by conservative Republicans for his betrayal of the tax pledge, and ultimately he was challenged for renomination on that ground by ultraconservative
Pat Buchanan. Unlike Carter, Bush did not press his case for independence
any further. To gain renomination, he felt compelled to negotiate a humiliat-
ing retreat. Awkwardly, he announced that he had come to agree with the
Republican faithful that his most significant domestic achievement had been
a mistake, and he pledged that he would, if reelected, replace his entire economic management team. Not only did Bush repudiate his own administration's handiwork in order to salvage his credentials as an orthodox innovator, but he also allowed the stalwarts who had denounced him to take control of the convention that was to renominate him. Commentators spoke at
the time of his de facto abdication of leadership. [20]

Bush had indeed tied himself in a knot, but it was hardly a unique one.
Of the twenty-four American presidents who have come to power affiliated
with an established set of governing commitments, only four (James Madison, James Monroe, Ulysses S. Grant, and William McKinley) have been
reelected to a second term, and two of those predate the rise of organized
opposition. Consider also that the seven presidents who have voluntarily
withdrawn from a second-term bid were all orthodox innovators. [21] Whatever might be said about Bush's lack of charisma or resolve, orthodox innovators like Bush have wielded a form of political authority that has always tended to dissolve in its own accomplishments. The difficulties Bush encountered
in trying to sustain his leadership authority are emblematic of the problems
inherent in trying to exercise the independent powers of the presidential
office in ways consistent with an established orthodoxy.

Bush's leadership was perhaps most typical in its practical political
effects. The characteristic political effect of orthodox innovation has been
schismatic. The actions of these presidents spark debilitating debates within
their own ranks over the true meaning of the faith, and the more they get

done, the deeper the factional disputes tend to become. By the end of their elected terms, even the greatest of the orthodox innovators—James Monroe, James Polk, Theodore Roosevelt, and Lyndon Johnson—found that they had built a house of cards. In erecting an imposing policy monument to political orthodoxy, each fractured his political base and put regime supporters at odds with one another. Purely constructive warrants for political leadership—warrants that are intended to affirm and extend the received order—may accomplish a lot in terms of public policy, but in the process the establishments that support them tend to succumb, at least momentarily, to internal bickering.

Today's postmodern institutional environment can only exacerbate the leadership problems that attend orthodox innovation. The basic problem in this leadership stance lies in the tension between the president's affiliation with an established and collective political project, on the one hand, and the president's constitutional independence and personal responsibility, on the other. As recent institutional developments have accentuated the independence of the office and the personal aspects of leadership, they have compounded the difficulties of sustaining any collective political identity. Certain particulars of Bush's efforts to pose as a faithful son of the Reagan Revolution illustrate the point quite plainly. Back in 1980, when Bush was waging a campaign in the Republican primaries for the presidential nomination, he publicly denounced Reagan's tax cut ideas as "voodoo economics" and the "free lunch" approach. Even after eight years as Reagan's vice president, doubts about Bush's faith in the new orthodoxy ran deep among true believers, and his best efforts to dispel these doubts—like his ludicrously iron-clad pledge on taxes at the 1988 Republican national convention—strained his identity to the point of caricature. Moreover, once in office Bush found himself hounded by the media for his failure to articulate his own "vision" for the nation. The "vision thing," as it became known, reflected the postmodern demand for personal leadership, the expectation that presidents will stand for their own distinctive priorities and purposes. But the idea of a personal vision runs contrary to a leadership project whose chief warrants entail adherence to an established orthodoxy.

The highly personalized, candidate-centered politics of today presents a minefield of dangers for the orthodox innovator. As contenders within the same party are prompted to build their own organizations, to differentiate themselves from their fellow partisans, and to stand on their own priorities, shared political identities become more difficult to assert and sustain. Leaders saddled with a faltering political project, as Carter was, may appreciate this new autonomy; leaders who draw authority more directly from their attachment to the established orthodoxy will not. They will find that the most potent institutional resources of the postmodern presidency serve only to complicate their leadership credentials as the steward of a robust ideological movement and to undermine their warrant to serve the cause faithfully. In the more party-centered politics of the nineteenth and early twentieth centuries, orthodox innovators were better able to submerge their own identities in the collective identities of the political organizations they presumed to represent. Not so today. The postmodern presidency seems to have turned this most common of leadership stances into something of an anachronism.

Bill Clinton and Other Preemptive Leaders

In his rise to power, it was clear that Bill Clinton was not, like Ronald Reagan, the great repudiator of a governing regime in collapse. Nor was he, like George Bush, the faithful son of an unfinished revolution. A Democrat seeking the presidency in the post-Reagan era, Clinton sought to preempt the Republican revolution by promising a "third way."

To talk about a third way in 1992 was to acknowledge the Democrats' three consecutive losses to liberal-bashing Republicans and to attempt to adjust the Democratic alternative to the new political standards that had been established by the Reagan Revolution. The idea was to dispel the aura of illegitimacy that had surrounded the Democratic Party's posture in national politics since the Carter debacle and to redefine the choices at hand so that the Republicans no longer posed the only alternative to discredited liberalism. To meet this challenge, Clinton cast himself firmly in the mold of an opposition leader. The practical problems he addressed were not those of a regime with which he was politically affiliated, but those of the new regime that had replaced liberalism. Clinton pegged the nation's woes to twelve years of Republican rule, exploited new divisions arising within the Republican coalition, and committed himself to a "new course" that would "put people first." At the same time, however, he acknowledged the Republicans' redefinition of the terms and conditions of legitimate national government. To escape the burdens of older Democratic identities, he rejected the liberal label outright, turned a cold shoulder to familiar icons of the left, and openly proclaimed himself the leader of a "New Democratic Party." By actively disassociating himself from the standard that Reagan had so effectively driven from the field, Clinton promised to take the discussion of political alternatives beyond what he called "the stale, failed rhetoric of the past."[22] His new party was, he said, "neither liberal nor conservative but both and different."[23]

It was, to be sure, a subtle, complicated, and equivocal message. Clinton did not assume the authority to challenge fundamentally the terms in which legitimate national government had come to be understood.[24] His opposition was more preemptive than reconstructive. Characteristically, the clarity of purpose achieved by the great repudiators gives way in such circumstances to leadership that is co-optive, ad hoc, and ultimately indeterminate in its fundamental purposes. What Clinton drew from this opposition stance was a good measure of independence in crafting and altering his political positions. Preemptive leaders have more room to maneuver around received commitments than do orthodox innovators or late-regime affiliates. They are far less beholden to those within their own ranks for their doctrinal purity or for the consistency of their actions with established party priorities. To put it another way, preemptive leaders are not out to establish, uphold, or salvage any political orthodoxy. Theirs is an unabashedly mongrel politics: an aggressive critique of the prevailing political categories and a bold bid to mix them up.

The "third way" finds its distinctive opportunities in the very schisms within the ranks of the dominant coalition that orthodox innovators are at such pains to assuage. By taking advantage of these schisms, preemptive leaders bid to appropriate much of the field of action carved out by those who built the regime. They threaten to take over their opponents' most attractive positions and to leave them holding the most extreme ones. The political contest is thus framed by the president's purposeful blurring of received political identities and by the opponents' stake in keeping those older identities intact. The corresponding risk these presidents run is that in trying to establish their third way, they may appear wholly lacking in political principles and come across as unscrupulous and cynically manipulative.

Preemptive leaders can be found throughout American history. Woodrow Wilson and Richard Nixon are prime examples. Like Clinton, they first reached the presidency in a three-way race that featured a major schism within the dominant party, and each won with about 40 percent of the popular vote. But third-way appeals have been heard from other presidents as well: Zachary Taylor, the military hero of the Mexican War elected by the antiwar Whigs; Grover Cleveland, the first Democrat to win the presidency in the aftermath of Civil War reconstruction; and Dwight Eisenhower, the first Republican to come to power after the New Deal reconstruction. Deep historical antecedents of this stance may be traced to John Tyler and Andrew Johnson—accidental presidents whose position on the national ticket reflected one party's effort to secure majority status by nominating a vice president from a disaffected faction of the other party. (Tyler, a disaffected Democrat, was elected vice president by the Whigs in 1840; Johnson, also a disaffected Democrat, was elected as vice president by the Republicans in 1864.) All of these presidents rode to power with a party opposed to the previously established regime, but once in office each was at pains to assert his independence from the dominant ideological factions in both parties.

Hyphenated party labels, hybrid agendas, personal leadership, and independent appeals are the emblems of the preemptive leadership stance. Taylor's "No Party" brand of Whiggery, Johnson's "War Democrats," Cleveland's "liberal reform Democracy," Wilson's "progressive Democracy," Eisenhower's "Modern Republicans," the "new Nixon" who spoke for the "silent" or "new" majority, Clinton's "New Democrats"—all exemplify political stances carefully crafted to sidestep established conceptions of the nation's political alternatives and to reach out beyond the president's traditional party base toward some new and largely inchoate combination.

Note further that this preemptive style of opposition has traditionally proven quite effective at the polls. Except for Taylor, who died in the middle of his first term, all of the third-way presidents who were elected to the presidential office were reelected to a second term. This record stands in stark contrast to that of the orthodox innovators, and it suggests the seriousness of the political threat that third-way appeals pose to ideologues of all stripes, especially to those still committed to completing the agenda of the most recent reconstruction in a more orthodox manner.

Observe, however—and this with an eye to the results of the 2000 election—that third-way alternatives have never proven durable. Preemptive leaders, with their "neo" parties having hybrid agendas, have characteristically held only a loose grip on the terms and conditions of national politics, and they have wielded only a temporary influence over its future course. This stance may support a personal success like Eisenhower's, or a virtuoso performance like Wilson's, but it is just as likely to foment a constitutional test of wills culminating in a showdown over presidential authority, as it did for John Tyler, Andrew Johnson, Woodrow Wilson, Richard Nixon, and Bill Clinton. Historically, no "third way" has ever outlasted the president who articulated it. Such leadership efforts have been highly individualized, and the political contests they set up have tended to become radically personalized. Although preemptive presidents may be quite successful in pressing their advantages, their political alternatives have never cut very deep.

Setting Clinton's experience against that of other preemptive presidents recasts understanding of both the typical and extraordinary aspects of his leadership. Although the convulsive character of the Clinton administration stands out among recent presidencies, it fits a recurrent pattern of extraordinary volatility in pursuit of a third way. Preemptive leaders are the wild cards of presidential history. They lack the repudiative authority to forge a new regime, but possess an independence that seems to threaten the regime-based structure of politics itself. In exercising this independence, they provoke intense political struggles in which their personal codes of conduct take center stage. Other presidents may be labeled apostates or incompetents, but these presidents are often judged moral degenerates, congenitally incapable of rising above nihilism and manipulation.

Consider in this regard Wilson's reputation among his critics as "the reversible president" who was "constantly changing, moving another way, and turning about."[25] At issue in this characterization were Wilson's stunning shifts on several major public policy issues, as well as his determination, especially after 1914, to find his own way through the Democratic-Progressive-Republican divisions of his day. Theodore Roosevelt, the nominal leader of the Progressives, and Henry Cabot Lodge, the stalwart Senate Republican, engaged in a relentless backstairs campaign of character assassination against Wilson. Taking direct aim at Wilson's legitimacy, they charged that he was a man wholly lacking in core commitments. Roosevelt mercilessly derided Wilson's "adroit, unscrupulous cunning, his pandering to those who love ease . . . his readiness to about-face, his timidity about any manly assertion of our rights, his lack of all conviction and willingness to follow every gust of opinion." Wilson's "soul," Roosevelt said, was "rotten through and through"; he had not "a thought for the welfare of the country; or for our honor; or for anything except his own mean personal advancement."[26] Lodge echoed these diatribes, charging that Wilson was "shifty," "furtive," and "sinister," a man whose "passionate absorption in himself and his own interests and ambitions" overshadowed all other considerations. As Lodge makes clear in his memoirs, Wilson went into the fateful fight over the League of Nations with this reputation for willful deceit, unbridled self-promotion, and false idealism already firmly fixed among his opponents.[27]

The centrality of individual character in preemptive leadership helps to account for the wide variation in how character issues have played out politically. The candidacies of Taylor and Eisenhower were conspicuous in putting character above politics. Each presented a record of disinterested service to the nation that drew attention away from his rather murky ideological commitments and political objectives. Cleveland joined the character issue directly. Dogged by charges of personal immorality in his rise to the presidency, he turned the tables on his opponents by charging them with corruption in the administration of government and promising "absolute cleanliness" in his own.[28] When Clinton, like "Tricky Dick" Nixon and "Shifty Tom" Wilson before him, took his stand exclusively on the political attractiveness of his third way, his opponents quickly labeled him "Slick Willy."

Shifty Tom, Tricky Dick, Slick Willy—all of these characterizations are of a type, a political type, not a personality type. They are characteristic of the personalization of politics that occurs when a president seeks to preempt established conceptions of the alternatives and substitute a third way. Determined to sustain their contention that Clinton's "New Democratic Party" was really a ploy masking a rearguard defense of liberalism, Republicans deftly transposed the question of ideology into a question of character. Character flaws offered an explanation for Clinton's repeated forays onto conservative ground; they accounted for his use of the presidency to mask his party's true leanings and selectively incorporate his opponents' most attractive positions. As Clinton challenged received definitions of liberal and conservative, of Democrat and Republican, and of Left, Right, and Center, opponents compiled evidence from his personal life to suggest that he really had no standards at all, that he was wholly lacking in principles. By showing Americans a man who never cared much for the truth, who had proven incapable of standing by any commitment, and who had no higher purpose than his own self-indulgence, Clinton's opponents found a way to preserve the truth that they wished to promote—namely, that Democrats remained a desperate party of discredited ideas and debased leadership while the Republicans remained the only legitimate exponents of national solutions.

The extraordinary convulsiveness and character-centeredness of preemptive leadership are revealed most strikingly in the prominent use of impeachment threats against third-way threats. John Tyler, Andrew Johnson, Richard Nixon and Bill Clinton are not a random set of presidents who happened to have blundered into impeachment crises. Rather, they were all third-way leaders who threatened received conceptions of the political alternatives. Their shared leadership stance suggests the primacy of political, rather than strictly legal, factors at work in these proceedings. The impulse has been to dislodge the threat to a more orthodox rendition of the governmental agenda by personalizing the political challenge it poses and stigmatizing it as an assault on constitutional government itself.

But if Clinton's leadership unfolded in ways true to the preemptive type, it also set itself apart by its extraordinary buoyancy in weathering these storms. Other preemptive leaders were isolated and crushed in showdown confrontations with their adversaries. By contrast, Clinton repeatedly eluded his opponents' efforts to corner and stigmatize him. The "comeback kid" survived a devastating policy defeat on health care, his signature issue, as well as a historic and seemingly decisive midterm loss of his party's control of Congress in 1994. He then went on to deftly turn the tables on his opponents in the government shutdown crisis of 1995–1996 and again in the impeachment crisis of 1998. And then, even in the wake of impeachment, he nearly broke the historic pattern among third-way leaders by coming so close to passing power to his own hand-picked successor, Vice President Al Gore.

In all this, Clinton doubtlessly reaped the benefits of a strong national economy. But he showed as well how thoroughly the postmodern presidency resonates with the preemptive appeal. If the orthodox innovator has been rendered something of an anachronism in the new political environment, the preemptive leader seems right at home. In its basic political structure, preemptive leadership has always been ideologically detached, highly personalized, and aggressively independent. Now, with the rise of a governmental system characterized throughout by a more atomized, entrepreneurial style of politics—one in which the leading actors build personal organizations and construct their own networks of support—the preemptive president is no longer the odd man out. Of all the different political ambitions brought to the presidency in recent years, it is this leadership stance that seems to fit the political opportunities and constraints of the day most closely.

This chapter has described the ways in which the recent evolution of American government and politics has complicated the tasks of reconstructive presidents and orthodox innovators. The strong suit of the reconstructive leader—forthright repudiation of a politically vulnerable establishment—has been undermined by the larger scope and greater fragmentation of the institutional environment. The strong suit of the orthodox innovator—affiliation with a still-robust ideological agenda—has been undermined by the personalization of political power and responsibility. By contrast, a preemptive leadership stance built on loose affiliations and ad hoc opposition can thrive in the postmodern political environment. The distinctive tools available to contemporary presidents for monitoring public opinion, massaging messages, manipulating images, and targeting support are all instrumental to this stance. They facilitate a preemptive strategy of mixing and matching commitments to particular and momentary demands, thereby allowing the president to float more freely and instrumentally among the central issues of the day. Preemptive leadership may remain by historical standards volatile, superficial, and unresolved, but the larger lesson in Clinton's performance seems to lie in the evolution of governing arrangements in America that accommodate, even encourage, such qualities.

After Clinton: Continuity and Change in the Politics of Leadership

Presidential leadership at the end of the twentieth century was neither all of a piece nor categorically different from what it has been throughout American history. The century's last four presidents adopted very different leadership stances. Each took account of what immediately preceded him and crafted his bid for leadership authority with an eye to the new situation left to him by his predecessor. Facing different political challenges, each articulated a different premise for national political action, and each set up a different sort of political contest in the process. As different as they were from one another, however, these efforts were far from idiosyncratic. The recent sequence of presidents has, in all its variety, replayed leadership contests that have been part of American politics from the start. In large part, the political ambitions and practical effects of recent presidents have confirmed traditional patterns and, with them, the historical range and institutional boundaries of the American presidency as an instrument of national political transformation.

Changes in the mode of governmental operations commonly associated with a categorical shift to a postmodern presidency are not without significance, but they are best understood as an overlay upon the traditional leadership postures. Rather than displace the traditional postures, these changes have modified the prospects of each in a particular way. As we have seen, the new governing environment does not comport especially well with the ambitions of reconstructive leaders, and it seems even less compatible with those of orthodox innovators. At the same time, preemptive leaders have been so enhanced with resources for independent action that these traditional wild cards are now in a position to control the play.

Or nearly control it. Election Day 2000 yielded nothing quite so definitive. In fact, the historic pattern prevailed again, though just barely. Eight years of Republican agitation aimed at discrediting the great preemptor had set the stage for a return to "normalcy," and in George W. Bush the party found the perfect symbol of restoration. But even though Clinton's preemption ultimately went the way of all others before it, it did not do so in a typical manner. Clinton's chosen successor won the popular vote, and although the Bush campaign promised to bring honor, decency, and comity back to Washington, it relied for its postelection victory on the residuum of Republican muscle at key sites.

Of all those caught in these crosscurrents, Al Gore stands out as the signal historical figure. Eyeing the robust economy, most commentators assumed that the 2000 election was Gore's to lose, and they charged his defeat either to his shortcomings as a candidate or to the mistakes in his campaign. But due regard to the priority of authority in leadership raises questions about these assumptions and conclusions. Gore may have been the candidate of continuity in economic policy in this election, but in his bid to follow Clinton, he was pursuing wholly new possibilities for presidential leadership. Never has a preemptive leader, not to say an impeached one, been able to pass power to a chosen successor. Rather than allege that Gore squandered a clear advantage, commentators might have done well to mark a Gore victory as a prospect without precedent. Notwithstanding the robust economy, such an outcome would have indicated a categorical shift in the boundaries of presidential politics and a rare triumph for subtlety in the crafting of a political identity. As it stands, Gore's popular vote margin suggests a considerable loosening of traditional constraints on the preemptive appeal.

The force of postmodern factors at work in modifying standard leadership patterns was manifested most strikingly in Gore's efforts to detach the promise of continuity in policy from the burdens of his political affiliation with Bill Clinton. Of special interest in this regard were his refusal to run on Clinton's record, his conspicuous efforts to distance himself from the administration in which he had been a full partner, and his avowed determination to stand as "his own man." It may be argued, as many have, that these were strategic mistakes, that a candidate cannot run away from his political affiliations and had better make the best of them. Be that as it may, the dilemmas Gore had to negotiate in trying to succeed a presidency painted by his opponents as a national disgrace were daunting, and the fact that Gore felt he had an option more attractive than the role of faithful son is revealing. The vice president's campaign testifies both to the growing weakness of affiliation as a factor in crafting leadership stances today and to the growing attraction of projecting a wholly personal appeal. By the same token, a Gore victory would not have transformed Clinton post hoc into a reconstructive leader. The Gore campaign was interesting precisely because it tried to go Clinton one better, to preempt the great preemptor.

George W. Bush comes to power in far less novel circumstances. In fact, the victory of the candidate of change in this election sets up a familiar leadership contest. This first unified Republican government in the post-Reagan era is opening a pivotal episode in orthodox innovation. With the new president rests the conservatives' vision of a great society and the challenge of realizing some semblance of it without sending the Republican Party into a sectarian tailspin. As we have seen, the most potent challenges to the leadership of orthodox innovators typically come from those within their own ranks who can speak with authority about the true meaning of the faith and question their president's version of the gospel. Even under the most favorable conditions, orthodox innovators have their hands full trying to deliver on past promises, balance new commitments with old, and forestall sectarian schisms among their allies.

As it turns out, circumstances for Bush are not especially favorable. Among the possibilities with important implications for this analysis, three stand out for special attention. The most obvious, and likely, is that Bush will explore the potential for orthodox innovation and see what he can get done for the cause. A full court press à la Lyndon Johnson would defy the odds. The Republicans' razor-thin margins of control in Congress combined with the dubious mandate of the presidential contest have raised questions about whether any significant leap forward on the conservative agenda is at hand. But Bush brings into office a compelling mix of old and new themes on which conservatives and moderates alike might join. A skillful orthodox innovator might deliver at least as much as John F. Kennedy with his carefully limited advances and promises of more to come. The test will be how far Bush might proceed in these precarious circumstances toward a policy achievement that rivals the great episodes of orthodox innovation in the past and, ultimately, how he handles the fallout from any final reckoning with long-standing conservative commitments. The ultimate triumph would be for Bush to realize the dream that eluded the likes of Lyndon Johnson and James Monroe: to turn his party into "the party for all Americans" and to usher in an "era of good feeling" on his conservative principles. Not coincidentally, these ideals are perfectly consistent with Bush's campaign rhetoric.

A more sobering possibility is that the Bush presidency will simply implode in a hapless struggle for credibility and foment a systemic crisis of political legitimacy in the process. Given the dubious authority Bush takes from his election, it is possible that any concerted leadership effort will not simply fracture the Republican ranks but also catalyze the formation of a new and more potent opposition movement. If the past is any guide, however, this possibility is likely to turn as much on how the president's opponents proceed as on how the president himself performs. At present, there is no insurgency on the horizon, and the leadership and program for a truly reconstructive politics are difficult to discern. Such an outcome would, however, cast a significantly different light on Bill Clinton's political accomplishments, suggesting that even if he did not himself reconstruct American politics, he did cut short the viability of a conservative regime and hasten the advent of a robust alternative.

The most interesting prospect is that Bush will try himself to escape the limitations of affiliated leadership and press the postmodern alternative. During the postelection contest, it was widely speculated that Bush might assert his political independence by using the unsettled circumstances of his election to distance himself from Republican orthodoxy and, in a manner more fitting a preemptive leader, begin to speak the language of the third way. Such a course might become even more attractive if there is any adverse change in the precarious balance of party power in Congress. A concerted move in this direction would present a historic test of the potential for bucking standard patterns, a test of whether orthodox innovation has become not just a contemporary anachronism but a complete irrelevance. At present, however, a Republican president actively resisting a Republican Congress at its moment of fulfillment seems a bit much to expect, even of the postmodern presidency.

Notes

1. Bruce Miroff, "The Presidency and the Public: Leadership as Spectacle," in *The Presidency and the Political System,* ed. Michael Nelson (Washington, D.C.: CQ Press, 1998), 299–323. Also see Elizabeth Drew, *White House Showdown: The Struggle between the Gingrich Congress and the Clinton White House* (New York: Simon and Schuster, 1996).
2. This chapter draws on and updates my analysis in *The Politics Presidents Make: Leadership from John Adams to Bill Clinton* (Cambridge: Harvard University Press, 1997).
3. See for example: Theodore Lowi, *The Personal President: Power Invested, Promise Unfulfilled* (Ithaca: Cornell University Press, 1985); Richard Rose, *The Post-Modern Presidency* (Chatham, N.J.: Chatham House, 1988); Samuel Kernell, *Going Public: New Strategies of Presidential Leadership* (Washington, D.C.: CQ Press, 1986); and Benjamin Ginsberg and Martin Shefter, *Politics by Other Means: Politicians, Prosecutors, and the Press from Watergate to Whitewater* (New York: Norton, 1999).
4. Bob Woodward recently located Clinton in a contemporary pattern of investigation-wracked administrations. *Shadow, Five Presidents and the Legacy of Watergate* (New York: Simon and Schuster, 1999).
5. See in particular Rose, *Post-Modern Presidency*; and Lowi, *Personal President.*
6. I do not mean to suggest that these sequences unfold independent of presidential leadership efforts. Quite the contrary—leadership efforts are themselves formative of these sequences: they help shape and drive the observed patterns of institutional reconstruction and political decay. Use of these historic patterns, however, allows me to draw on the past more directly to illuminate significant changes and continuities in the politics of leadership.
7. *The Presidential Campaign 1976,* Vol. I, Part 1: Jimmy Carter (Washington D.C.: Government Printing Office, 1978), 244.
8. *Ibid.,* 174, 203, 298.
9. See, for example, Emmet John Hughs, "The Presidency vs. Jimmy Carter," *Fortune,* December 4, 1978; Sidney Weintraub, "Carter's Hoover Syndrome,"*New Leader,* March 24, 1980; and James Sundquist, "The Crisis of Competence in Our National Government,"*Political Science Quarterly* (summer 1980).
10. "Energy and National Goals, July 15, 1979," *Public Papers of the Presidents of the United States: Jimmy Carter* (Washington, D.C.: Government Printing Office, 1977–1981), 1235–1239.
11. "Speech Accepting the Republican Nomination," *New York Times,* July 18, 1980, 8.
12. "Inaugural Address, Jan. 20, 1981," *Public Papers of the Presidents of the United States: Ronald Reagan,* Vol. 1 (Washington, D.C.: Government Printing Office, 1982), 1.
13. "At Peoria Illinois" (Oct. 16, 1854), *Collected Works of Abraham Lincoln,* ed. Roy P. Basler (New Brunswick, N.J.: Rutgers University Press, 1953), 2:276; and "A House Divided," *Collected Works of Abraham Lincoln,* 2:461–469.
14. "Inaugural Address" (March 4, 1933), *The Public Papers and Addresses of Franklin Roosevelt,* Vol. 2, ed. Samuel Rosenman (New York: Random House, 1938–1950), 14–15.

15. "Speech Accepting the Republican Nomination in 1984," *Public Papers of the Presidents of the United States: Ronald Reagan,* Vol. 2 (Washington, D.C.: Government Printing Office, 1982), 1180.

16. The significance of Reagan's less direct and more limited assault on the substantive commitments of the old-order regime would not become clear until long into the Clinton administration. In any thinking about the political impact of the Reagan deficit, however, a more general point is important: as a rule, America's reconstructive presidents have not been much better than any of its other presidents at solving national problems. Jefferson's alternative to the economic and military policies of the Federalists left his successors defenseless in the face of British power; Jackson's alternative to the fiscal policies of the National Republicans turned out to be financial disaster; and FDR's New Deal failed to pull the nation out of the depression. What reconstructive presidents have done, and what other presidents have been unable to do, is to replace old standards of legitimate national government and to redirect the search for solutions to governing problems toward a new set of ideas. This Reagan did uniquely among contemporary presidents.

17. "Speech to the Republican National Committee," January 18, 1989, Federal News Service.

18. Walter Dean Burnham, "The Politics of Repudiation in 1992, Edging toward Upheaval,"*American Prospect* (winter 1993): 22–23.

19. "Acceptance Speech before the Republican National Convention," *New York Times,* August 19, 1988.

20. A. M. Rosenthal, "Mr. Bush Steps Aside," *New York Times,* October 13, 1992.

21. The seven presidents who have voluntarily withdrawn from second-term bids are James K. Polk, James Buchanan, Rutherford B. Hayes, Theodore Roosevelt, Calvin Coolidge, Harry S. Truman, and Lyndon B. Johnson.

22. Vernon Van Dyke, *Ideology and Political Culture* (Chatham, N.J.: Chatham House, 1995), 274–283.

23. For example, Robin Toner, "Arkansas' Clinton Enters the '92 Race for President," *New York Times,* October 4, 1991, 1.

24. Even on his health care initiative, Clinton felt compelled to try to accommodate the altered standards of legitimacy set by the Reagan Revolution. On this point see Theda Skocpol, *Boomerang: Clinton's Health Security Effort and the Turn against Government in U.S. Politics* (New York: Norton, 1996).

25. "Our Reversible President," *Collier's Weekly,* April 18, 1914.

26. *The Letters of Theodore Roosevelt,* Vol. 8, ed. Elting Morrison (Cambridge: Harvard University Press, 1954), 1031, 1199.

27. Henry Cabot Lodge, *The Senate and the League of Nations* (New York: Scribners, 1925), 79–80, 212–213, 216–226.

28. Geoffrey Blodgett, "The Political Leadership of Grover Cleveland," *South Atlantic Quarterly* 82 (summer 1983): 290–291; and Pearl Louise Robertson, *Grover Cleveland as a Political Leader* (Chicago: University of Chicago Libraries, 1939).

2

The Nominations:
The Return of the Party Leaders

Harold W. Stanley

On March 15, 1999, more than nineteen months before Election Day 2000, Vice President Al Gore made his first excursions of the 2000 campaign into New Hampshire and Iowa. Former senator Bill Bradley of New Jersey was Gore's principal opponent for the Democratic nomination; every other possible challenger had passed up the race. Although almost a dozen Republicans had declared their candidacy for the presidential nomination or were preparing to do so, political pundits anticipated a general election battle between Gore and Texas governor George W. Bush.[1]

Despite the ultimate accuracy of this prediction, the results of the 2000 nomination process were far from determined before the primary and caucus season began. Both Gore and Bush, viewed widely as the front-runners, had problems to overcome. A successful challenge to either or both in an early primary or caucus—the conventional strategy for challengers[2]—would jeopardize their front-runner status and their nominations. Early polling had Gore trailing two Republicans, Bush and Elizabeth Dole, the former head of the American Red Cross and a cabinet official in the Ronald Reagan and George Bush administrations. In his quest for the Democratic nomination, Bradley could perhaps capitalize on Gore's general election vulnerability. Bush, a fresh face but an untested national candidate whose understanding of the issues and qualifications for the presidency might be found wanting, could stumble, giving Dole or other candidates an opening. Challengers jockeyed for position to exploit such an opportunity.

Beginning in the late 1960s, Democratic Party reforms of the presidential nominating process opened the process to causes and candidates not embraced by the party establishment. The relatively closed Democratic Party encountered by Minnesota senator Eugene McCarthy in his 1968 antiwar protest campaign was reformed by national party rules regulating the timing and manner in which delegates to the party's national nominating conventions could be selected. The new rules did not call for additional state primaries, the most visible consequences of the reforms, but most state parties and legislatures opted for them as the most palatable way of complying. As a result, the number of primaries rose from fifteen in 1968 to around forty by 1992. Democrats led the way in making these reforms, but Republicans were affected as well, because Democratic state legislatures often changed Republican rules in order to keep the party processes similar.

Vice President Hubert Humphrey won the 1968 Democratic presidential nomination without entering a single primary. But with the new rules, that scenario became an unlikely if not an impossible one to replicate. Candidates not backed by the party establishment—insurgents such as South Dakota senator George McGovern in 1972, Georgia governor Jimmy Carter in 1976, California governor Ronald Reagan in 1976 and 1980, and Colorado senator Gary Hart in 1984—fared well in the reformed nomination process.

Ironically, despite these reforms to open the party nominating contests, by 2000 the reformed process had evolved into one in which the candidates with extensive party leadership backing—Bush and Gore—enjoyed considerable advantages. Such backing might not have proved decisive, but candidates without it faced obstacles far more formidable than those confronting McGovern, Carter, Reagan, or Hart in previous elections. Front-loading—the tendency of state political leaders to move their primaries and caucuses toward the start of the election year in order to gain greater leverage and attention in presidential politics—meant that a candidate needed substantial financial and organizational resources before the voting even began. Broad backing from party leaders was the key to securing these resources.

In 2000, California, Michigan, and Ohio joined the parade of states that had for years been creeping toward the front of the calendar. The greater extent of front-loading in 2000 compared with earlier years is evident in the length of time required to select a majority of convention delegates after the first primary or caucus. In 1976, almost four months elapsed; in 1980 three and a half months; in 1992 the Democrats took just under two months, the Republicans two and a half months; and in 2000 both parties took less than two months (forty-eight days for the Democrats and fifty for the Republicans).[3] The more leisurely pace of earlier elections had given way to an accelerated, transcontinental race for delegates.

In the front-loaded calendar, front-runners hoped to survive the early, small-state contests in Iowa, New Hampshire, and, for Republicans, South Carolina, and then benefit from a run-everywhere strategy that placed a premium on superior financial and organizational resources. An insurgent candidate who counted on winning the hearts and minds of voters in an early small state as a prelude to riding the resulting enhanced media coverage and greater fund-raising to victory in subsequent contents might come to grief in the compressed schedule. Insurgents bravely interpreted front-loading as being in their favor: so many events in such a short time could prevent the front-runners from regaining momentum if they slipped. After all, front-runners had stumbled before. The insurgents' best hope was to do what they could to provoke such a stumble and be ready to benefit if that happened.

As this chapter will reveal, the story of the 2000 nominations was one in which, contrary to the initial intentions behind the reforms of the nominating process in the 1960s and 1970s, the party leaders returned to positions of considerable influence over the nominations. The extensive party backing of Bush and Gore helped the front-runners to prevail but did not rule out surprisingly strong challenges by Bill Bradley and Republican senator John McCain of Arizona. An appreciation of the dynamics of the 2000 nomination contests requires a chronological account of the candidates, contexts, and strategies leading up to the conventions.

The "Invisible" Primary of 1999

Even before the primary and caucus voting begins, the standings and likely success of presidential candidates are established through trial heat surveys designed to determine their support and name recognition and through evidence of their fund-raising prowess. Although scholars call this period the "invisible primary," the run-up to the 2000 nominations proved to be highly visible as the candidates sought to establish themselves as viable contenders.[4] The heavily front-loaded nomination calendar added to the importance of the pre-voting period. Expectations that the nominations would be settled by mid-March 2000 made a strong start all the more essential.

The 1998 congressional elections also had implications for candidates seeking the 2000 presidential nominations. The Republican-led impeachment inquiry triggered by President Clinton's sexual relationship with White House intern Monica Lewinsky galvanized Republican conservatives but turned off most voters. Democratic gains in the 1998 elections unified the Democrats, demoralized the Republicans, and shored up Clinton's centrist New Democratic direction. All this redounded to the benefit of Gore as Clinton's heir apparent. The midterm results also boosted Bush, the favorite of a Republican establishment irritated by the party's damaged image and eager for new leadership to win back the White House in 2000. As the public assessed the would-be leaders, its political cynicism and yearning for something other than politics-as-usual deepened. Prosperity removed the economy as a pressing problem, freeing the voters to pay greater attention to leadership character.

Months before the Iowa caucus, the dynamics of the 2000 presidential nominations was already taking shape. Events in 1999 winnowed candidates such as Elizabeth Dole, former Tennessee governor Lamar Alexander, and former vice president Dan Quayle from the Republican field; solidified Bush's status as the Republican front-runner while raising questions about his political stature; established John McCain rather than magazine publisher Steve Forbes as the principal challenger to Bush; and confirmed Bradley as a credible challenger to Gore.

Bush and Campaign Finance

George W. Bush took presidential campaign finance to a new level by raising a record-breaking $67 million in 1999 alone. In a mere four months,

Bush surpassed the previous record set by the 1996 Republican nominee, Sen. Robert Dole, who raised $31.2 million over eighteen months in 1995–1996. Bush's success cemented the notion that he was the front-runner, provoking his Republican opponents to argue that his fund-raising signaled a political problem, not a political strength. Forbes contended that Bush proved not so much that he could raise money, but that he was "inextricably tied to Washington lobbyists and special interests." McCain promised to make campaign finance reform central to his campaign against "an elaborate influence peddling scheme in which both parties conspire to stay in office by selling the country to the highest bidder."[5] Despite these charges, the cold, hard fact was that Bush entered the election year with $31.4 million in the bank, or more than four times McCain's campaign chest.

Bush not only outstripped his fellow Republican candidates in money raised but also squeezed several of them out of contention. Upon setting up an exploratory committee for his candidacy in March 1999, Bush immediately snagged most of his party's top fund-raisers, stunning his Republican rivals.[6] By contrast, Elizabeth Dole, a distant second to Bush in the national polls, had a faltering campaign start. Her months-long inability to enlist a national fund-raising chair vividly illustrated her weak start, and anemic fund-raising continued to plague her promising but short-lived campaign.[7] Quayle and Alexander cut staff and lowered fund-raising targets. As Melvin Sembler, the Republican National Committee finance chairman, observed, "What's happened is Bush is sucking the wind out of everybody's sails."[8]

Bush's fund-raising prowess in a time of economic prosperity stemmed from a variety of factors: a home-state advantage that allowed him to tap wealthy Texas backers; strong support from fellow Republican governors; the national network of financial backers who had supported his father's previous presidential campaigns; and the hunger of Republicans to return to the White House.[9] Why did this hunger lead so many to settle on Bush? His landslide reelection in 1998 as governor of Texas had exalted Bush in national Republican circles. He had won 69 percent of the vote, including 49 percent from typically Democratic Hispanic voters. Bush's huge win and the contrasting setback for Republicans in the congressional elections prompted many Republican leaders to urge the party to unite behind this rising political star from outside Washington. Bush's presumed ability to connect with voters commended him, as did an approach to government that he called "compassionate conservatism." In Bush's view, Republicans needed to put a "compassionate face" on their conservative philosophy, because "people think oftentimes that Republicans are mean-spirited folks. Which is not true, but that's what people think." Bush contended that his Texas record indicated that he was capable of reaching out to Hispanics, blacks, and working-class Catholics without forsaking conservative ideology or alienating core Republican voters. Whether or not the compassionate conservative image won over many voters in these groups, it benefited Bush among white moderates: "He doesn't come across as one of these southern, Christian Coalition, right-wing-nut Republican candidates. So white suburbanites, especially white suburban women, who are looking for someone who is reasonable can support him." [10] As a general election strategy, compassionate conservatism had strong promise. Republicans would need to mobilize their conservative partisan base but also would need to reach to the center to avoid losing as they had in 1992 and 1996. Bush intended to run a centrist campaign.

Bush's early gathering of Republican support was all the more impressive because he was not yet highly visible nationally and his issue positions were still largely unknown. As political scientist David Magleby noted, "He's so untested and undefined, but the Republican elite have in an extraordinary way rallied to this candidate." [11] Marla Romash, the deputy chairwoman of Gore's campaign, put a more partisan slant on things: "I think you're seeing a lot of people writing a blank check to a blank slate." [12]

Bush's unprecedented fund-raising allowed him to refuse federal matching funds (the federal campaign finance law allows the federal Treasury to match the first $250 of each individual contribution to a candidate during the preconvention period).[13] Candidates in 2000 who qualified under the law could each receive up to $16.5 million in matching funds. By forsaking these funds, Bush did not have to abide by the law's strict state-by-state spending limits ($1.16 million in Iowa, for example, and $0.66 million in New Hampshire) or by its overall preconvention spending limit of $33.8 million.[14] Bush was, however, subject to the $1,000 contribution limit from individual donors.

Bush's decision to refuse federal funds was especially important because Forbes was expected to forgo matching funds again, financing his presidential campaign with his vast personal fortune. In 1996, Forbes had spent $37 million of his own money, hammering Bob Dole in attack ads. Bush, not bound by spending limits, could respond in kind to such a barrage.[15]

Pundits anticipated a big-spending campaign for the Republican nomination, with only Bush and Forbes having the resources to compete. Front-loading meant that candidates subject to the spending limits could be hitting the overall limit in the middle of the primaries, as Dole had done in 1996, or, worse yet, could be broke by early March, just when expensive states such as California, New York, and Ohio held their primaries. Moreover, the early scheduling of so many delegate-rich primaries raised the risk inherent in any challenger strategy that counted on early success to boost contributions for later primaries and caucuses.

For Bush, then, front-loading suggested the advisability of saying no to matching funds and avoiding spending limits. Forgoing matching funds also would avoid the problems faced by Bob Dole in 1996; he sewed up the nomination early but hit the overall spending ceiling in April, months before the Republican convention. Although the national Republican Party had tried to take up the slack by spending millions on issue ads featuring Dole, the Clinton-Gore campaign, having faced no primary challenge, was able to roll out an advertising campaign that gave it an enduring lead. In July 1999, Bush noted, "I'm mindful of what happened in 1996 and I'm not going to let it happen to me. I'm going to win."[16]

Among Democrats, fund-raising provided additional evidence of the threat Bradley could pose to Gore. Bradley tapped into donors who were disenchanted with the Clinton administration and with Gore as its heir apparent. Although Clinton had won the presidency twice, his "New Democrat" move toward the center of the political spectrum had left some Democrats pining for a return to more traditional liberal party principles. In the end, though, neither Gore nor Bradley gained a critical early advantage over the other through fund-raising. After Bradley raised twice the amount Gore raised in the last quarter of 1999, each began the election year with about $19 million in cash on hand.[17]

Endorsements

Bush's front-runner status stemmed in part from his numerous endorsements by Republican Party officials and officeholders. Bush started gathering endorsements early. When Elizabeth Dole stepped down as American Red Cross president in January 1999 to crank up her presidential campaign, she found that her calls to line up support were already too late. McCain faced the same problem. By February 2000, Bush enjoyed the backing of 26 fellow Republican governors, 39 senators, and 175 House members, in sharp contrast to McCain's backing from no governors, 4 fellow Republican senators, and 7 House members.[18]

Broad-based party backing provided Bush with sizable benefits, especially in view of the front-loaded calendar, but it also carried a price. Although Bush ran on his record as governor of Texas, the strong embrace by the Republican establishment eroded his fresh-faced, Washington-outsider status. Ironically, McCain, a three-term senator, became the candidate with the outsider image.

Among Democrats, Bradley received a small number of endorsements from political figures in his party such as Sen. Daniel Patrick Moynihan of New York. Basketball superstar Michael Jordan, making his first political endorsement, also came out in support of Bradley, as did several other sports figures. But Gore's eight years as vice president, toiling in the vineyards of the party, paid off to give him a strong edge in endorsements from Democratic Party and elected officials.

The Iowa Straw Poll, August 14

In August 1999, the Iowa state Republican Party staged a fund-raising event that turned into an early test of the candidate strengths. Most candidates used the nonbinding popularity contest, which had no direct effect on the state's delegate selection caucuses in 2000, as an opportunity to display their political muscle. The rules favored candidates with financial resources plentiful enough to mobilize their supporters. Iowa residents who would be of voting age in November 2000 could, upon payment of a $25 fee, register their preference among the Republican presidential candidates. Campaigns paid the fees, the state Republican Party profited, and the 24,000 participants backed the candidates in this order: George W. Bush, 31 percent; Steve Forbes, 21 percent; Elizabeth Dole, 14 percent; Gary Bauer, the former head of the Family Research Council, 9 percent; commentator Pat Buchanan, 7 percent; Lamar Alexander, 6 percent; former ambassador Alan Keyes, 5 percent; Dan Quayle, 4 percent; and Sen. Orrin G. Hatch of Utah, 2 percent. McCain did not compete, because he could not keep up financially with his main opponents. Forbes spent almost $2 million on the straw poll, Bush about $750,000, and Dole $250,000.[19] Bush had spent relatively little time campaigning in Iowa, relying instead on a well-financed organization to turn out his supporters. His first-place finish demonstrated his front-runner status, but his mere ten-percentage-point victory confirmed an earlier reminder by one Bush backer, "Bush has to win the nomination. He's not going to get it on a silver platter."[20]

Although the media interpreted the Iowa straw poll as a boost for Elizabeth Dole's campaign, she failed to capitalize on her success. Organizational turmoil did not help her cause: she lost two spokesmen in September alone. The only female candidate in the campaign, she also suffered from fundraising that never exceeded one-tenth of the Bush intake.[21]

In the weeks after the Iowa straw poll, Alexander, Dole, and Quayle dropped out of the race, claiming that fund-raising difficulties inhibited their ability to get their message out. Buchanan bolted to the Reform Party later in the fall.[22]

Polling

According to the national polls in 1999, Gore and Bush were the preferred Democratic and Republican nominees of their parties. But state polls in the critical early states, particularly New Hampshire, suggested that Bradley and McCain might derail the front-runners, triggering a dynamic that could conceivably win them their parties' nominations. [23] Voting in the nominating process proceeds state by state, and the early states looked uncertain for the front-runners.

Bush, who initially thought his main challenge would be to head off the conservative Steve Forbes for the nomination, found over the course of 1999 that his strongest opponent was likely to be McCain. Before declaring for the presidency, McCain, a former fighter pilot, mounted a book tour for his best-selling memoir, which chronicled his years as a prisoner of war in Vietnam. A military hero with a famous temper, McCain struck a chord with voters eager for change. His plain-speaking promise that "I will never lie to you" was reminiscent of the 1976 politically appealing pledge that presidential candidate

Jimmy Carter made in the wake of Watergate scandal. McCain also offered
an alternative to voters who were not yet ready to embrace Bush as firmly as
he had been embraced by the Republican establishment. McCain skipped the
Iowa caucuses to concentrate on the other early states, starting with New
Hampshire. The idea was to get a sling shot effect from early wins that would
counter the Bush advantages in finance, organization, and endorsements in the
later primaries and caucuses.[24] Polls suggested that these early wins were within McCain's reach.

In the Democratic camp, Gore's political strength had frightened away
almost all would-be challengers, inadvertently elevating Bradley into a one-
on-one contest with the vice president. A former National Basketball Association star with the New York Knicks, a Rhodes Scholar, and a former senator from New Jersey, Bradley sought to raise the level of political discourse
by not stooping to the sniping and negativity characteristic of many campaigns. But Bradley, like Gore, was not a scintillating speaker. Indeed, according to one observer, both were "right up there with Calvin Coolidge and
Walter F. Mondale in the deadpan derby."[25] Although not easily compart-
mentalized ideologically, Bradley challenged Gore from the left, looking to
reenergize the liberal Democratic coalition. For Democratic voters with
misgivings about Gore, Bradley was the only alternative. And many voters
wanted to distance themselves from the scandals of the Clinton administration, however unfair it might be link those scandals to Gore.[26]

Gore found Bradley a more challenging opponent than he had anticipated. Throughout most of his 1999 campaign, Gore seemed listless, unable
to make appreciable headway. His desire to impress audiences sometimes led
to statements that were easily ridiculed, such as his claim that he "took the
initiative in creating the internet."[27] After a September poll showed Bradley
pulling even in New Hampshire, Gore moved his campaign headquarters
from Washington to Nashville, reshuffled his campaign organization, and
went on the attack against Bradley.[28]

Candidate Debates

Bush's front-runner status encountered turbulence in the presidential
debates among the Republican candidates during the fall of 1999. Appearing to be the inevitable nominee works for a while, but, as Bush learned, it
soon requires supporting evidence. Because front-runners are expected to do
very well, evidence to the contrary is seized upon by political opponents as
well as by a press corps more interested in covering a competitive, newsworthy contest than a coronation.[29] At first, Bush skipped the Republican
debates, a common strategy for front-runners. When he did take part he was
cautious and sometimes awkward, often repeating lines from his campaign
speeches that were topically remote from the questions he was asked. Such
"debating" left many supporters wondering about Bush's ability to endure
the rigors of the long haul and led some to suspect he might not be up to the

challenge. Bush recovered from his early lackluster performances, but the concerns lingered.[30]

In the fall of 1999, when Gore realized that his front-runner strategy of ignoring Bradley was not working, he challenged his opponent to frequent debates. In those contests, Gore attacked the details of Bradley's proposals, especially his national health plan, and questioned Bradley's leadership ability, all the while presenting an image of himself as a leader who would "stay and fight." Bradley's initial reluctance to respond to Gore's attacks left the impression that Bradley would not stand up for his positions. Gore's candidacy slowly rebounded.[31]

Media Coverage

The newsworthiness of the 2000 presidential nominations, as measured by coverage in the ABC, CBS, and NBC evening newscasts, declined from that evident in 1996. Both parties had contested nominations in 2000, but in 1996 only the Republican nomination had been up for grabs. Yet during the first eleven months of 1999, the network evenings news programs gave only half as much airtime to the nomination contests as they had four years earlier—six hours, forty-two minutes, from January through November 1999, as compared with thirteen hours, fourteen minutes, during the same period in 1995.

Although reduced from 1996, the networks' coverage of the campaign, particularly its tone, focus, and quantity, was politically significant. As political scientist John H. Aldrich has noted, "The amount of coverage candidates receive in the media is itself a [campaign] resource."[32] In 1999, front-runners fared better than challengers: of 256 presidential nomination stories, Bush (86) and Gore (73) were featured in considerably more than their main challengers, McCain (17) and Bradley (40). The content of the news stories can be categorized by their coverage of each candidate's viability ("horse race" judgments about the probability a candidate will become president) and desirability (positive and negative assessments of the candidates by news sources). Overall, the tone of comments about desirability was positive. Bush and McCain each received primarily positive evaluations in on-air opinions from sources and reporters—63 and 58 percent, respectively. Evaluations of electoral viability were more favorable for Bush (91 percent), although McCain received a noteworthy 65 percent. On the Democratic side, nightly network news coverage in 1999 reflected the political reality of the Democratic contest—Gore was in deep trouble. Although Gore received more favorable comments on desirability (66 percent positive) than Bradley (51 percent), Bradley topped Gore in network coverage about viability: Bradley 86 percent positive, Gore only 35 percent.

Critics fault news coverage that focuses more on the horse race aspects of an election than on the substance of the candidates' records, policies, personal character, and political performance. Television network news coverage in 1999 was grist for these critics' mill. Of the 456 evaluative statements about Bush, 53 percent concerned his political viability and only 14 percent discussed his performance in office or his stands on the issues. Of the 303 evaluative statements about Gore, 46 percent addressed his viability and only 14 percent dwelled on his performance as vice president or his stand on issues.[33]

Election Year 2000

Both McCain and Bradley counted heavily on early wins to establish momentum against their front-running opponents. In presidential primaries and caucuses, a "better-than-expected" showing by a candidate can translate into momentum for the campaign, often in the form of more favorable media coverage and a hike in campaign contributions. The momentum then heightens the candidate's prospects for later victories. Jimmy Carter's 1976 campaign, in which he rose from obscurity to capture the Democratic nomination, illustrates this pattern. Gary Hart's near-toppling of Democratic front-runner Walter F. Mondale in 1984, however, shows that even considerable momentum may not be enough to secure victory.[34]

In 2000, Iowa, New Hampshire, and Super Tuesday towered over the nomination landscape, with South Carolina and Michigan also looming large for Republicans (see Tables 2-1 through 2-4, pages 38–41). Understanding the dynamics of the 2000 nominations requires a chronological discussion of these vital contests.

Iowa, January 24

Any attempt to set standards for judging success in a primary or caucus is always a struggle between the press and the candidates. The Bush campaign convinced the press that the threshold Bush had to exceed in the Iowa caucus was the strongest showing ever achieved in Iowa by a Republican— Robert Dole's 37 percent in 1988. Bush succeeded, gaining 41 percent of the vote (Table 2-2). Forbes placed a strong second with 30 percent, but the surprisingly strong finish of Alan Keyes with 14 percent kept Forbes from claiming credibly that he had emerged as the sole conservative challenge to Bush.[35]

McCain skipped Iowa, husbanding his resources to campaign extensively in New Hampshire and to a lesser degree in South Carolina. (He justified this to the press by contending that his stance against ethanol subsidies would rankle Iowa voters.) New Hampshire, with its tendency to back mavericks against establishment candidates and its rules that allow independents to vote in party primaries (these are called open primaries), seemed friendlier territory than Iowa. Momentum gained by upsetting Bush in New Hampshire could then reverberate helpfully in South Carolina if McCain laid the groundwork there.

In the end, McCain's absence from Iowa devalued Bush's victory. The standard for the two candidates was not the same. As the front-runner Bush was expected to run well in all states. McCain, as a challenger, had a freer hand (at least in the early going) to pick and choose states in which to battle Bush.

On the Democratic side, Bradley spent more time campaigning in Iowa than did Gore (fifty-nine to forty-one days, respectively), but Gore dashed Bradley's hopes for an upset or even a promising showing, crushing him by 63 percent to 35 percent (Table 2-4).[36] Even before the caucus voting, Bradley explained his lagging poll numbers in Iowa by bemoaning the difficulty of toppling a candidate with broad party backing. "We're up against entrenched power," Bradley said of Gore. "Anytime somebody has the president of the United States backing him because he was loyal to the president, loyalty's returned. Anytime you have someone who has the Democratic National Committee leadership and most of the big Democratic fundraisers and the leadership of organized labor, and arrives on *Air Force Two,* that is entrenched power."[37] Gore's revamped campaign had put Bradley on the defensive and cast Gore as a fighter. Bradley was slow to respond to Gore and lackluster in organizing to get out the vote.[38]

New Hampshire, February 1

The New Hampshire results upset the Republican front-runner but not the Democratic one. Bradley, contending that Iowa with its time-consuming caucus rewarded "entrenched power," claimed to prefer traditional contests such as the New Hampshire primary.[39] Bradley nearly won New Hampshire, but the result, measured against earlier surveys that showed him leading, did not provide him with the boost he needed. Gore edged out Bradley 50 percent to 46 percent (Table 2-3). Independents backed Bradley over Gore 56 percent to 41 percent, but there were not enough of them (40 percent) to overcome Gore's edge among Democrats, who made up 56 percent of the voters and split 59–41 for Gore. Attitudes toward the president influenced the voters' choices: most of those disapproving of Clinton as a person (54 percent) voted for Bradley but not enough to offset Gore's more lopsided support from those approving of the president as a person.

The New Hampshire loss dealt Bradley a blow from which he would never recover. Lacking the lift of an early win, Bradley would have to clash with Gore in states less hospitable to his challenge. And making matters worse, in the five weeks after New Hampshire there were seven Republican but no Democratic primaries or caucuses. During those five weeks, Bradley's struggle against Gore was overshadowed by the Bush-McCain battle. Bush and McCain received five times more nightly network news coverage than did Gore and Bradley.[40]

Bradley's narrow loss in New Hampshire contrasted poorly with McCain's substantial win over Bush in the state's open Republican primary; the vote was 49 percent to 30 percent. (Forbes managed only 13 percent; see Table 2-1.)[41] Non-Republican voters gave McCain the edge by more than

Table 2-1   2000 Republican Presidential Primary Results

	Date	Turnout	Bush	McCain	Keyes	Others
New Hampshire	Feb. 1	238,206	30.4%	48.5%	6.4%	14.7%
Delaware	Feb. 8	30,060	50.7	25.4	3.8	20.0
South Carolina	Feb. 19	573,101	53.4	41.9	4.5	0.2
Arizona	Feb. 22	322,669	35.7	60.0	3.6	0.7
Michigan	Feb. 22	1,276,770	43.1	51.0	4.6	1.4
Virginia	Feb. 29	664,093	52.8	43.9	3.1	0.3
Washington	Feb. 29	491,148	57.8	38.9	2.4	0.9
California	March 7	2,847,921	60.6	34.7	4.0	0.7
Connecticut	March 7	178,985	46.3	48.7	3.3	1.7
Georgia	March 7	643,188	66.9	27.8	4.6	0.6
Maine	March 7	96,624	51.0	44.0	3.1	1.9
Maryland	March 7	376,034	56.2	36.2	6.7	1.0
Massachusetts	March 7	501,951	31.8	64.7	2.5	1.0
Missouri	March 7	475,363	57.9	35.3	5.7	1.0
New York	March 7		51.0	43.4	3.3	2.3
Ohio	March 7	1,397,528	58.0	37.0	4.0	1.1
Rhode Island	March 7	36,120	36.5	60.2	2.6	0.8
Vermont	March 7	81,355	35.3	60.3	2.7	1.7
Colorado	March 10	180,655	64.7	27.1	6.6	1.6
Utah	March 10	91,053	63.3	14.0	21.3	1.4
Florida	March 14	699,503	73.8	19.9	4.6	1.6
Louisiana	March 14	102,912	83.6	8.9	5.7	1.8
Mississippi	March 14	114,979	87.9	5.4	5.6	1.0
Oklahoma	March 14	124,809	79.1	10.4	9.3	1.2
Tennessee	March 14	250,791	77.0	14.5	6.7	1.7
Texas	March 14	1,126,757	87.5	7.1	3.9	1.5
Illinois	March 21	736,857	67.4	21.5	9.0	2.1
Pennsylvania	April 4	643,085	73.5	22.7	—	3.9
Wisconsin	April 4	495,769	69.2	18.1	9.9	2.8
Indiana	May 2	406,664	81.2	18.8	—	—
North Carolina	May 2	322,517	78.6	10.9	7.9	2.7
Dist. Of Columbia	May 2	2,433	72.8	24.4		2.8
Nebraska	May 9	185,758	78.2	15.1	6.5	—
West Virginia	May 9	109,404	79.6	12.9	4.8	2.8
Oregon	May 16	349,831	83.6	—	13.4	3.0
Arkansas	May 23	44,573	80.2	—	19.8	—
Idaho	May 23	158,446	73.5	—	19.1	7.4
Kentucky	May 23	91,323	83.0	6.3	4.7	5.9
Alabama	June 6	203,079	84.2	—	11.5	4.2
Montana	June 6	113,671	77.6	—	18.3	4.1
New Jersey	June 6	240,810	83.6	—	16.4	—
New Mexico	June 6	75,230	82.6	10.1	6.4	0.8
South Dakota	June 6	45,279	78.2	13.8	7.7	0.3
Total		17,147,304	63.2%	29.8%	5.3%	1.6%

Source: Rhodes Cook, *America Votes 2000* (Washington, D.C.: CQ Press, 2001).

Notes: "—" indicates that the candidate was not listed on the ballot or that votes for the candidate or others were not tabulated separately. Turnout figures were not available for New York Republicans. Write-in vote figures were not available for Pennsylvania. Results are based on official returns except for Arkansas, Indiana, Massachusetts, and North Carolina.

Table 2-2 2000 Republican Caucus Results

	Date	Turnout	Bush	McCain	Keyes	Others
Iowa	Jan. 24	87,233	41.0%	4.7%	14.2%	40.0%
Alaska	Jan. 24	4,330	36.3	9.5	9.5	44.8
Hawaii	Feb. 7					
North Dakota	Feb. 29	9,066	75.7	18.9	5.3	0.0
Minnesota	March 7	18,390	62.7	17.4	19.9	0.0
Washington	March 7	—	80.0	15.3	3.3	1.3
Wyoming	March 10	944	77.5	10.3	11.7	0.5
Nevada	Feb.–Mar.					
Montana	April					
Kansas	May 25					

Source: Rhodes Cook, *America Votes 2000* (Washington, D.C.: CQ Press, 2001).

Notes: "—" indicates that the candidate was not listed on the ballot or that votes for the candidate or others were not tabulated separately. For Washington the percentages shown are based on the county convention delegates won by the candidate. Caucus results are not available for Kansas, Montana, and Nevada. No vote was taken in Hawaii. Turnout figures were not available for Washington.

three to one, and McCain almost matched Bush among the slight majority of primary voters who considered themselves Republicans. Among conservative voters, McCain matched Bush's support.[42]

McCain had devoted considerable effort to New Hampshire. He spent sixty-one days there to Bush's thirty-two, held 114 town hall meetings, and shook hands with an estimated one of every twenty state residents.[43] Bush banked more on media buys and organizational support from the state party.[44] McCain also excelled in courting the press. He traveled between campaign stops on a bus, "The Straight Talk Express," in which he was in constant conversation with reporters. Greater press access to McCain may have paid off in more favorable coverage of his candidacy.[45]

Within days of his New Hampshire victory, McCain made the cover of the three major news weeklies: *Time, Newsweek,* and *U.S. News and World Report.* The win invigorated his campaign fund-raising: he quickly raised $2.5 million through his Web site alone, a sum that compared favorably with Bush's in-flow and indicated how quickly momentum can shift in a presidential campaign.

The New Hampshire loss, especially its unexpectedly large size, sent the Bush campaign into a tailspin. And Bush's win with 51 percent in Delaware the next week was of little help—McCain received 25 percent without even campaigning there. In mid-February, the Bush campaign was floundering, having already spent nearly $50 million and still spending at a rate of almost $3 million a week.[46] The only Bush wins had come in states where McCain did not compete. Polls had Bush and McCain evenly matched in upcoming primaries in South Carolina and Michigan. Even fund-raisers for Bush were anxious, wondering how many more $1,000 donors could be found and how so much money could have been spent for so little gain.[47]

Table 2-3 2000 Democratic Presidential Primary Results

	Date	Turnout	Bradley	Gore	Others
New Hampshire	Feb. 1	154,639	45.6%	49.7%	4.7%
Delaware	Feb. 5	11,141	40.2	57.2	2.6
Michigan	Feb. 22	44,850	—	—	100.0
Washington	Feb. 29	297,001	31.4	68.2	0.4
Connecticut	March 7	177,301	41.5	55.4	3.0
Maine	March 7	64,279	41.3	54.0	4.7
Maryland	March 7	507,462	28.5	67.3	4.2
Massachusetts	March 7	570,074	37.3	59.9	2.8
New York	March 7	974,463	33.5	65.6	0.9
Rhode Island	March 7	46,844	40.6	57.2	2.2
Vermont	March 7	49,283	43.9	54.3	1.8
Missouri	March 7	265,489	33.6	64.6	1.8
Ohio	March 7	978,512	24.7	73.6	1.7
Georgia	March 7	284,431	16.2	83.8	—
California	March 7	2,654,114	18.2	81.2	0.6
Colorado	March 10	88,735	23.3	71.4	5.3
Utah	March 10	15,687	20.1	79.9	—
Arizona	March 11	86,762	18.9	77.9	3.2
Florida	March 14	551,995	18.2	81.8	—
Louisiana	March 14	157,551	19.9	73.0	7.1
Mississippi	March 14	88,602	8.6	89.6	1.8
Oklahoma	March 14	134,850	25.4	68.7	5.8
Tennessee	March 14	215,203	5.3	92.1	2.6
Texas	March 14	786,890	16.3	80.2	3.4
Illinois	March 21	809,648	14.2	84.3	1.4
Pennsylvania	April 4	704,150	20.8	74.6	4.6
Wisconsin	April 4	371,196	8.8	88.5	2.7
Indiana	May 2	293,172	21.9	74.9	3.1
North Carolina	May 2	544,922	18.3	70.4	11.3
Dist. of Columbia	May 2	19,417	—	95.9	4.1
Nebraska	May 9	105,271	26.5	70.0	3.6
West Virginia	May 9	253,310	18.4	72.0	9.6
Oregon	May 16	354,594	—	84.9	15.1
Arkansas	May 23	246,900	—	78.5	21.5
Idaho	May 23	35,688	—	75.7	24.3
Kentucky	May 23	220,279	14.7	71.3	14.1
Alabama	June 6	278,527	—	77.0	23.0
Montana	June 6	87,867	—	77.9	22.1
New Jersey	June 6	378,272	—	94.9	5.1
New Mexico	June 6	132,280	20.6	74.6	4.8
South Dakota	June 6				
Total		14,041,651	19.9%	75.7%	4.4%

Source: Rhodes Cook, *America Votes 2000* (Washington, D.C.: CQ Press, 2001).

Notes: "—" indicates that the candidate was not listed on the ballot or that votes for the candidate or others were not tabulated separately. Turnout figures were not available for New York. Write-in vote figures were not available for Pennsylvania. Results are based on official returns except for Arkansas, Indiana, Massachusetts, and North Carolina. No vote was taken in South Dakota.

Table 2-4   2000 Democratic Caucus Results

	Date	Turnout	Gore	Bradley	Other
Iowa	Jan. 24	61,000	63.4%	34.9%	1.7%
Hawaii	March 7	1,364	79.8	17.4	2.8
Idaho	March 7	1,500	62.8	33.0	4.2
North Dakota	March 7	2,291	77.7	21.7	0.6
Washington	March 7		68.4	28.2	3.4
South Carolina	March 9	7,519	92.2	1.9	5.8
Michigan	March 11	19,160	82.7	16.3	1.0
Minnesota	March 11	10,764	74.2	14.2	11.7
Nevada	March 12	1,089	90.2	2.2	7.6
Texas	March 14				
Wyoming	March 25	581	85.4	4.8	9.8
Delaware	March 27	800	100.0	—	—
Virginia	April 15	10,000	96.0	—	4.0
Alaska	April 22				
Kansas	May 6	566	95.6	—	4.4

Source: Rhodes Cook, *America Votes 2000* (Washington, D.C.: CQ Press, 2001).

Notes: "—" indicates that the candidate was not listed on the ballot or that votes for the candidate or others were not tabulated separately. Turnout figures were not available for Washington; caucus results were not available for Texas or Alaska. Turnout was estimated in Iowa, Idaho, Delaware, and Virginia. Percentages reflect the candidate preferences of caucus attenders except in certain states, in which the percentages reflect shares of the following won by the candidate: Delaware and Idaho (state convention delegates), Virginia (congressional district and state convention delegates), and Washington (legislative and county convention delegates).

McCain's candidacy thwarted Bush's plan to secure the nomination with a centrist campaign. Bush now complained about McCain's strategy of using support from Democrats and independents to gain the Republican nomination, even though such outreach would be essential for his own victory in the general election. Yet to continue to challenge Bush, McCain would need greater support from Republicans. Although some states had open primaries in which non-Republicans could participate, more states had closed primaries limited to Republicans voters.

South Carolina, February 19

After New Hampshire, the next major McCain-Bush contest was in South Carolina. The primary was open to non-Republicans, which seemed to favor McCain. But South Carolina's strong social conservatism and influential religious right presented Bush with advantages he needed to counter McCain's momentum out of New Hampshire.

Bush used the two weeks between the New Hampshire and South Carolina primaries to retool his campaign, de-emphasizing talk of "compassionate conservatism" and stressing in a new slogan that he, unlike McCain, was "A Reformer with Results." To court South Carolina voters, Bush turned sharply to the right: he made his first stop after New Hampshire at Bob Jones University, a religiously conservative school in Greenville widely criticized for its anti-Catholic views and ban on interracial dating.

Bush also went on the attack. A Bush ad depicted McCain, who chaired the Senate Commerce Committee, as a senator who "solicits money from lobbyists with interests before his committee and pressures agencies on behalf of contributors."[48] McCain then blundered by running a television ad of his own that said Bush "twists the truth like Clinton." For many Republicans, McCain's charge was overkill. Bush cried foul, taking umbrage at the attack on his honor, and McCain pulled the ad, promising to stick to his previous pledge to mount a positive campaign. As Darrell M. West, a Brown University expert on political advertising, noted, McCain "doesn't have the money to put on a saturation negative campaign of his own. So it's probably better for him to call a cease-fire and get the benefit of that."[49] Unfortunately for McCain, Bush refused to join the cease-fire and escalated his own attacks. By not counterattacking, McCain handed Bush an opportunity to define him in the voters' minds.

When they finally had their say, voters handed the state to Bush, 53 percent to 42 percent. For McCain, who was relying on early momentum to counter Bush's advantages in organization and finances, the loss in South Carolina was extremely disappointing. Republicans made up 60 percent of the primary voters, and Bush carried them by 69 percent to 26 percent. (McCain's advantage among the rest was 64 percent to 30 percent.) McCain partially blamed his South Carolina defeat on Bush's big spending: "One of the reasons why we had a little trouble getting our message out in South Carolina—because we were outspent 5, 6, 10 to 1."[50] Also, the campaign's growing negativity hurt McCain more than Bush, tarnishing his fresh, heroic image by the resort to politics-as-usual. As one account put it: "McCain's captivating image as a straight-talking, politically muscular reformer began slowly to suffer as he dived headlong into a bitter, boyish back-and-forth fight over campaign etiquette and fairness in advertising—a fight that would grow nastier and, for McCain, more distracting, right up until the end."[51]

Michigan, February 22

South Carolina had voted on Saturday, February 19. Michigan would vote three days later, on Tuesday, February 22. In those three days the campaign turned even nastier. McCain phone banks called Michigan voters with a "Catholic Voter Alert" to inform them of Bush's visit to Bob Jones University and to suggest that Bush was anti-Catholic. McCain first denied and then later acknowledged that his campaign was behind the calls, further damaging his reputation for straight talk. Michigan voters also received taped phone calls backing Bush from religious right leader Pat Robertson. The calls accused McCain of being a threat to unborn children and religious freedom.

Bush, banking on the strong support of Michigan governor John Engler, had touted the Michigan primary as his "firewall" against a surging McCain. As a result, the Bush forces were stunned when McCain won there, 51 percent to 43 percent.

Super Tuesday, March 7

On Super Tuesday, March 7, Republicans held eleven state primaries and two caucuses; Democrats held eleven primaries and four caucuses. The huge number of delegates at stake on March 7 made it highly desirable for candidates to have momentum going into Super Tuesday. Possessing the resources to run everywhere had its rewards: the advantages to Bush of waging a national campaign began registering the week before Super Tuesday. On February 29, Bush racked up wins in North Dakota, Virginia, and Washington. Despite an open primary in Virginia, McCain was unable to defeat Bush there and so gained no delegates in the winner-take-all contest. The sweep added helpfully to Bush's delegate total, as had wins over the previous weekends in three U.S. territories and Puerto Rico.

The day before the Virginia primary, McCain had lashed out at the religious right, a formidable group in the Republican coalition. In doing so, McCain took on two leaders of the religious right, Pat Robertson and Jerry Falwell, labeling them "agents of intolerance." The next day, on the Straight Talk Express, McCain escalated that epithet to "forces of evil"—later explaining what had not been obvious at the time, that he had been joking. In response, Christian conservatives mobilized, turning out to help Bush beat back McCain in Virginia and later primaries.[52]

On March 2, McCain admitted that his campaign had gotten off message and promised a solution: "I'm going to try to keep it on the issues and not get bogged down in this tit-for-tat kind of thing."[53] But the Bush campaign and its allies vexed McCain with new ads. One Bush campaign commercial accused McCain of not supporting breast cancer research, even though McCain's sister was a breast cancer survivor. Wealthy individuals and well-heeled groups can run ads independently of a candidate's campaign, advocating issue positions but not making an overt, candidate-specific "vote for" or "vote against" pitch. One independent ad criticized McCain and praised Bush's environmental record; a wealthy Texas backer of Bush paid $2.5 million to run the ad in California, Ohio, and New York in the days leading up to Super Tuesday.[54] Plainly unhappy, McCain railed against these ad tactics, which were crowding out his own message of reform and openness.

On Super Tuesday, Bush won nine states, including California, New York, and Ohio. McCain won only the four New England states. These results, in combination with the delegates Bush had gained from his seven previous wins (McCain had only three previous wins) and Bush's greater organizational and financial strength in the contests that lay ahead, prompted McCain to suspend his campaign on March 9. In withdrawing, McCain congratulated Bush but stopped short of endorsing him.[55]

Meanwhile, in the Democratic camp Gore kept Bradley winless on Super Tuesday by sweeping all fifteen primaries and caucuses with strong majority support. Bradley had once led Gore in Massachusetts and New

York, but Gore carried those states by 60 and 65 percent, respectively. Desperate for a boost before Super Tuesday, Bradley had spent six days campaigning in Washington State, hoping to top Gore in a presidential preference primary (no delegates were at stake) on February 29. But Bradley failed there as well, losing to Gore by a two-to-one margin.

Like McCain, Bradley withdrew two days after Super Tuesday. He said that he would "support" Gore and even campaign for him, but he refrained from using the word *endorse*. When asked about Gore's campaign, Bradley was critical, referring to "distortions and negativity."

The promise of Bradley's campaign, which seemed so great in the fall of 1999, had faded in the face of too many missed opportunities. The Democratic calendar gave him no place to go after New Hampshire. Bradley seemed too cerebral and detached, unable to connect tellingly with voters. He made little headway against Gore whose roughly similar issue positions were accompanied by, in Bradley's words, the "politics of a thousand promises and a thousand attacks." Unfortunately for Bradley, Gore's tactics spurred many Democratic voters to see the vice president as someone willing to fight for his beliefs.[56]

The Nominations Decided, the Primaries and Caucuses Continue

Once the nominations were settled, Bush moved into a general election mode of campaigning. Gore seemed relatively unfocused and adrift as Bush effectively seized the political center, adopting a moderate stance and moving away from the more conservative positions he had taken in South Carolina.[57] Outlining policy proposals on issues such as education, Social Security reform, and Medicare, Bush sought to reduce the traditional Democratic advantage on these issues.

The lack of an aggressive response from Gore during the spring helped Bush. He worked hard to yoke Gore to Clinton, contending that the election was about the end of the Clinton-Gore era and promising to restore integrity to the White House. Bush also pledged to sustain economic prosperity and spread its benefits more widely.[58] Despite his short time on the national scene, having only been elected as governor of Texas in 1994 and 1998, Bush appeared to the public as the stronger leader.[59]

The vice presidency can be—and proved to be for Gore—a difficult position from which to demonstrate strong leadership qualities. As one political scientist has observed, "The public that values loyalty in a vice president disdains that quality as soon as he bids to become president."[60] Gore labored under the handicap of being vice president to a president whose job performance garnered the public's high approval but whose personal conduct did not. Although Gore was an exceptionally influential vice president, credit for Clinton administration successes eluded him, while attacks for the administration's shortcomings tended to stick. Gore's fund-raising zeal in the 1996 campaign raised legal questions, and his strong defense of the president at a postimpeachment rally of Democratic members of Congress (Clinton "will be regarded in the history books as one of our greatest presidents") seemed more loyal than accurate. Gore backers took consolation in the fact that Reagan in 1980, Bush in 1988, and Clinton in 1992 had all trailed in spring surveys but won at the polls in November.

Miscues compounded Gore's difficulties in finding his footing for the general election.[61] For example, in late March Gore parted with administration policy on the deportation of Elián Gonzàlez, a six-year-old Cuban refugee, contending that Elián should be permitted to stay in the United States. Gore was widely regarded as pandering to predominantly Republican Cuban American voters in Florida, a battleground state for the general election. Even Democrats took issue with Gore's position, and his image as a leader took another hit.[62]

Outside the Two Major Parties

Both major party nominees had reason to be concerned about third parties in 2000 With the general election expected to be close, minor parties could siphon critical votes away from a major party. Bush, by running a centrist campaign, ran the risk of alienating the Republican right and fueling a conservative third-party candidacy that could cost the Republicans support in the general election. The prospect of a Reform Party candidacy by Pat Buchanan raised this specter. Democrats faced a kindred threat from the left in the person of Green Party nominee Ralph Nader.

Third-party candidates sought to capitalize on the discontent roused by H. Ross Perot in 1996 when he ran as the Reform Party nominee and in 1992 when he ran as an independent candidate. The Reform Party nomination was worth fighting for in 2000. Perot had established the party in 1996. His 8 percent showing that year, down from 19 percent in 1992, entitled the Reform candidate to $12.6 million in federal funds for the 2000 general election. Jesse Ventura, a former professional wrestler who had been elected governor of Minnesota on the Reform Party ticket in 1998, considered seeking the party's presidential nomination for 2000. In February of that year, however, he quit the party in disgust, contending that it was "totally dysfunctional" and "unworthy of the support of the American people."[63]

His defection left Buchanan and John Hagelin, a physicist who also was the nominee of the Natural Law Party, to battle it out. Buchanan ultimately triumphed at a bitterly divisive party convention in August, gaining legal right to the $12.6 million. But his general election campaign was seriously hampered by the intraparty feuding, much to the relief of Republican partisans.[64]

The Democrats fared less well with the minor parties in 2000. The Green Party nominated consumer advocate Ralph Nader, who maintained his political independence by refusing to join the party. Nader had run for president in 1996 but not very seriously, spending less than $5,000 on his campaign. In 2000, Nader campaigned actively and hit hard with his environmental and anticorporate themes. The possibility that Nader might corral enough potential Gore supporters to cost the vice president victory in a close general election contest loomed ominously for Democrats.

The National Conventions

In recent years, the greater proportion of pledged delegates selected in primaries has transformed national conventions into ratifying assemblies rather than deliberative bodies that choose the nominees.[65] Nevertheless, conventions constitute one of the best opportunities for the newly nominated candidates to offer their views and visions to the voters. Benefiting from live television coverage, the subsequent news stories, and the opposition party's temporary quiescence, a party's national convention provides a prime-time opportunity to convert voters and shore up existing support.

The vice-presidential choices of the major party candidates were greeted with praise by convention delegates and others. Bush tapped Richard B. Cheney, an oil company executive and former secretary of defense, member of the House of Representatives, and White House chief of staff. Gore turned to Joseph Lieberman, a veteran senator from Connecticut. Cheney brought Washington experience to the Republican ticket, leavening Bush's Washington outsider status. Gore's pick of Lieberman, the first Jewish candidate on a major party ticket and a Clinton critic, was viewed as a bold, innovative move that displayed leadership.[66]

Conventions can produce positive "bumps" in a candidate's poll numbers, however fleeting they may prove to be in the later heat of the campaign, and both Bush and Gore secured favorable boosts from their conventions. The Republicans went first, meeting from July 31 to August 3 in Philadelphia. The Democrats met August 14–17 in Los Angeles.

The Republican convention was marked by a unity unmatched since 1984, as well as by an unprecedented inclusiveness. Bush had consistently kept his distance from congressional Republicans, whose preoccupation with impeachment had cost them public favor. The convention's themes and roster of speakers reflected this distance. To the disgruntlement of some religious conservatives, an openly gay Republican congressman spoke on international trade in prime-time. The three convention cochairs were a woman, an African American, and a Hispanic. Even if such an approach yielded little support from the racial, ethnic, and social constituencies that usually turned a cold shoulder to Republicans, it was sure to hit home among moderate voters, taking the edge off the party's reputation for hard-edged conservatism. In the end, then, the convention enhanced Bush's poll standings; indeed, he moved into one of his largest leads of the year shortly afterward.[67]

Both Bradley and McCain, despite the negativity of the nomination campaigns, made convention appearances in support of their parties' nominees. In the weeks after McCain suspended his candidacy on March 9, Bush and McCain forces had worked to heal the wounds of a bitter campaign and to bridge the differences in their policy agendas. Although testy at times, the two smoothed matters over. McCain endorsed Bush on May 9 and emerged at the convention as a loyal supporter of the ticket, adding immensely to the image of the Republicans as a highly unified party.[68]

Bush's strong showing put pressure on Gore to make the most of the Democratic convention to turn his sagging political fortunes around. And Gore did. One of the delicate tasks demanded of Gore as vice president was to separate himself from Clinton just enough to avoid being blamed for the president's failings and yet remain close enough to receive credit for his achievements. Gore excelled in his acceptance speech, reviewing the administration's record of prosperity, then proclaiming, "I stand here tonight as my own man." He laced his speech with populist appeals, contrasting the powerful for whom the Republicans would fight with the people for whom he would do battle. Even the kiss he gave his wife, Tipper, on his way to the podium occasioned considerable press and public commentary; it was more passionate and spirited than political protocol required.[69] With the speech and the kiss, Gore, a candidate many had found too "wooden," helpfully energized his campaign. For almost two years Gore had, with rare exceptions, lagged behind Bush in the polls. In the aftermath of the convention, Gore drew even with Bush, then pulled ahead.

Conclusion: How Well Did the Process Work?

The early clinching of the nominations rendered many primaries and caucuses irrelevant. Although Bush and Gore achieved convention delegate majorities on March 14 (Table 2-5), the decisions by McCain and Bradley to withdraw on March 9 meant that the Republican nomination was essentially settled before the voters in twenty-seven states and the District of Columbia had voted to select national convention delegates. The Democratic nomination was settled before the voters in thirty states and D.C. had done so. Whether keeping presidential nominations open longer would help build the parties or hurt by leaving them battle-scarred is an open question. Nevertheless, in 2000 Republican Party elites, fearful that more states might seek even earlier slots in the 2004 primary calendar, considered reforming the rules of the nomination process. Any changes in the rules for 2004 would have had to be adopted by the Republican national convention in 2000. Democrats took an aloof stance, citing the election of Clinton in 1992 and 1996 as proof that the process did not need fixing.

After holding hearings, the GOP Advisory Commission on the Presidential Nominating Process rejected proposals for a national primary or a series of regional primaries with the order of regional voting rotating from election to election. Instead, the commission recommended a plan that would schedule voting in the states according to their population size—that is, the

Table 2-5 Nomination-Clinching Dates for Presidential Nominees

Year	Candidate (Party)	Date
2000	George W. Bush (R)	March 14
	Al Gore (D)	March 14
1996	Bill Clinton (D)	March 12
	Robert Dole (R)	March 26
1992	George Bush (R)	April 28
	Bill Clinton (D)	June 2
1988	George Bush (R)	April 26
	Michael Dukakis (D)	June 7
1984	Ronald Reagan (R)	May 8
	Walter F. Mondale (D)	June 5
1980	Ronald Reagan (R)	May 26
	Jimmy Carter (D)	June 3
1976	Jimmy Carter (D)	July 14[a]
	Gerald Ford (R)	August 19[a]
1972	George McGovern (D)	July 12[a]
	Richard Nixon (R)	August 22[a]

Sources: 1972–1996: Associated Press, "Dates on which Candidates Clinched the Nomination for the Presidency in Their Parties," March 15, 2000 (Lexis-Nexis); 2000: Ceci Connolly, "Bush, Gore Clinch Nominations," *Washington Post*, March 15, 2000, A6.

[a] Nomination clinched at party convention.

small and medium-sized states would vote from February or March through May, and the largest states would vote on the first Tuesday in June. The delegates at stake in the largest states would constitute a near-majority of the convention.

The recommendation failed. Large states had particular misgivings about going last in the nominating process, fearing that the field of candidates would be markedly winnowed and the contest effectively decided before they could vote. The traditional Republican reluctance to decree national rules for the state parties was another source of opposition.[70] Bush, anxious to avoid conflict at the convention, kept the reform proposal from reaching the floor. Republicans did not revise their presidential selection process for 2004.

As for the race for the top spots on the party tickets, both Gore and Bush, the presumptive front-runners before the primary and caucus voting began, were pressed to prove themselves worthy of nomination. On the Democratic side, Bradley failed to score an early upset and proved unable to turn back Gore's momentum and strong party backing. Gore successfully replaced his imperious, heir-apparent campaign of early 1999 with a scrappy, attacking campaign in which he presented himself as a fighter for working families against the large special interests such as drug companies and health maintenance organizations. Although Gore won the nomination, he failed to solve the puzzle of how to distance his candidacy from the Clinton administration's scandals while running on the Clinton administration's record.

Bush's relatively quick clinching of a delegate majority should not obscure the peril his candidacy faced after McCain won the primaries in New Hampshire and Michigan. Nevertheless, Bush's financial and organizational advantages proved overwhelming. McCain's challenge forced Bush to run a more conservative campaign than he had intended, but Bush was able to move toward the political center once the race was settled in mid-March.

Ironically, the various rules reforms of the 1960s that were intended to open up the Democratic Party and wrest control from its entrenched leaders had, with the stampede of states to the front of the delegate selection process, made those leaders once again critically influential. With so many primaries and caucuses scheduled so early in the process, candidates had to be able to wage, from day one, a cross-country campaign that could easily exceed the resources of any candidate not favored by a broad spectrum of party officials, donors, and officeholders. McCain's candidacy revealed that a serious insurgency was still possible. Its failure likewise revealed the formidable obstacles that such an insurgency faces in a front-loaded nominating process.

Notes

1. Dan Balz, "Starting Early and Urgently," *Washington Post,* April 4, 1999, A1.
2. Stephen J. Wayne, *The Road to the White House 2000: The Politics of Presidential Elections* (Boston: Bedford/St. Martin's, 2000), 137–138; and James W. Davis, *U.S. Presidential Primaries and the Caucus-Convention System* (Westport, Conn.: Greenwood Press, 1997), 90–98.
3. This shortening of the effective nominating season reflects the growing number of delegates selected in primaries as well as the movement of state primaries toward the start of the process. In 1972, 60 percent of the Democratic delegates and 53 percent of the Republican delegates were selected in primaries. See Howard L. Reiter, "The Evolution of the Presidential Nominating Process: Slouching toward a Nationwide Primary," H-Pol, October 5, 1996, online at http://h-net.msu.edu/~pol/ssha/netnews/f96/reiter.htm. By 2000, the percentage was over 80 percent for both parties.
4. Emmett Buell, "The Invisible Primary," in *In Pursuit of the White House: How We Choose Our Presidential Nominees,* ed. William G. Mayer (Chatham, N.J.: Chatham House, 1996), 1–43; and Arthur Hadley, *The Invisible Primary* (Englewood Cliffs, N.J.: Prentice Hall, 1976).
5. Richard L. Berke, "Bush Announces a Record Haul, and Foes Make Money an Issue," *New York Times,* July 1, 1999.
6. Don Van Natta Jr., "Bush's Network for Cash Was Set Up in '98 at Lunches in Texas Capital," *New York Times,* May 16, 1999.
7. Dole's problems were not helped when her husband, former Republican presidential nominee Rorbert Dole, suggested that he might send a check to one of her opponents, Senator McCain. Don Van Natta Jr., "Aura of Invincibility Shrinks Gifts to Bush Rivals," *New York Times,* June 10, 1999.
8. Ibid.
9. Richard L. Berke, "Flush Times and Hungry Republicans Generate Bush Campaign Windfall," *New York Times,* July 4, 1999.
10. David Bositis of the Joint Center for Economic and Political Studies, quoted in Terry M. Neal, "Bush's Message Reflects Hispanic Demographics," *Washington Post,* September 15, 1999, A3.

11. Berke, "Flush Times and Hungry Republicans."
12. Berke, "Bush Announces a Record Haul."
13. For a discussion of presidential campaign finance, see Anthony Corrado, *Paying for Presidents: Public Financing in National Elections* (New York: Twentieth Century Fund Press, 1993).
14. The law's exemption of 20 percent of a campaign's fund-raising expenses essentially raises the overall spending limit candidates may spend in the preconvention period to $40.54 million. Federal Election Commission, "FEC Announces 2000 Presidential Spending Limit," March 1, 2000, online at http://www.fec.gov/press/preslimits2000.htm.
15. Don Van Natta Jr., "Bush Foregoes Federal Funds and Has No Spending Limit," *New York Times,* July 16, 1999.
16. Ibid. Clinton's advertising campaign for 1996 began in the summer of 1995 and continued through to the Democratic national convention in August 1996; he focused on swing states. Wayne, *Road to the White House 2000,* 134–135. The "soft money" raised by the political parties—large contributions that fall outside federal election law limits—can finance such issue advertising but cannot include a direct "vote for" or "vote against" message. In 1996, soft-money fund-raising by the two major parties exceeded $250 million. Jill Abramson, "Bush's Big Bankroll and What It Means," *New York Times,* July 2, 1999.
17. John M. Broder, "Bush's Money Machine Lost No Steam in Last Quarter," *New York Times,* December 31, 1999.
18. Margaret Warner, "Identity Crisis," *News Hour with Jim Lehrer,* February 24, 2000, online at http://www.pbs.org/newshour/bb/election/jan-june00/gop_identity_2-24.html.
19. Dan Balz and David S. Broder, "Bush Wins Iowa Straw Poll, Forbes Second," *Washington Post,* August 15, 1999, A1; and Janine Yagielski, "They're Off: Iowa Straw Poll Sets GOP Race in Motion," August 15, 1999, online at http://www.allpolitics.com
20. Haley Barbour, former chairman of the Republican National Committee, quoted in Katharine Q. Seelye, "Bush Adds $800,000 to Election Bank Account in Sweep through Washington Area," *New York Times,* July 15, 1999.
21. Cathleen Decker, "Dole Slow to Capitalize on Unusual Second Chance," *Los Angeles Times,* August 20, 1999, A14.
22. Dan Balz, "Alexander Quits a Long Quest," *Washington Post,* August 17, 1999, A4; Katharine Q. Seelye, "Low on Cash, Dole Withdraws from G.O.P. Race," *New York Times,* October 21, 1999; Todd S. Purdum, "Facing Reality, Quayle Ends Dream of Returning to White House," *New York Times,* September 28, 1999; and Francis X. Clines, "Buchanan Bolts G.O.P. for Reform Party Run," *New York Times,* October 25, 1999, A1.
23. Ronald Brownstein, "Bush, Gore Hold Big Leads in Nation but Not in New Hampshire," *Los Angeles Times,* November 21, 1999.
24. Alison Mitchell, "With 'Patriotic Challenge,' McCain Makes Run Official," *New York Times,* September 28, 1999.
25. R. W. Apple Jr., "Notion of a New Al Gore Begins to Take Root," *New York Times,* October 11, 1999, A12.
26. David S. Broder, "Script for an Upset," *Washington Post,* April 25, 1999, B7. Gore was tainted by allegations of improprieties in the 1996 campaign such as his fund-raising appearance at a Buddhist temple. His defense when questioned about certain of these improprieties—namely, that "no controlling legal authority" ruled them out—was widely viewed as clumsy.
27. "Gore Chuckles at His Internet Claim," *New York Times,* March 21, 1999, 29.
28. Susan Feeney, "Saying 'Tough Fight' Ahead, Gore Moves Campaign to Nashville," *Dallas Morning News,* September 30, 1999.

29. "In fact, one explanation for the allure of the McCain and Bradley insurgencies is that some journalists, as well as ordinary voters, seem charmed by them personally—and have a hankering for some drama." Richard L. Berke, "Nominees May Be Chosen Quickly in Rare Competitive Primary Season," *New York Times,* January 2, 2000, 22.

30. Frank Bruni, "Jabs at Bush Put Focus on Question of Intellect," *New York Times,* December 8, 1999; and Richard L. Berke, "Some Unease in G.O.P. over Bush in Debates," *New York Times,* December 10, 1999.

31. Ronald Brownstein, "Gore Deals a New Strategy to Out-Democrat Bradley," *Los Angeles Times,* October 20, 1999, A1; and Dan Balz, "Rivalries Surge as Forces Shift Near Primaries," *Washington Post,* December 5, 1999, A1.

32. John H. Aldrich, *Before the Convention: Strategies and Choices in Presidential Nomination Campaigns* (Chicago: University of Chicago Press, 1980), 108.

33. "Campaign 2000—Early Returns: Network News Coverage of the Campaign Preseason," *Media Monitor* 13 (November/December 1999), online at http://www.cmpa.com/Mediamon/mm111299.htm.

34. For an analytical discussion of momentum as well as its application to the 1976, 1980, and 1984 nominations, see Larry M. Bartels, *Presidential Primaries and the Dynamics of Public Choice* (Princeton: Princeton University Press, 1988).

35. After finishing a disappointing sixth behind a fifth-place McCain who did not even campaign in Iowa, Senator Hatch ended his presidential campaign on January 26. Helen Dewar, "Hatch Ends Presidential Bid, Backs Bush," *Washington Post,* January 27, 2000, A7.

36. The total is a count of days the candidates spent in Iowa beginning on March 15, 1999. "Visit Tally: Who Will Be Able to Say 'Time Well Spent,'" *The Hotline,* January 21, 2000.

37. Bradley on "Face the Nation," CBS, January 23, 2000, quoted in "Bradley: Holds Out Hope for 'Surprise,' Touts Endorsement in Ad," *The Hotline,* January 24, 2000.

38. James Dao, "The Challenger: Bradley Says Campaign Is on the Right Path," *New York Times,* January 25, 2000, A21; and Thomas B. Edsall, "Iowa Loss Puts New Pressure on Bradley," *Washington Post,* January 25, 2000, A1.

39. Walter R. Mears, "Bradley, Gore Appeal to N.H. Voters," Associated Press, January 20, 2000 (Lexis-Nexis).

40. "Campaign 2000—The Primaries: TV News Coverage of the Democratic and GOP Primaries," *Media Monitor* 14 (March/April 2000), online at http://www.cmpa.com/Mediamon/mm111299.htm.

41. Bauer dropped out on February 4 after a poor showing in New Hampshire in which he secured only 1 percent of the vote. "Bauer Endorses McCain for President," February 16, 2000, online at http://www.cnn.com/2000/ALLPOLITICS/stories/02/16/bauer.cnn/.

42. "GOP Primary: New Hampshire" and "Democratic Primary: New Hampshire"—these and subsequent exit poll results were retrieved online at http://www.cnn.com.

43. "Visit Tally: McCain Far and Away Most Frequent Visitor," *The Hotline,* January 28, 2000; and Eric Slater and T. Christian Miller, "On Big Stage, McCain Couldn't Live Up to His Own Billing," *Los Angeles Times,* March 10, 2000, A16.

44. Even by October 1999, McCain had made seventeen trips to New Hampshire, Bush only four. Melinda Henneberger, "New Hampshire Warns Bush, 'Don't Be a Stranger Hee-ahh,'" *New York Times,* October 23, 1999.

45. "McCain: Media Darling?" *The Newshour with Jim Lehrer,* February 14, 2000. But such media access had its risks. For example, before the New Hampshire

primary, when asked how he would respond if his fifteen-year-old daughter said she was pregnant and wanted an abortion, he replied that his family would discuss the matter but that the final decision would be his daughter's. McCain, with a consistent antiabortion voting record, faced intense questioning about his answer, and he ultimately revised it to say that the decision would be his family's, not his daughter's alone. Edward Walsh, "The Ride of His Political Life; Despite Bumps, McCain Enjoyed the Trip," *Washington Post,* March 11, 2000, A6.

46. John M. Broder and Don Van Natta Jr., "Once Flush, Bush Is Facing a Dwindling Coffer," *New York Times,* February 16, 2000.

47. "Bush fund-raisers said they were especially upset by the decision to spend $2 million in Arizona, Mr. McCain's home state, which Bush did not visit. 'We spent $2 million, and McCain spent zero, and we lost by 26 [sic] points,' a longtime Bush fund-raiser said. 'It's embarrassing, and it's a complete waste.'" Quoted in Don Van Natta Jr., "The Money: A Daunting Edge in Campaign Cash Narrows for Bush," *New York Times,* February 25, 2000, A1. Also see Broder and Van Natta, "Once Flush." The other big spender, Forbes, having spent about $37 million on his campaign, got far less. Forbes dropped out on February 10 after trailing the noncampaigning McCain with a dismal 20 percent of the vote in Delaware, a state Forbes had carried in 1996. In 2000, Forbes spent about $32 million of his own money and $5 million in donations. In 1996, he had spent $37.4 million. Leslie Wayne, "Forbes Spent Millions, but for Little Gain," *New York Times,* February 20, 2000, A26.

48. Frank Bruni, "Bush and McCain, Sittin' in a Tree, D-I-S-S-I-N-G," *New York Times,* February 9, 2000.

49. Quoted in Mark Z. Barabak and Doyle McManus, "McCain Drops Negative TV Ads: The Arizona Senator Calls on Front-runner Bush to Do the Same but Texas Governor Rejects the Invitation as a 'Trick,'" *Los Angeles Times,* February 12, 2000, 11.

50. Don Van Natta Jr. and John M. Broder, "With a Still-Ample Treasury, Bush Builds a Green 'Fire Wall' against McCain," *New York Times,* February 21, 2000.

51. Slater and Miller, "On Big Stage."

52. In the February 29 Virginia primary, the religious right made up 20 percent of voters, and 80 percent of them backed Bush. (Earlier, in South Carolina, the religious right also made up 20 percent of voters, and 70 percent of them voted for Bush.)

53. Slater and Miller, "On Big Stage."

54. Richard W. Stevenson with Richard Perez-Pena, "Major Bush Donor Reveals He Ran Anti-McCain Ads," *New York Times,* March 3, 2000.

55. Edward Walsh, "McCain Withholds Bush Endorsement, Calls on GOP to Adopt Reform Message," *Washington Post,* March 10, 2000, A1.

56. Dana Milbank, "He's Here! And There! Heading in All Directions Won't Get Al Gore Where He Wants to Go," *Washington Post,* December 19, 1999, B1.

57. Dan Balz, "Bush Advances by Leaving Primaries Behind," *Washington Post,* April 23, 2000, A4; and Dan Balz, "Outmaneuvered by Bush, Gore Faces Questions," *Washington Post,* May 28, 2000, A1.

58. Dan Balz, "Gore and Bush Camps Awash in Confidence," *Washington Post,* March 26, 2000, A1.

59. Richard L. Berke with Janet Elder, "Poll Shows Bush Ahead of Gore, with Leadership a Crucial Issue," *New York Times,* May 16, 2000, A1.

60. Michael Nelson, "The Curse of the Vice Presidency," *American Prospect,* July 31, 2000, online at http://www.prospect.org.

61. Katharine Q. Seelye, "Gore's Post-Primary Pace Worries Some Democrats," *New York Times,* May 25, 2000, A26.

62. James Dao, "Democrats Criticize Gore for Position on Cuban Boy," *New York Times,* April 1, 2000, A9.
63. Dan Lerner, "Ventura Quits Reform Party," *Financial Times,* February 12, 2000, 2.
64. Thomas B. Edsall, "Buchanan Declares Culture War; With New Funds, Reform Party Nominee Begins Belated Run," *Washington Post,* September 19, 2000, A9.
65. James W. Davis, *U.S. Presidential Primaries and the Caucus-Convention System* (Westport, Conn.: Greenwood Press, 1997), 241–244.
66. Terry M. Neal and Dan Balz, "GOP Hails Cheney's Inclusion on Ticket: Democrats Prepare to Fight 'Big Oil,' " *Washington Post,* July 26, 2000, A1; and Ceci Connolly, "Gore Picks Senator Lieberman: Running Mate to Be First Jew on Major Ticket," *Washington Post,* August 8, 2000, A1.
67. Connolly, "Gore Picks Senator Lieberman."
68. Dan Balz, "McCain Endorses Bush—Softly," *Washington Post,* May 10, 2000, A1.
69. "This Morning: Sealed with 'The Kiss,' "*The Hotline,* August 21, 2000.
70. Robin Toner, "The Process: Just How Well Did the System Work?" *New York Times,* March 12, 2000, 40; and Adam Clymer, "The Primary Schedule: G.O.P. Panel Seeks to Alter Schedule of Primary Voting," *New York Times,* May 3, 2000, A1.

3

The Election: Ordinary Politics, Extraordinary Outcome

Michael Nelson

Virtually everything that was said and written in the aftermath of the presidential election of 2000 emphasized how unusual it was. No one would deny that an election whose outcome was not resolved until more than a month after the voters went to the polls had some distinctive elements. Most obviously, the election was astonishingly close. Only one popular vote out of every two hundred cast separated Al Gore, who received 51.0 million votes, from George W. Bush, who received 50.5 million votes. In the electoral vote, which is decisive, Bush won by 271–266. His margin of victory was the closest since the Hayes-Tilden election of 1876, a contest that also remained unresolved until long after Election Day. Not since 1888 had the popular vote winner lost to his opponent, as Gore did in 2000.

Other elements of the 2000 election were unusual as well. Because the defeat of the Gore-Lieberman ticket allowed Joseph Lieberman to continue serving as a U.S. senator from Connecticut, the Senate was evenly divided between the two major parties for the first time since 1880. Gore's selection of Lieberman as his running mate was itself historic. Lieberman was the first Jew—indeed, the first non-Christian—ever to be nominated by a major party for president or vice president. In another development, Republicans retained control of the House of Representatives for the fourth consecutive election, the first time they had done so since the 1920s. The first first lady in history to run for office, Hillary Rodham Clinton, was elected to the Senate by the voters of New York. Distressed by Gore's defeat, she immediately announced her intention to sponsor a constitutional amendment that would replace the electoral college with a system of direct election.

The extraordinary always distracts from the ordinary. Not surprisingly, the unusual qualities that marked the elections of 2000 mask the influence of several steadier, more enduring, and arguably more important aspects of American politics. These ordinary and enduring aspects include the elevation of the vice presidency as the prime stepping-stone to a presidential nomination, the unifying character of national party conventions, the rise of third-party candidates, the enhanced vice-presidential selection process, quadrennial debates between the presidential and vice-presidential candidates, low voter turnout, the importance of the electoral college, and divided government. Because the unusual elements of the 2000 presidential election are treated extensively elsewhere in this book—especially in Chapter 9, "The Postelection Election"—this chapter focuses on the more enduring ones.

Vice Presidents as Presidential Candidates

Until the election of George Bush (the elder) as president in 1988, no incumbent vice president had been elected president since Martin Van Buren in 1836. Appropriately, Bush opened his first postelection press conference by saying, "It's been a long time, Marty." [1] Yet it is also true that, starting with Harry S. Truman in 1945, five of the last eleven presidents—nearly half— have been former vice presidents: Truman, Lyndon B. Johnson, Richard Nixon, Gerald Ford, and Bush. Death or resignation accounts for the ascensions of Truman, Johnson, and Ford, but each of them except Ford won at least one presidential election on his own. Clearly, the vice presidency is a political riddle. The riddle can be stated simply: What office is the best political stepping-stone to the presidency—and also the worst?

The roots of the vice presidency's puzzling political status are embedded deeply in the Constitution and in more than two centuries of history. [2] The Constitutional Convention of 1787 created the vice presidency as a weak office, but also a prestigious one. The Constitution empowered the vice president only to be "president of the Senate, but shall have no Vote, unless they be equally divided." The office's prestige derived from the way vice presidents were elected. Every four years, presidential electors were charged to cast two votes for president. The first-place finisher in the electoral college won the presidency, and the person who finished second became the vice president. In awarding the vice presidency to the runner-up in the presidential election, the Constitution made the vice president the presumptive heir to the presidency. The nation's first two vice presidents, John Adams and Thomas Jefferson, were elected as its second and third presidents.

The arrival on the national scene of political parties nominating not just candidates for president but also vice-presidential candidates rendered this system unworkable. The breakdown came in 1800 when all of the Democratic-Republican Party's electors faithfully discharged their duty to vote for both Jefferson and his vice-presidential running mate, Aaron Burr, only to produce a tie vote for president. The House of Representatives took weeks to resolve the dispute in Jefferson's favor.

The Twelfth Amendment, which was passed in time for the 1804 election, solved this problem neatly by instructing electors to cast one vote for president and a separate vote for vice president. But the amendment had a disastrous unintended side effect on the vice presidency: it left the office weak and, by stripping the vice president of any claim to being the country's second most qualified person to be president, took away nearly all of its prestige as well. The nineteenth century was not a happy time for the vice presidency. Talented political leaders shunned the office. Those who occupied it received little respect or responsibility from the presidents they served.

The vice presidency is still a constitutionally weak office. But the contrast between the political prestige of the nineteenth-century version of the vice presidency and the twentieth-century version is stark. Although four nineteenth-century vice presidents succeeded to the presidency when the elected president died, none of them was then nominated to run for a full presidential term in his own right. The best of the four—Chester A. Arthur—was a mediocre president in the eyes of his contemporaries and of historians.[3] The other three—John Tyler, Millard Fillmore, and Andrew Johnson—ran the gamut from bad to awful. By contrast, not only were all five of the twentieth century's successor presidents—Theodore Roosevelt, Calvin Coolidge, Truman, Johnson, and Ford—subsequently nominated to run for president by their party, but all except Ford (who came very close) were elected. As a group, historians actually rank them higher than the twentieth century's elected presidents.[4]

The vice presidency has become especially prestigious since the end of World War II. Starting with Nixon in 1960, every elected vice president except Dan Quayle has led in a majority of the Gallup polls that measure the party rank and file's preconvention preferences for president.[5] Again excepting Quayle, all eight of the postwar vice presidents who have sought their party's presidential nomination have won it.

As an additional measure of political prestige, the roles and resources of the vice presidency have grown in recent years. The office is larger and more prominent than in the past—in the terminology of political science, it has been "institutionalized." As recently as the mid-1970s, vice presidents had their offices in the Capitol and the Executive Office Building, arranged their own housing, and had to borrow speechwriters and other staff from the White House as best they could. Today they enjoy a large and professional staff, a West Wing office, a separate line item in the executive budget, and a grand official residence—the Admiral's House at the Naval Observatory. The office also has been institutionalized in the broader sense that more—and more substantial—vice-presidential activities are now taken for granted. These include regular private meetings with the president, a wide-ranging role as senior presidential adviser, membership on the National Security Council, full intelligence briefings, access to the Oval Office paper flow, public advocacy of the administration's programs and leadership, a role in the party second only to the president's, sensitive diplomatic missions, attendance at cabinet meetings, and liaison with congressional leaders and interest groups.

The reasons for the growing prestige of the vice presidency in politics and government are varied. At the turn of the twentieth century, the rise of national news media (mass-circulation magazines and newspaper wire services) and a new style of active political campaigning elevated the visibility of the vice president, which in turn made the office more appealing to a better class of political leaders than the weak and scorned nineteenth-century version of the vice presidency had been. In the 1900 election, the Republican nominee for vice president, Theodore Roosevelt, won widespread publicity and accumulated political IOUs from local politicians in almost every state by becoming the first vice-presidential candidate in history to campaign vigorously across the country. During the 1920s and 1930s, the roster of vice presidents included a Speaker of the House, a Senate majority leader, and a Nobel Prize–winning cabinet member.

In 1940, Franklin D. Roosevelt, who had run for vice president himself in 1920 (he lost), successfully claimed for presidential candidates the right to name their running mates. In the past, party leaders had made that decision. For the sake of party unity, they typically had used the occasion to pair the nominee for president with a vice-presidential candidate from the opposite wing of the party, thereby discouraging the president from ever trusting the vice president personally or entrusting him with useful responsibilities in office. In general, voters want vice presidents to be loyal to the president almost as much as presidents do. Allowing presidential candidates to choose their running mates virtually assured that such loyalty would be forthcoming.

After 1945, the combination of Truman's woefully unprepared succession to the presidency when Roosevelt died (Truman was at best dimly aware of the existence of the atom bomb and the Allies' plans for the post–World War II world) and the proliferation of nuclear weapons heightened public concern about the vice presidency. Citizens wanted vice presidents who were ready and able to step into the presidency at a moment's notice.

During the second half of the twentieth century, the Constitution was altered in ways that have redounded to the benefit of the vice president. The Twenty-fifth Amendment, which was enacted in 1967, made the vice president the crucial actor in determining whether a president is disabled. It also provided that whenever the vice presidency becomes vacant (by 1967, this had happened sixteen times during the nation's first thirty-six presidencies), the president will nominate a new vice president pending congressional confirmation. So prestigious had the vice presidency become that in 1976 Americans barely noticed that their national bicentennial celebration was presided over by two men, President Gerald Ford and Vice President Nelson A. Rockefeller, who had attained their offices not through election but by being appointed vice president.

Equally significant in constitutional terms was the Twenty-second Amendment, which in 1951 imposed a two-term limit on presidents. Just as Congress had not meant to damage the vice presidency politically when it enacted the Twelfth Amendment in 1804 (but did), neither was Congress trying to enhance the vice president's political status when it placed a ceiling on presidential tenure (but did). The two-term limit has made it possible for the vice president to step forward as a presidential candidate early in the president's second term rather than have to wait in the wings until the president decides what to do. All three vice presidents who have served second-term presidents since the Twenty-second Amendment was enacted have made good use of this opportunity: Nixon in 1960, Bush in 1988, and Gore in 2000.

Gore inherited an impressive office when he became vice president in 1993. He contributed to the power and prestige of the vice presidency as well: he headed up the administration's Reinventing Government initiative, served as an important diplomatic channel to Russia and other former Soviet republics, filled the bureaucracy with talented political allies, deflated strong opposition to the North American Free Trade Agreement when he shredded H. Ross Perot in a televised debate, developed the Telecommunications Act of 1996 and persuaded Congress to pass it, and stiffened the president's spine at crucial moments. "You can get with the goddamn program!" Gore famously told Clinton when the president was vacillating on his 1993 economic plan—and Clinton did.[6] No vice president in history was more influential than Gore.

Still, the question remains: Is being vice president a blessing or a curse for a talented political leader who is trying to win the presidency? The answer comes in two parts, with the easy part first. Service as vice president is clearly the most direct route to winning a party's presidential nomination. In addition to the opportunity for early fund-raising and organization building that the Twenty-second Amendment affords, vice presidents derive two other important political benefits from the office in their pursuit of a presidential nomination. One is that their ongoing activities as party leader—campaigning across the country during elections, raising funds at other times—and as public advocate of the administration and its policies uniquely situate them to win friends among the political activists who typically dominate the nominating process. Such campaigning also is good experience for a presidential candidacy. The other important political benefit is that the recent growth in the governmental responsibilities and resources of the vice presidency has made both the office and its occupant seem more presidential. Substantive matters like international diplomacy and symbolic ones like the mansion, *Air Force Two,* and even the new vice-presidential seal that displays a wingspread eagle with a claw full of arrows and a starburst at its head (the eagle in the old seal seemed rather sedentary) attest to the prestige of the office.

In sum, the modern vice president typically is an experienced and talented political leader who is loyal to the president and admired by the party—an ideal formula for securing a presidential nomination and one that Gore executed skillfully in 2000. Exit surveys during the Democratic primaries and caucuses showed Gore winning overwhelming support from voters who approved of Clinton's performance as president. Needless to say, such voters made up the vast majority of those who turned out at the polls.[7] Gore's worst moment in the nomination campaign was, in a sense, the exception that demonstrated the rule. The vice president's zeal as a fund-raiser for Clinton and the Democratic National Committee in 1995 and 1996 gave former senator Bill Bradley, Gore's opponent for the Democratic nomination, an opening among independent voters. But it also strengthened Gore's bond with Democratic activists, which turned out to be much more important.

Winning the party's nomination for president is no small thing, but it is not the main thing. For all their advantages in getting nominated, vice presidents have had an unusually hard time closing the deal in November. To be sure, the so-called Van Buren syndrome can be overstated: of the thirty-four vice presidents who served between Van Buren and Bush, only seven even tried to run for president,[8] and two of them—Nixon in 1960 and Hubert H. Humphrey in 1968—came very close to winning. Nonetheless, vice presidents carry burdens into the general election campaign that are as firmly grounded in their office as the advantages they bring to a nominating contest.

Indeed, some of the activities of the modern vice presidency that are most appealing to party activists may repel other voters. Days and nights spent fertilizing the party's grass roots with fervent, sometimes slashing rhetoric can alienate those who look to the presidency for leadership that unifies rather than divides. Gore's blurt to a postimpeachment rally of Democratic members of Congress that Clinton "will be regarded in the history books as one of our greatest presidents" undoubtedly roused the spirits of his fellow partisans, but it seemed wildly excessive to almost everyone else.[9] As for the woodenness that many people attributed to Gore, it was partly a longstanding trait of his but mostly an artifact of the hundreds of vice-presidential moments he spent standing motionless and silent in the background while Clinton spoke animatedly to the television cameras.

Certain institutional qualities of the modern vice presidency also handicap the vice president–turned–presidential candidate. Vice presidents must work hard to gain a share of the credit for the successes of the administration. But they can count on being attacked by the other party's presidential nominee for all of the administration's shortcomings. Such attacks allow no effective response. A vice president who tries to stand apart from the White House may alienate the president and cause voters to wonder why he did not speak up earlier. Gore did himself no good, for example, when he spent the evening of his official announcement for president telling the "20/20" television audience that Clinton's behavior in the Monica Lewinsky affair was "inexcusable." [10]

The vice president's difficulties are only compounded when it comes to matters of substantive public policy. During the campaign, every time Gore tried to identify a problem he wanted to solve as president, Bush would step forward to chastise him for not persuading Clinton to solve it earlier. For example, when during the first debate Gore mentioned his proposal to extend prescription drug benefits to seniors, Bush replied, "Four years ago they campaigned on getting prescription drugs for seniors. And now they're campaigning on getting prescription drugs for seniors. It seems like they can't get it done." [11]

Vice presidents can always say that loyalty to the president forecloses public disagreement, but that course is no less perilous politically. The public that values loyalty in a vice president values different qualities in a potential president. Strength, vision, and independence are what they look for then—the very qualities that vice presidents almost never get to display.[12] Polls that through much of the election year showed Gore trailing Bush in the category of leadership were less about Bush and Gore than about the vice presidency. So were the Election Day exit polls showing that voters who regarded strong leadership as the personal quality they wanted most in a president supported Bush by 64 percent to 34 percent.[13]

The political handicaps that vice presidents carry into the general election are considerable, but they need not be insurmountable. As with all things vice-presidential, much depends on vice presidents' relationships with the presidents they serve. One of the main reasons Nixon and Humphrey lost, for example, is that their presidents were so unhelpful. Almost every Poli Sci 101 student knows what Dwight D. Eisenhower said when a reporter asked him to name a single "major idea" of Nixon's that he had adopted as president: "If you give me a week, I might think of one."[14] A few years later, Lyndon Johnson treated Vice President Humphrey spitefully as soon as it became clear that the 1968 Democratic convention was not going to draft the president for another term despite his earlier withdrawal from the race.

In contrast, Van Buren benefited enormously from his association with President Andrew Jackson, who regarded his vice president's election to the presidency as validation of the transformation he had wrought in American politics. Ronald Reagan was equally committed to George Bush's success in 1988, putting ego aside to praise (even inflate) the vice president's contributions to what the president began calling the "Reagan-Bush administration." Reagan's popularity was of even greater benefit to his vice president. Bush won the votes of 80 percent of those who approved Reagan's performance as president; he lost nine to one among those who disapproved.[15] Eighty percent of many is more than 90 percent of few: Bush was elected.

Although Clinton said in 2000 that he wished he could run for a third term (and identified Gore condescendingly as "the next best thing"),[16] he had to content himself with adopting Andrew Jackson's belief that his legacy was closely tied to his vice president's political success. Clinton passed on to Gore Reaganesque approval ratings and a strong economy. At the September 2000 meeting of the American Political Science Association, seven political scientists forecast the outcome of the 2000 presidential election using models that incorporate measures of economic growth and presidential approval. The winner, they unanimously predicted, would be Gore, by a margin of anywhere from 6 percent to 20 percent of the major-party popular vote.[17] For four years the economy had grown at an annual rate of at least 4 percent and Clinton's job approval rating had stayed above 60 percent—the highest and most consistent ratings for a second-term president in the history of polling. In addition, unemployment had fallen during every year of Clinton's presidency, eventually dropping below 4 percent; the average annual rate of inflation during the Clinton years was the lowest since the early 1960s; and the enormous budget deficits that Clinton had inherited from his predecessor had become enormous budget surpluses.

Why were the political scientists wrong? One reason is that they overlooked the difference between the voters' approval of Clinton's performance as president and their disapproval of Clinton as a person. The 2000 exit polls indicated that 57 percent of voters approved of the job Clinton was doing: these voters supported Gore by 77 percent to 20 percent. But 60 percent said they had an unfavorable opinion of Clinton himself, and they supported Bush by 70 percent to 26 percent.[18]

The more important reason Gore lost, however, is that he distanced himself from both Clinton the president and Clinton the person. Heeding a New Age adviser's recommendation that he must challenge the president if he was to emerge from his vice-presidential image as a "beta male" and replace Clinton as the nation's "alpha male," Gore went overboard.[19] Telling the voters in his acceptance speech at the Democratic convention that "I stand here tonight as my own man" was appropriate and political beneficial.[20] Rejecting Clinton's repeated offers to campaign for him, which party leaders pleaded with Gore to accept, was not.[21] Even worse, instead of emphasizing the national prosperity that had marked the Clinton-Gore years, Gore ran a populist-style "people, not the powerful" campaign more appropriate for a candidate challenging an incumbent in economic hard times than for a vice president seeking to extend his party's control of the presidency in good times. Gore's strongest political advantage in 2000 was his ability to ask the voters: If eight years of Democratic rule has produced peace and prosperity, why elect a Republican? Yet as *Slate* editor Michael Kinsley wrote, the theme of the Gore campaign was, "You've never had it so good, and I'm mad as hell about it."[22] In the three nationally televised debates with Bush, Gore never mentioned Clinton. "We might have blown it," a Gore aide said near the end of the campaign. "We didn't remind people of how well off they are."[23]

The closeness of the election underscores how winnable it was for Gore. As Figure 3-1 indicates, Gore nearly swept the Northeast, the upper Midwest, and the Pacific Coast. The exit poll data reported in Table 3-1 reveal that he ran more strongly among certain demographic groups—including unmarried women (63 percent), African Americans (90 percent), members of union households (59 percent), liberals (80 percent), gay and lesbian voters (70 percent), voters with incomes below $30,000 (55 percent), city dwellers (61 percent), voters who seldom or never attend religious services (56 percent), Democrats (86 percent), and highly educated voters (52 percent)—than any Democratic presidential candidate since Johnson in 1964. Gore also did well among those who shared his support for legalized abortion (66 percent), Medicare-provided prescription drugs for seniors (60 percent), and stricter gun control laws (62 percent). Finally, Gore drew strong support from those who regarded the candidates' stands on the issues as more important than their personal qualities (55 percent), those who thought

Figure 3-1 2000 Presidential Election, by Region

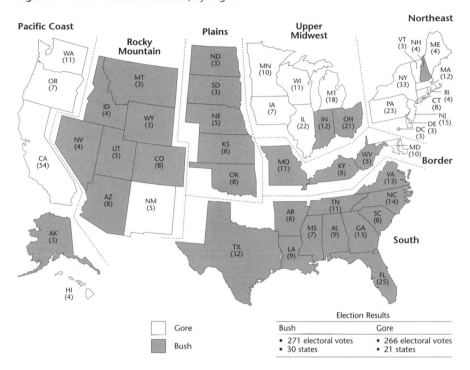

managing the government was a higher presidential priority than providing moral leadership (61 percent), and those who judged the environment to be more important than economic growth (59 percent).[24]

But Gore paid a price for his decision not to stress the peace and prosperity of the Clinton years in his campaign. Voters who said that world affairs were what concerned them the most actually supported Bush by 54 percent to 40 percent. As for the economy, although voters who thought it was in excellent condition supported Gore by 53 percent to 46 percent, those who said it was good favored Bush by 53 percent to 38 percent. Gore overwhelmingly carried the 28 percent of voters who said that Clinton was "very responsible" for the economy, 79 percent to 18 percent. But the 40 percent of voters who judged Clinton "somewhat responsible" supported Gore over Bush by only 52 percent to 43 percent.[25] "More than anything else," political scientist Gary C. Jacobson concluded, "Gore's inability to exploit his biggest asset, the Clinton economy, effectively cost him a clear-cut victory." [26]

Table 3-1 How People Voted in 2000

	Gore	Bush	Nader
All (100)	49%	48%	3%
Men (48)	42	53	3
Women (52)	54	43	2
White (81)	42	54	3
African American (10)	90	9	1
Hispanic (7)	62	35	2
Asian American (2)	55	41	3
Other (1)	55	39	4
No high school degree (5)	59	39	1
High school graduate (21)	48	49	1
Some college (32)	45	51	3
College graduate (24)	45	51	3
Post-graduate degree (18)	52	44	3
Family income			
Under $15,000 (7)	57	37	4
$15–30,000 (16)	54	41	3
$30–50,000 (24)	49	48	2
$50–75,000 (25)	46	51	2
$75–100,000 (13)	45	52	2
Over $100,000 (15)	43	54	2
Union member in household (26)	59	37	3
Gay or lesbian (4)	70	25	4
City (29)	61	35	2
Suburb (43)	47	49	3
Rural (28)	37	59	2
Protestant(54)	42	56	2
Catholic (26)	50	47	2
Jewish (4)	79	19	1
Other (6)	62	28	7
None (9)	61	30	7
Attend religious services			
Weekly or more than weekly (42)	39	59	2
Monthly (14)	51	46	2
Seldom or never (42)	56	39	4
Married			
Men (32)	38	58	2
Women (33)	48	49	2

(Continued)

Table 3-1 *Continued*

	Gore	Bush	Nader
Unmarried			
Men (16)	48%	46%	4%
Women (19)	63	32	3
Republican (35)	8	91	1
Democrat (39)	86	11	2
Independent (27)	45	47	6
Liberal (20)	80	13	6
Moderate (50)	52	44	2
Conservative (29)	17	81	1
1996 presidential vote			
Clinton (46)	82	15	2
Dole (31)	7	91	1
Perot (6)	27	64	7
Other (2)	26	52	15
Did not vote (13)	44	52	3

Source: Voter News Service "Exit Polls," online at http://cnn.com/ELECTION/2000/results/index.epolls.html.

Unifying Conventions

In recent years, the politics of presidential nominations has stabilized to such an extent that it falls safely under the rubric of ordinary rather than extraordinary politics. Nominations for president in the contemporary era are typically sewn up by the winning candidate long before the national party convention meets in July or August of the election year. The convention, in turn, has become a kind of coronation, used to launch the general election campaign from a foundation of party unity rather than to make any real, and thus potentially divisive, decisions. The result, in almost all cases, is a post-convention "bounce" in the polls for the presidential nominee that gets the campaign off to a strong start.

National party conventions have gone through three eras since they first appeared in the 1830s. In the first era, from 1832 to 1952, conventions were the arena in which presidential nominations usually were fought and won. Party leaders from around the country assembled, wheeled and dealed, and decided on a nominee. As one measure of their contentiousness, twenty-eight of the sixty-one Democratic, Whig, and Republican conventions that took place in this 120-year period were multiballot affairs. The 1924 Democratic convention needed 103 ballots to choose its nominee; eight other conventions required ten or more ballots.

The second era began with the 1956 election and lasted through 1980. None of the fourteen major-party conventions in this quarter-century period needed more than one ballot to nominate its candidate. The blossoming of presidential primaries, which advanced the beginning of the nominating contest to much earlier in the election year, and the presence of live television cameras at the conventions, which rendered closed-door dealing in smoke-filled rooms impossible, invariably led to the emergence of a nominee some time (often shortly) before the convention met. But the tradition of the convention as an important decision-making body was not entirely lost. Conventions in this period were frequently marked by open battles about the party platform, the convention rules, delegate credentials, and other matters. In 1964, for example, conservative supporters of Arizona senator Barry Goldwater shouted down Nelson Rockefeller, the liberal governor of New York, during a platform debate. In 1980, Sen. Edward M. Kennedy fiercely battled President Carter over a rule that bound the delegates to vote for the candidate they had been elected to support in their state's primary or caucus.

Beginning in 1984, conventions entered their third era. Not only are modern conventions strictly one-ballot events; they also are planned and even scripted by the nominee. Such choreography is politically desirable, because, as political scientist Martin P. Wattenberg has shown, parties that present a united front to the country gain an advantage over parties that place their divisions on display.[27] It is politically possible, because the recent "front-loading" of the delegate-selection process toward the first three months of the election year invariably produces an early winner in the fight for the party's nomination. In 1976, after New Hampshire voted in February, only five states held primaries in March; by 2000 thirty-four states did, including nearly all of the large states with the richest delegate prizes. To ensure that a nominee emerges from this blizzard of winter primaries and that the party can unite long before the convention, party leaders and fund-raisers rally to the candidate who takes the early lead, rendering effective opposition to the front-runner nearly impossible.

At the convention itself, platform, credentials, and rules fights are either suppressed (under recently adopted party rules, no challenge to a committee's decision is allowed on the convention floor unless at least 25 percent of its members demand it) or shunted into off-hours sessions, outside the gaze of the television networks. Prime-time is devoted to speeches, celebrity appearances, and videos whose content is strictly controlled by the nominee. The delegates are little more than a studio audience. In sum, the modern convention is "a huge pep rally, replete with ritual, pomp, and entertainment—a made-for-TV production. From the perspective of the party and its nominee, the convention now serves primarily as a launching pad for the general election."[28] Some of those launches have been spectacular. Clinton, for example, went from trailing Bush by eight percentage points before the 1992

Democratic convention to leading him by twenty-two points afterward.[29]

Like Gore's capture of the 2000 Democratic convention, Bush's march to the Republican nomination followed the modern script closely. Next to being vice president, service as governor of a state has become the leading stepping-stone to a presidential nomination.[30] This has not always been the case. At times, Washington experience has been favored: for example, in the four elections that took place between 1960 and 1972, every Republican and Democratic nominee for president was or had been a senator. Voters during that period seemed to value the knowledge that senators derive from dealing with national concerns, especially foreign policy. Since former Georgia governor Jimmy Carter's entry on the national scene in 1976, however, governors or former governors have won every presidential election but one: Carter in 1976, Reagan in 1980 and 1984, Clinton in 1992 and 1996, and Bush in 2000. (Bush's father was the exception in 1988.) Governors have benefited politically from the nation's anti-Washington mood in the post-Vietnam, post-Watergate era, as well as from the value voters place on the experience governors gain as chief executives. Governors who run for president also find it easy to launch a campaign with money raised in their own states. Contractors who do business with the state government realize that even if the governor does not become president, he or she will remain governor.[31]

As Harold W. Stanley points out in Chapter 2, Bush raised an extraordinary amount of money for his nomination campaign—so much, in fact, that he was able to eschew federal funding and ignore the ceiling on spending that comes with it. Although Bush's massive campaign treasury made him vulnerable to attacks by Arizona senator John McCain, his chief rival for the Republican nomination and the Senate's leading advocate of campaign finance reform, it also enabled him to run the sort of fifty-state campaign that is essential to victory in the front-loaded delegate-selection process. Thematically, Bush presented himself to the voters as a "compassionate conservative" who believes that the federal government can most effectively address the problems that afflict those in need by supporting church-sponsored programs.[32] The Republican Party's economic conservatives liked Bush's emphasis on a smaller federal government. Its religious conservatives harkened to his call for a faith-based approach to national problems.

Centrist swing voters were the intended audience for the Bush-orchestrated Republican convention, which assembled in Philadelphia at the end of July. Other than Bush and his vice-presidential running mate, Richard B. Cheney, nearly all of the speakers who were featured in prime-time during the convention were African Americans, Latinos, women, or, in one case, a gay Republican member of Congress. Bush clearly hoped to increase Republican support among the groups of voters represented by these speakers, as he had done during his successful Texas gubernatorial campaigns in 1994 and, especially, in 1998. But Bush's greater purpose was to assure moderate, independent voters that he was not a conservative extremist. He underscored this purpose in his acceptance speech at the Republican convention and throughout the general election campaign by emphasizing issues such as education and Social Security reform and by promising that he would seek to govern in a bipartisan spirit. "I have no stake in the bitter arguments of the last few years," Bush told the delegates and, more important, the large television audience. "I want to change the tone of Washington to one of civility and respect." [33]

Bush's postconvention five-percentage-point bounce in the polls gave him his biggest lead of the campaign. Two weeks later, Gore closed the gap with a ten-point bounce after a Democratic convention in Los Angeles that was at least as appealing to the voters as the Republican convention had been. Gore dispelled his reputation for woodenness not only by giving a fighting acceptance speech but also by passionately kissing his wife onstage just before delivering it. The campaign between Bush and Gore remained closely fought until—and even after—November 7.

On Election Day, Bush won nearly all of the traditionally Republican Plains and Rocky Mountain states (see Figure 3-1). He swept the South, including Gore's home state of Tennessee and three other southern states that Clinton had won four years earlier. Finally, Bush won three of the four border states, all of which Clinton had carried in 1996, along with Ohio (another Clinton state), Indiana, New Hampshire, and Alaska. Bush also outpaced Gore among some groups of voters that had supported Clinton, such as political independents (47 percent).

As the exit poll results in Table 3-1 indicate, Bush did nearly as well among men (53 percent) as Gore did among women. He enjoyed stronger support from white voters (54 percent), college-educated voters (51 percent), Republicans (91 percent), and conservatives (81 percent) than any Republican presidential candidate since his father in 1988. Bush's 35 percent support among Hispanic voters, although far from a majority, was a marked improvement from 1992, when his father received 25 percent of the Hispanic vote, and 1996, when Sen. Robert J. Dole received 21 percent.

Other than party affiliation and political ideology, the major divisions among Bush and Gore voters were economic and, perhaps more important, cultural. A strong correlation existed between voters' annual income and their support for Bush. His share of the vote rose steadily as income rose—from those who earn $15,000 or less (37 percent) to those who earn $100,000 or more (54 percent). Voters who preferred an across-the-board tax cut to Gore-style targeted tax cuts favored Bush by 68 percent to 29 percent. Those who valued economic growth over the environment supported him by 58 percent to 39 percent. [34]

Bush received even stronger support from cultural conservatives. The more religious voters claimed to be, the more likely they were to vote for Bush: 59 percent of those who attend services at least once a week supported him, compared with 39 percent of those who seldom or never attend.

Married men (58 percent) and married women (49 percent) supported Bush, as did gun owners (61 percent), self-identified members of the religious right (80 percent), Protestants (63 percent), voters who valued "moral leadership" in a president over "managing the government" (70 percent), those who said the country's moral condition is on the "wrong track" (62 percent), small town and rural residents (59 percent), those for whom "honest/trustworthy" was the personal presidential quality that mattered most (80 percent), and opponents of stricter gun control laws (74 percent) and legalized abortion (71 percent).[35]

Third-Party Candidates

Since 1968, third-party candidates have become a familiar and significant part of the presidential landscape.[36] Five of the past nine presidential elections, including each of the last three, have featured such candidates. In 1968, George Wallace received 14 percent of the national popular vote and forty-six electoral votes. Twelve years later, in 1980, John Anderson won 7 percent of the popular vote. Perot received 19 percent of the popular vote in 1992 and 8 percent in 1996. In 2000, Ralph Nader won 3 percent. The average share of the national popular vote received by minor-party candidates during this period was 6.7 percent per election, four times the 1.6 percent that such candidates averaged in the nine preceding elections of 1932 through 1964.

To be sure, extended periods of significant third-party activity have occurred before, notably during the twelve years from 1848 to 1860 and the thirty-two years from 1892 to 1924. But the contemporary era of third-party presidential politics may last longer. One reason is that some of the historical barriers to third-party candidacies recently have been weakened. Another is that many voters have become detached from the major parties.

Weakened Historical Barriers

Three main barriers historically have stood in the way of third parties: the high hurdles to ballot access that many state legislatures, controlled by a two-party duopoly of Republicans and Democrats, have imposed on them; the difficulties, reinforced by the Federal Election Campaign Act of 1974, encountered in raising enough money to wage a credible national campaign; and the legal and constitutional biases that inhere in America's system of single-member district, simple-majority elections and, in particular, in the electoral college.

All three of these barriers have been eroded to some extent in recent years. Lawsuits brought by Wallace, former senator Eugene J. McCarthy (who ran as a third-party candidate in 1976), and Anderson successfully challenged onerous ballot access laws. Although Perot and other third-party candidates needed 716,000 signatures to get on all fifty state ballots in 1992, that was considerably fewer than the 1.2 million that Anderson had to gather in 1980. Perot's success in turn benefited the Reform Party, which Perot founded, and the Green Party as they sought spots on the nation's ballots in 2000.

As for the campaign finance law, although it places limits on the fund-raising ability of third-party candidates, it also guarantees that those parties that win 5 percent or more of the popular vote in one election receive time-ly and ample federal funding in the next one. Because Perot, as the Reform Party candidate in 1996, won more than 5 percent of the national popular vote, the party's 2000 nominee received $12.6 million in federal funds.

The bias against third parties inherent in the election system is less mutable. As Maurice Duverger argued in the 1950s when promulgating Duverger's Law ("the simple-majority, single-ballot system favors the two-party system"), the winner-take-all nature of American elections discourages third parties because even a large number of votes, if it is less than a plurali-ty, does not win their candidates any offices.[37] The consequence is that tal-ented political leaders, eager for victory, shy away from third parties, as do many voters, who fear that a third-party vote would be wasted on a candi-date who cannot win.

Perot fell prey to Duverger's Law in some ways but not others. His 19 percent of the popular vote in 1992 carried no states and therefore yielded no electoral votes. In the end, nearly one-fourth of the voters who thought Perot was the best candidate cast their ballots for either Bush or Clinton, depending, as they saw it, on which one was the lesser of two evils. In their view, only Bush or Clinton had a real chance of winning.[38] Yet in contrast to Duverger's Law, Perot's support actually increased during the general election campaign from 8 percent in early October to 19 percent on Election Day. Perot made another late surge in 1996, from around 4 percent to 8 percent. In both elections, Perot drew votes about equally from each of the major-party candidates, with many of his supporters saying they would not have voted had he not been on the ballot.

Oddly, perhaps, it worked to Perot's advantage that few doubted Clin-ton would win in 1992 and 1996. Voters who strongly preferred Perot but even more strongly dreaded that one or the other of the major-party candi-dates would win felt they could safely vote for the independent candidate. By contrast, Wallace's support fell off sharply in 1968, from a high of 21 percent to 13 percent on Election Day, and Anderson's dropped from 24 percent to 7 percent in 1980. Public opinion polls and most political pundits had fore-cast that both of these elections would be very close.[39] As a result, many Wal-lace and Anderson supporters peeled off to help defeat the major-party can-didate they disliked most intensely by voting for his opponent.

Proliferation of Independent Voters

Third parties have their greatest opportunity to do well when there is a large pool of voters who are not strongly attached to either of the two major parties. Such a pool has existed for more than a third of a century. During the 1950s and early 1960s, only about one-fifth of voters were classed as independents in the National Election Studies; by 1996 more than one-third were.[40] In recent elections, more new voters have registered as independents than as Democrats and Republicans combined.[41]

Historically, voters' ties to the major parties grow weaker—and their openness to third parties may grow stronger—the longer ago the realigning election that defined the era of party competition in which they live. The source of the dividing line between the parties, whether slavery in 1860 or the economy in 1896 and 1932, becomes less relevant with the passage of time, especially to new generations of voters who do not remember what the original controversy was all about.

Although every era of party competition has displayed this sort of fraying toward the end, none has become more attenuated than the contemporary era. In the past, party realignments occurred roughly every thirty years: 1800, 1828, 1860, 1896, 1932. Yet the last of these realignments took place nearly seventy years ago, and many scholars wonder whether another ever will occur.[42] Dealignment, the word usually used to describe the contemporary era, creates a fertile field in which third parties may flourish.

Third Parties in 2000

Ballot access, federal funding, and a large pool of independent voters may be necessary conditions for third-party success, but they are not sufficient ones. The Reform Party self-destructed in 2000 after Pat Buchanan captured its nomination. Buchanan, a conservative political commentator who had run strong campaigns for the Republican presidential nomination in 1992 and 1996, dropped out of the 2000 Republican race when he did poorly in the August 1999 Iowa straw poll. He refocused his presidential ambitions on capturing the Reform nomination after associates of Ross Perot, who had decided not to run a third time, invited him to do so. Buchanan shared some traditional Reform positions, especially strong opposition to free trade, but he spoke out more frequently on social and cultural issues that divided the party, such as abortion, affirmative action, and gay rights—all of which Buchanan strongly opposed. Buchanan's nomination at the Reform convention provoked the only Reformist ever to be elected to high government office, Gov. Jesse Ventura of Minnesota, to abandon the party. Perot, who had expected Buchanan to downplay his stands on social and cultural issues, endorsed Bush. The combination of a fractured party and Buchanan's recovery from gall bladder surgery, which kept him off the campaign trail during much of the fall, ruined his candidacy. Buchanan received less than 1 percent of the national popular vote on Election Day. His strongest showing was in North Dakota, where he received 3 percent of the vote, and Alaska and Idaho, where he received 2 percent. The exit polls found that only 1 percent of those who had voted for Perot in 1996 voted for Buchanan in 2000.

Instead, they supported Bush over Gore by 64 percent to 27 percent and gave 7 percent of their votes to Ralph Nader, the Green Party nominee.[43]

Nader ran a much stronger campaign than Buchanan. Nationally, the longtime consumer activist won 3 percent of the popular vote, including 10 percent in Alaska, 7 percent in Vermont, and 6 percent in Hawaii, Maine, Massachusetts, Montana, and Rhode Island. But because the majority of Nader's votes came at Gore's expense, his influence on the election was felt most strongly in the larger and more closely contested states. In northern progressive states such as Minnesota, Wisconsin, Washington, and Oregon, Gore had to campaign much harder than he would have if Nader had not been on the ballot. More critically, Nader received 97,419 votes in Florida, many more than the 930 votes by which Gore lost the state—and the presidency—to Bush. The exit polls indicated that, nationally, Nader voters preferred Gore over Bush by 47 percent to 21 percent.[44]

Nader's main purpose in running was to win 5 percent of the national popular vote so the Green Party would be assured federal funding to pursue its environmentalist and anti–free trade agenda in the 2004 election. Liberal Democrats such as Jesse Jackson and Minnesota senator Paul Wellstone pleaded with Nader to throw his support to Gore, at least in states that were close. Some independent activists even launched a vote-trading campaign on the Internet to foster arrangements in which Gore supporters in states that were not close would agree to vote for Nader if Nader voters in closely contested states would vote for Gore. But Nader argued that Gore was at best the "lesser of two evils." The Democratic and Republican Parties, he charged, "are both so marginal on the great issue of the distribution of power and wealth, and the corruption of cash register politics, that whatever real differences they are willing to fight for pale in comparison to the major subjects that they are exactly on the same page on."[45] In the end, however, less than half of the 8 percent of voters who had expressed their intention to vote for Nader earlier in the campaign actually did so on Election Day.

Although Nader failed to win 5 percent, he earned widespread media coverage for the Green Party and energized its supporters at the grass roots. Unlike the Reform Party, the Greens had already preceded their entry into presidential politics with extensive efforts at the local level. Around seventy party members have been elected to local offices. In 2000, the party fielded more than 270 candidates in races ranging from town council member to U.S. senator.

Vice-Presidential Selection

Careful selection of vice-presidential nominees is another enduring feature of modern American politics. Winning votes on Election Day is still as much the goal as it always has been when candidates for president choose their running mates. What has changed is that modern presidential candidates realize that the voters now care more than they did in the past about competence and loyalty—a prospective vice president's ability to carry out a departed president's policies capably and faithfully should the need arise.[46]

As noted earlier, during the nineteenth century vice-presidential nominations were used almost exclusively to balance the ticket, partly to heal the party's divisions and partly to win additional support in the general election. Old-style ticket balancing usually paired candidates from different and often opposing factions of the party and regions of the country. Once elected, a vice president could expect to be replaced after one term, when an altered political setting would dictate the choice of a different vice-presidential candidate who could provide the ticket with a new set of electoral balances. Until James S. Sherman in 1912, no vice president was even nominated for a second term by a party convention. The prospect of spending four years presiding over the Senate, only to be unceremoniously dumped from the ticket, dissuaded most talented political leaders from accepting a vice-presidential nomination. Daniel Webster, declining the second spot on the Whig Party's ticket in 1848, said, "I do not propose to be buried until I am dead." [47]

The situation improved somewhat in the early twentieth century, when the rise of national political campaigning and a national media made the vice presidency a more visible and appealing office to a better class of politicians. In fact, every elected first-term vice president since Sherman in 1912 has been nominated to run for a second term.[48] But the seeds of a real transformation were planted with Truman's succession to the presidency in 1945. The dawn of the nuclear age heightened voters' concerns that the vice president be someone who is ready and able to step into the presidency at a moment's notice. Good government—namely, the selection of competent, loyal vice-presidential candidates—became good politics.

Little is left to chance in modern vice-presidential selection. Carter established a precedent in 1976 when he conducted a careful, organized pre-convention search for a running mate. A list of four hundred Democratic officeholders was compiled and scrutinized by aides, then winnowed down to seven finalists who were investigated and ultimately interviewed by Carter. He then tapped Sen. Walter F. Mondale at the convention. Mondale, Gov. Michael S. Dukakis, and Clinton followed similar procedures as the Democratic presidential nominees in 1984, 1988, and 1992, respectively. Reagan did nothing so elaborate in 1980 because he hoped to lure former president Ford onto the ticket, but he and his aides did give considerable thought to the kind of running mate they wanted before choosing George Bush. Bush in turn searched widely before choosing Sen. Dan Quayle in 1988, and Dole did the same before choosing former Housing and Urban Development secretary Jack Kemp in 1996.[49]

The fruits of both the new emphasis on loyalty and competence and the care that is invested in the selection process are evident in the roster of postwar vice-presidential nominees. The modern era has been marked by an almost complete absence of ideologically opposed running mates, and those vice-presidential candidates who have differed on certain issues with the heads of their tickets have hastened loyally to gloss over past disagreements and deny that any would exist in office. The record is even more compelling concerning vice-presidential competence. In recent years, as the office has expanded to include a significant range of responsibilities and resources and has developed into the main political stepping-stone to the presidency, a vice-presidential nomination has become attractive to nearly all political leaders. Since 1948, vice-presidential candidates as often as not have been more experienced in high government office than the presidential candidates who chose them, including Mondale in 1976, Sen. Lloyd Bentsen in 1988, Gore in 1992, and Cheney in 2000.

To be sure, no guarantee exists that reasoned, responsible vice-presidential nominations will be the unbroken rule. Politicians do not always see their interests clearly. In 1984, for example, many observers thought that Mondale was too eager to placate feminist groups within the Democratic Party when he selected Rep. Geraldine A. Ferraro, a three-term member of the House with no notable experience in foreign affairs, as his running mate. Four years later, Bush erroneously convinced himself that Quayle's youth and good looks would attract the votes of young and female voters.

What seems certain, however, is that the presidential candidate who pays insufficient attention to competence and loyalty in choosing a running mate will pay a price in the election. The news media will offer unfavorable critiques, the other party will run harsh commercials, and the now-traditional televised vice-presidential debate may reveal the nominee to be an unworthy presidential successor. Quayle's presence on the ticket in 1988 reduced Bush's margin of victory in the popular vote by as much as four to eight percentage points.[50] In contrast, although Clinton's selection of Gore in 1992 defied all the conventions of ticket balancing—like Clinton, he was a southerner, a Baptist, a moderate, and a baby boomer—Gore's obvious intelligence and ability appealed to many voters.[51]

Because the Republican convention preceded the Democratic convention in 2000, Bush had to choose his running mate before Gore did. To screen potential nominees, Bush established a vetting process headed by Richard Cheney, a veteran Washington politician with experience in the House of Representatives and in two Republican administrations, including prominent service as chief of staff in the Ford White House and secretary of defense under Bush's father. In the end, Bush chose Cheney himself. The selection was surprising in one way—most of the speculation had centered on Bush's fellow big-state Republican governors, such as Tom Ridge of Pennsylvania and John Engler of Michigan. But in a more important way, Bush's selection of Cheney was not surprising at all. Governors who are nominated for president—FDR in 1932, Alfred M. Landon in 1936, Thomas E. Dewey in 1944 (but not 1948), Adlai Stevenson in 1952 and 1956, Carter in 1976, Reagan in 1980, Dukakis in 1988, and Clinton in 1992—almost always choose experienced Washington figures for vice president. They do so to reassure the voters that their own inexperience in national government, especially in foreign policy, will be offset by the vice president's experience. Bush underlined this virtue of the Cheney nomination by declaring that he had chosen Cheney less to help win the election than to help him govern "as a valuable partner"—a shrewd tactic for helping Bush to win the election.[52]

Gore enlisted former secretary of state Warren Christopher to screen potential Democratic running mates, impressed by Christopher's skillful direction of the process that had led to Gore's own selection in 1992. Between February and July, Christopher and Gore whittled a list of around forty names down to four, all of them senators: John Edwards of North Carolina, John Kerry of Massachusetts, Bob Kerrey of Nebraska, and Lieberman, who was added at Gore's insistence.[53] From the beginning, Gore wanted to make a bold choice that would help to establish him in the voters' minds as a leader in his own right, not just as Clinton's loyal lieutenant. "This choice says everything about you—" Christopher reportedly told Gore at their final meeting, "what's in your heart, what's in your soul, what's in your mind."[54] No one doubted the boldness of Gore's decision to choose Lieberman, a deeply religious Jew who had publicly criticized Clinton's behavior during the Monica Lewinsky affair as "immoral" and "harmful."[55]

Bush's selection of Cheney and Gore's choice of Lieberman helped their tickets in offsetting ways. In the exit polls, the 4 percent of voters who were Jewish backed the Gore-Lieberman ticket by 79 percent to 19 percent, nearly the same margin of support they had given to Clinton in 1996. Seventy-two percent of all voters said that Lieberman's religion would make him neither a better nor a worse vice president, and of the remaining 28 percent, twice as many said they thought it would make him a better one. Asked about their preference for vice president, 46 percent of voters said Lieberman and 48 percent said Cheney, a statistical wash.[56] Cheney's main contribution to Bush was indirect. His great experience in foreign affairs helps to explain why most of the voters who regarded foreign policy as the most important issue in the election supported Bush, even though Bush's background in this area was considerably weaker than Gore's.

Presidential Debates

A fifth enduring element of contemporary American politics is the routine occurrence of live, prime-time, nationally televised debates between the presidential and vice-presidential candidates. The first presidential debates took place in 1960. One reason they occurred then was the rapid diffusion of television sets throughout the nation. In 1950, only about one-tenth of American homes had a television. By 1960, only about one-tenth did not. Another reason was that both of the major-party candidates had strong incentives to debate, Nixon because he fancied himself (mistakenly, as it turned out) the stronger debater and Kennedy because he wanted a forum in which he could overcome the widespread public perception that he was too young and inexperienced to be president.[57]

No debates accompanied the next three presidential elections, because one of the major-party candidates in each contest did not think he had anything to gain by debating his opponent. Johnson in 1964 and Nixon in 1968 and 1972 each held a strong lead over the other party's nominee and saw no reason to give him an opportunity to cut into it. Nixon also was chastened by his disappointing experience against Kennedy and, in 1968, was wary of sharing the stage with Wallace, the third-party candidate.

The political motivations that animate presidential candidates did not change in 1976 and 1980, but political circumstances did. In both elections, an unpopular incumbent president—Ford in 1976 and Carter in 1980—faced a popular challenger, Carter and Reagan, respectively. The president wanted to debate so he could overcome the challenger's lead. The challenger wanted to debate so he could, by sharing the platform with the incumbent, appear "presidential." Debates took place in both elections, but each had a unique feature. The 1976 election introduced the first debate between the vice-presidential candidates, Mondale and Dole. In 1980, one of the two presidential debates included the third-party candidate, Anderson.

The 1984 election was a landmark in the history of presidential and vice-presidential debates. As Sidney Kraus has argued, 1984 marked the "institutionalization" of debates as a standard part of the general election campaign.[58] From 1960 to 1980, debates had taken place only when the political interests of both major-party candidates coincided. In 1984, for the first time, a popular incumbent president, Reagan, debated his opponent even though he had nothing to gain by doing so, and he instructed his running mate, Bush, to do the same.

The fruits of institutionalization became apparent in 1988. By then, voters took debates for granted. A candidate who chose not to participate would pay a high political price. Although Bush had no desire to debate Dukakis or allow Quayle to debate Bentsen, he did so. In 1992, almost as a matter of course, Bush and his running mate debated Clinton, Perot, and their running mates. Similarly, in 1996 Clinton debated Dole, and Gore debated Kemp.

Sponsorship of the debates has become institutionalized as well. Until 1988, debates were sponsored by either the television networks or the League of Women Voters. In 1988, the newly formed Commission on Presidential Debates, a privately funded organization cochaired by the heads of the two major-party national committees, took charge. The ten-member commission, which consists entirely of Republicans and Democrats, decided to include in the debates only candidates who had a "realistic chance of election." (In 2000, that meant having at least 15 percent support in the polls.) In 1992, both Clinton and Bush insisted that Perot be invited, forcing the commission's hand. But in 1996, the commission judged Perot to have no realistic chance of winning, and the major-party candidates were divided: Clinton wanted to include him but Dole did not. In 2000, neither the commission nor either major-party candidate wanted to include Nader and Buchanan. Gore did not relish being attacked from the left by Nader and Bush had no desire to defend his right flank against Buchanan.

To say that debates have become institutionalized is not to say that they are self-executing. Every four years, the candidates argue about the number, timing, and format of the debates—the aptly named "debate about the debates." Gore carried a reputation into the 2000 campaign as an aggressive, experienced, and skillful debater, a reputation that Bush did not have.[59] As a result, Gore wanted more debates and Bush fewer, a stance that by itself made Gore appear confident and Bush timid in the minds of many voters. More important, Gore's quick acceptance of the commission's plan for three presidential debates and one vice-presidential debate in early- to mid-October appeared reasonable to many observers, while Bush's counterproposal for one commission-sponsored debate, along with joint appearances on CNN's "Larry King Live" and NBC's "Meet the Press," seemed like an effort to write his own rules. Bush television ads that attacked Gore for being afraid to debate struck even Bush's supporters as ludicrous. Realizing that in the court of public opinion he was losing the argument about how and when to debate, Bush caved in and accepted the commission's proposal.

Ironically, Bush benefited considerably more from the debates than Gore did. In the first debate, a formal affair in which both candidates stood before a podium, Gore treated his opponent with disdain, often speaking condescendingly when it was his turn and sighing and grimacing while Bush spoke. Chastened by the adverse public response, Gore was deferential, almost obsequious, during the second debate, a loosely structured event that placed the two candidates around a table with PBS's Jim Lehrer, who moderated all of the presidential debates. Gore hit his stride in the town meeting–style third debate, but the inconsistency of his behavior from one debate to the next fed voters' doubts about who Gore really was. Bush was not strongly impressive in any of the debates, but voters saw the same Bush in all three of them. They also heard Bush discuss foreign policy during the second debate with apparent poise and competence, easing some of their doubts about how well he would perform as president on diplomatic and security matters.

The vice-presidential debate between Lieberman and Cheney, which took place between the first and second presidential debates, also redounded to Bush's benefit. The two candidates discussed the issues reasonably and amicably and were equally impressive in doing so. But Cheney, a rusty campaigner who had gotten off to a slow start after he was nominated for vice president, had much more to gain in the minds of voters than did Lieberman, who had already demonstrated his appeal in several highly successful joint appearances with Gore.

Gore's verdict on his performance in the three presidential debates was that he had been, like the three bears' porridge, "too hot" in the first one, "too cold" in the second one, and "just right" in the third one.[60] One could just as easily say, however, that Gore had performed well in only one of the three debates and had performed consistently in none. Bush, who entered the debates trailing Gore by around five percentage points in the polls, came out of them with about a five-point lead. The Commission on Presidential Debates was the other winner. For the first time, all of the debates were held at the time and place of the commission's choosing. In the future, it will be hard for candidates to overturn this precedent and impose their own preferences on the debate schedule.

Low Voter Turnout

Low voter turnout is another ordinary feature of modern American politics. The percentage of the voting-age population that casts ballots has fallen steadily since 1960, when the turnout rate was 63 percent. In 1996, only 49 percent voted, the lowest share of the electorate since 1924, a year when most women, newly enfranchised by the Nineteenth Amendment, were unfamiliar with voting and many states had registration laws that discriminated against recent immigrants and African Americans. Although the 2000 election followed a closely fought campaign and guaranteed the choice of a new president, the turnout rate only increased to 51 percent.

The steady decline in voter turnout in the contemporary era has occurred despite several developments that should have led to greater turnout. Since 1960, it has become much easier for people to register to vote. In 1964, the poll tax was eliminated by the Twenty-fourth Amendment. In 1965, the Voting Rights Act largely ended discrimination against African Americans and other minorities. In addition, residency requirements have been greatly eased in response to Supreme Court decisions, and the states have instituted procedures such as mobile registrars, postcard registration, and, in some cases, Election Day registration. In 1993, the National Voter Registration Act, the so-called motor-voter bill, required all the states to allow registration by mail and at motor vehicle, welfare, unemployment, and other state offices. Political science professors who ask their students where they registered to vote have become accustomed to hearing most of them say that they registered at their high schools or at the motor vehicle office.

Voting also has become easier in recent years. Many states allow people to vote at their convenience during the weeks preceding the election. In Oregon, voters cast their ballots by mail. More important, education levels have been rising steadily in American society. Few things correlate as strongly with voting as education: the more of it citizens have, the more likely they are to vote. The reason, as political scientists Raymond E. Wolfinger and Steven J. Rosenstone observe, is that education "imparts information about politics . . . [and] increases one's capacity for understanding and working with complex, abstract, and intangible subjects, that is, subjects like politics."[61] The real puzzle is not why voter turnout has been declining since 1960, but why it has not been rising.

The solution to this puzzle is complex and, among scholars, much contested, involving elements as varied and seemingly nonpolitical as the age, marital, and religious structure of American society.[62] Young people, single people, and people who do not attend church regularly—all of whom have been growing in number since 1960—are less likely to vote than those who are older, married, and churchgoers. Certainly the 1971 enactment of the Twenty-sixth Amendment, which reduced the minimum voting age from twenty-one to eighteen, contributed to the six-percentage-point decline in the rate of voter turnout that occurred between 1968 and 1972. As Daniel Wirls points out in Chapter 4, older people are twice as likely to vote as younger people.

The controversy over the results of the 2000 presidential election in Florida revealed that ballot design and voting technology affect whether the voters who show up at the polls will actually have their votes counted. Nationwide, 2.1 million ballots—about 2 percent of all ballots cast—were marked either for more than one presidential candidate or for none, sometimes intentionally but often as a consequence of voters' confusion about voting procedures.

These errors were especially widespread among the 34 percent of voters whose states and counties use the old-style punch card system, in which a voter must punch through the pre-perforated square, or "chad," next to the name of the candidate of his or her choice. The 27 percent of voters whose ballots must be marked (SAT or ACT–style) in pencil and then read by an optical scanning device encounter fewer problems, as do the 9 percent who vote on ATM-like electronic touch screens and the 19 percent who vote by pulling a small lever next to their candidate's name in a mechanical voting machine.[63] Both the postelection furor over the outcome of the election in Florida and the Supreme Court's decision in *Bush v. Gore* to open the voting process to judicial scrutiny under the equal protection clause of the Constitution augured a national effort to ensure that voters can easily and accurately express their intentions in the voting booth.[64] Civil rights groups were especially incensed that the less-expensive, more error-prone punch card system is more prevalent in poor and minority precincts than in affluent jurisdictions.

But the more important explanations for declining voter turnout are political, not mechanical. As noted earlier, voters in the contemporary era of partisan dealignment tend to be less strongly committed to a political party than in the past. The consequences for turnout are clear. Just as strong party attachments typically increase one's psychological involvement in politics and reduce the time and effort needed to decide how to vote, weak attachments tend to distance one from politics and raise the costs of voting. To the extent that candidates and political parties devote their budgets to saturating the airwaves with commercials rather than mobilizing people to vote, they aggravate this situation.[65]

Equally important, Americans' sense of their own political effectiveness—what political scientists call "external efficacy"—has been in steep decline since 1960. Fewer voters see a connection between what they do on Election Day and what the government does afterward.[66] According to a

2000 study by political scientist Thomas E. Patterson, only around 14 percent of nonvoters would like to vote but, for reasons of health or travel, cannot. The rest are either "apathetic" (the 35 percent of nonvoters who are
uninterested in politics and feel no civic obligation to vote), "alienated" (the
26 percent who are angrily disgusted with politics), or "disenchanted" (the
25 percent who are not permanently estranged from the political process but
who distrust politicians).[67]

The Electoral College

During the 1980s, much was heard about a "Republican lock" on the
electoral college that all but guaranteed victory in presidential elections to the
Republican nominee regardless of what happened in the national popular
vote.[68] The lock theory simply noted that Republican candidates for president had carried twenty-one states with 191 electoral votes in every presidential election from 1968 to 1988, and that Democrats had consistently
won only the District of Columbia, with three electoral votes. Broadening the
standard to include states that had supported the same party in at least five
of these six elections only widened the disparity: 318 electoral votes (thirty-
three states) for the Republicans and 13 electoral votes for the Democrats
(the District and Minnesota). With 270 votes needed for victory, the electoral
college seemed to some to be so imbued with a Republican bias as to practically rig the election.

Clinton's victory in the 1992 election laid the Republican lock theory to
rest: Democrats carried eighteen states (198 electoral votes) that had gone
Republican either five or six times since 1968. His reelection in 1996, however, gave birth to a new but equally implausible lock theory, this one favoring the Democrats. Noting that Clinton carried twenty-nine states with 346
electoral votes both times he ran, White House political director Douglas
Sosnik claimed, "We are seeing the beginning of a Democratic electoral college advantage, making us better positioned for a generation of presidential
campaigns to come."[69] Political scientist Larry Bartels estimated in 2000 that
if one assumes a "50–50 split of the national popular vote, and assumes that
the distribution of states around that average will be similar to what it has
been in the last three presidential elections," the Democratic candidate will
win the electoral vote by 272 electoral votes to 266.[70]

The truth is that, almost without exception, the electoral college "mag-
nifies" the national popular vote—that is, the candidate who wins a plurality of the people's votes wins a large majority of the electoral votes. Magnification of this kind occurred in every presidential election from 1892 to 1996.
Sometimes the magnification was small—in 1976, for example, Carter's 50
percent of the popular vote translated into 55 percent of the electoral vote.
More often the magnification was great. Nixon in 1972 and Reagan in 1984
received 61 percent and 59 percent of the popular vote, respectively. But
Nixon won 97 percent of the electoral vote, and Reagan won 98 percent. In

the twenty-seven presidential elections that took place between 1892 and 1996, the winning candidate's average 53 percent of the popular vote became 76 percent of the electoral vote.

Nonetheless, as critics of the electoral college have often pointed out, no guarantee exists that the popular vote winner will be elected president. Theoretically, a candidate could narrowly carry the eleven largest states, lose all of the other states overwhelmingly, and win a 270–268 electoral college victory with less than 30 percent of the popular vote. In 1888, Benjamin Harrison lost the national popular vote to Grover Cleveland by 48 percent to 49 percent. But by carrying six of the seven largest states, Harrison prevailed in the electoral college by 233 to 168 and was elected president.

In the modern political era of constant public opinion polling, candidates who are far behind as Election Day approaches typically give up the effort to win a national popular vote plurality and run campaigns aimed at carrying just enough states to eke out a narrow victory in the electoral college. Trailing Nixon in 1972, McGovern spent nearly all of his time and money during the final month of the campaign trying to win the twelve largest states. In mid-October 1988, Dukakis decided to pursue an eighteen-state strategy for victory. Late in the 1996 campaign, Dole tried to employ the same strategy but with different tactics. He wrote off all but twenty-nine mostly small and medium-sized states that, taken together, had 278 electoral votes, eight more than he needed to win.

Gore's prospects of winning the 2000 election in the accepted way—that is, seek votes everywhere and rack up both popular and electoral vote majorities—were reasonably strong during most of the election year. But when Gore proved unable to close the five-point deficit in the polls with which he had stumbled out of the debates, Democratic strategists quietly embraced the McGovern-Dukakis-Dole strategy. By election eve, most of them were explaining off the record that they planned to pull out a victory by winning almost all of the big states narrowly while Bush was carrying the rest of the country solidly.[71] They premised this plan on the huge popular vote majority that Bush was expected to win in his home state of Texas, an "inefficient" victory that would pad his national popular vote plurality but earn him no more electoral votes than would a narrow victory.

Ironically, Gore became the victim of his own strategy. He, not Bush, won the national popular vote. But Bush won the electoral vote and the presidency. As indicated in Table 3–2, Texas did go strongly for Bush—he carried it by a margin of 1,367,521 votes. But of the six states that went for either candidate by 400,000 votes or more, Texas was the only one to prefer Bush. Gore carried the other five, including New York by 1,531,833 votes and California by 1,283,638 votes.[72]

Although Senator-elect Hillary Rodham Clinton and several other members of Congress quickly called for a constitutional amendment that would replace the electoral college with direct election, the future of the electoral college seems secure. The amendment process outlined in Article V of the

Table 3-2 2000 Popular Vote for President, by State

State	Bush Vote	%	Gore Vote	%	Nader Vote	%	Buchanan Vote	%	Other Vote	%
Alabama	943,799	57	696,741	42	18,055	1	6,317	*	7,532	*
Alaska	136,068	59	64,252	28	22,789	10	4,254	2	3,304	1
Arizona	715,112	51	635,730	45	41,937	3	11,478	1	1,054	*
Arkansas	472,120	51	420,424	45	13,275	2	10,960	1	10,159	1
California	4,437,557	42	5,721,195	54	405,722	4	43,751	*	71,352	1
Colorado	884,047	51	738,470	42	91,482	5	10,479	1	14,122	1
Connecticut	545,954	39	795,861	56	60,644	4	4,398	*	12,884	1
Delaware	137,081	42	180,638	55	8,288	3	775	*	1,088	*
District of Columbia	17,020	9	162,004	86	9,925	5	—	—	641	*
Florida	2,911,872	49	2,910,942	49	97,419	2	17,472	*	19,759	*
Georgia	1,416,085	55	1,110,755	43	—	—	10,921	1	36,473	1
Hawaii	137,785	38	205,209	56	21,609	6	1,071	*	2,125	*
Idaho	336,299	69	138,354	28	—	—	7,687	2	6,132	1
Illinois	2,019,256	43	2,588,884	55	103,754	2	16,106	*	13,748	*
Indiana	1,242,372	57	899,836	41	—	—	17,374	1	16,780	1
Iowa	634,225	48	638,355	49	29,352	2	5,731	1	6,236	*
Kansas	616,829	58	392,867	37	35,706	3	7,277	1	7,086	1
Kentucky	869,946	57	637,518	41	23,125	2	4,181	*	5,897	*
Louisiana	924,670	53	789,837	45	20,817	1	14,478	1	10,007	1
Maine	284,724	44	316,109	49	37,842	6	4,324	1	3,784	*
Maryland	770,911	40	1,093,344	57	51,078	3	4,067	*	5,856	*
Massachusetts	876,906	33	1,610,175	60	173,758	6	11,086	*	19,182	1
Michigan	1,947,100	47	2,141,721	51	83,838	2	—	—	19,716	*
Minnesota	1,110,290	46	1,168,190	48	126,586	5	22,268	1	10,963	*
Mississippi	549,426	57	400,845	42	7,899	1	2,237	*	5,640	*
Missouri	1,189,521	51	1,110,826	47	38,488	2	9,806	—	10,501	*
Montana	239,755	58	137,264	34	24,487	6	5,735	1	3,557	1
Nebraska	408,719	63	215,616	33	22,975	3	3,431	1	2,991	1
Nevada	301,539	49	279,949	46	15,004	2	4,747	1	7,660	2
New Hampshire	273,135	48	265,853	47	22,156	4	2,603	*	3,058	1
New Jersey	1,253,791	41	1,747,445	56	92,184	3	6,919	*	10,382	*
New Mexico	286,417	48	286,783	48	21,251	4	1,392	*	2,762	*
New York	2,235,776	35	3,767,609	60	223,547	4	33,356	1	40,913	1
North Carolina	1,607,238	56	1,236,721	43	—	—	8,971	*	12,284	1
North Dakota	175,572	61	96,098	33	9,530	3	7,330	3	1,345	*
Ohio	2,294,167	50	2,117,741	46	114,482	3	25,980	1	17,591	*
Oklahoma	744,335	60	474,326	38	—	—	9,014	1	6,502	*
Oregon	712,705	47	719,165	47	77,186	5	7,043	*	12,143	1
Pennsylvania	2,264,309	47	2,465,412	51	102,453	2	16,879	*	26,916	*
Rhode Island	132,535	32	254,500	61	24,194	6	2,256	1	1,077	*

(continued)

Table 3-2 *Continued*

State	Bush Vote	%	Gore Vote	%	Nader Vote	%	Buchanan Vote	%	Other Vote	%
South Carolina	804,826	57	578,143	41	21,008	2	3,540	0	7,913	*
South Dakota	190,515	60	118,750	38	—	—	3,314	1	3,444	1
Tennessee	1,056,480	51	977,789	48	19,694	1	4,218	*	5,954	*
Texas	3,796,850	59	2,429,329	38	137,716	2	12,426	*	23,166	1
Utah	512,168	67	201,734	26	35,661	5	9,277	1	7,005	2
Vermont	119,273	41	148,166	51	19,810	7	2,182	1	1,128	*
Virginia	1,431,654	52	1,221,094	45	59,270	2	5,592	*	16,417	1
Washington	1,101,621	45	1,240,302	50	101,906	4	7,117	*	17,863	1
West Virginia	329,708	52	291,088	46	10,440	2	3,101	*	2,280	*
Wisconsin	1,235,035	48	1,240,431	48	93,553	4	11,379	*	9,483	*
Wyoming	147,674	69	60,421	28	—	—	2,724	1	2,607	2

Source: http://www.cnn.com/ELECTION/2000/results/index.president.html.

Note: An asterisk indicates a vote total of less than 1 percent; a dash indicates that the candidate was not on the ballot in that state.

Constitution is arduous. A proposed amendment can be blocked by one-third plus one of either the House of Representatives or the Senate or by one-fourth plus one of the state legislatures. Controversial proposals to amend the Constitution find it almost impossible to survive this process, and the electoral college is highly controversial. Small states like it because they get a larger (albeit still tiny) voice in presidential elections than their populations would warrant, and big states like it because their large bundles of electoral votes secure them virtually all of the candidates' attention during the campaign. Lobbyist organizations that represent African Americans, Latinos, Jews, and unionized workers—groups that are more prevalent in the big states than elsewhere—also tend to support the electoral college.[73]

To be sure, a strongly mobilized public could sweep these obstacles to reform aside. For decades, polls have indicated that large majorities of Americans have opposed the electoral college. But because the electoral vote mirrored or magnified the popular vote in every twentieth-century election, the issue was never salient enough to mobilize many of them to pick up the phone or take pen in hand and express their views to members of Congress. Scholars had long assumed that only an election such as the one in 2000, in which the candidate who became president lost the popular vote, would convert the public's passive opposition to the electoral college into the sort of active opposition that would make reform possible.

But two aspects of the 2000 election prevented such a mobilization from occurring. One was that the five-week-long controversy over which candidate had won Florida overshadowed every other aspect of the election. Gore's popular vote plurality was seldom mentioned during this period, especially after he expressly downplayed its importance in his first postelection news conference.[74] The other is that Gore, far from being the victim of an opponent's strategy to manipulate the electoral college, was himself the candidate who tried to manipulate it. The futility of Gore's strategy did little to arouse either public support for him as the true winner of the election or public opposition to the electoral college as the institution that had brought about his defeat.

A constitutional amendment that might attract broader support would bar "faithless electors" from the process by recording the electoral votes of each state automatically—the so-called automatic plan that presidents Kennedy and Johnson urged Congress to approve during the 1960s. Historically, only ten electors have broken faith with the voters and cast their electoral vote for a different candidate than the one who received a plurality in their state on Election Day. In no case have their votes affected the outcome of the election. But the frequency of faithless voting has increased from one elector in every twenty elections from 1789 to 1944 to more than one in every two elections since 1948. Around half the states outlaw faithless voting by electors, but because the Constitution imposes no such constraint, these laws are of doubtful constitutionality. In 2000, an elector from the District of Columbia abstained rather than vote for Gore, who had carried the District by 85 percent to 9 percent. She withheld her vote to protest the District's lack of representation in Congress. No elector had ever used his or her vote in such a way. Nor had any elector ever done so in such a close election.

Divided Government

The recent pattern of divided government is the final aspect of ordinary American politics to be discussed in this chapter. United government, with the same political party in control of both the presidency and Congress, was until recently the norm in Washington. From 1900 to 1968, united government prevailed 79 percent of the time. From 1969 to 2000, it prevailed only 19 percent of the time—the four years of Carter's presidency and the first two years of Clinton's first term, when the Democrats controlled both of the elected branches.

Perhaps the obvious explanation for the modern prevalence of divided government is the accurate one: the voters elect a divided government because they do not wish to entrust complete control to either major party.[75] Certainly a majority of voters in most recent elections have said they hoped divided government would be the outcome. Even though only a minority, usually 20 percent to 30 percent, split their ticket between the presidential candidate of one party and the congressional candidate of the other,[76] that is a substantial number of voters in a close election, especially when they are motivated, as some are, by an active desire to bring about divided control.[77]

During much of the contemporary era, divided government has meant a Republican president and a Democratic Congress; indeed, from 1968 to 1992 that was the only form that divided government took. Several theories emerged to explain this pattern. For example, one theory held that many voters regarded a Democratic Congress as the best safeguard of their desire for an active federal government and a Republican president as insurance against their corresponding dread of higher taxes.[78] Another looked to the nature of the two parties: a heterogeneous Democratic Party that satisfied a variety of constituencies at the congressional level but seldom could unite behind a single presidential candidate, and a homogeneous Republican Party that found it easy to rally around its standard-bearer for president but difficult to tailor its appeals to a wide range of states and congressional districts.[79]

From 1994 to 2000, however, divided government meant a Democratic president and a Republican Congress. Theories to explain the new pattern were in short supply. It may be that the "southernization" of the Republican Party simultaneously made it harder for the Republicans to win the presidency and, joined with the decennial reallocation of House seats from the north to the more conservative south, easier for them to win Congress.[80] Or it may be that the new pattern was a fluke, no more or less likely than any other combination of presidents and Congresses would have been in an era that is so closely divided between the parties. At no point in the 1990s, for example, did the Democrats win more than 49 percent of the national popular vote for president or the Republicans more than 53 percent of the House of Representatives. As for "the public's own divided and self-contradictory preferences, nothing fundamental has changed," notes Jacobson. Voters continue to want both the "low tax rates, low inflation, less intrusive government, greater economic efficiency, and strong national defense" that they associate with the Republican Party and the "middle-class entitlements and other popular domestic programs" that they associate with the Democrats.[81]

The outcome of the elections of 2000—a Republican president and a Republican Congress, for the first time since 1952—was united government, but of a sort that mocks the very concept of united government. The Republican majorities were tiny even by contemporary standards: 5 electoral votes (out of 538) in the presidency, 9 seats (out of 435) in the House, and an exactly even divide in the Senate, with only Vice President Cheney's power to break ties enabling the Republicans to claim majority status. To make matters worse, the Democrats strongly believed that they had been cheated out of the presidency in an unfair Florida recount and, consequently, that Bush's authority to govern was less legitimate than that of any president in more than a century. Even before Bush was inaugurated in January 2001, the Democrats had begun campaigning to regain control of Congress in November 2002. Thus, despite Bush's efforts during the preinauguration transition period and afterward to reach out to the Democrats, and the Democrats' clenched-teeth promise to respond in a bipartisan spirit, divided government in Washington was the reality regardless of the form.

Historically, the consequences of divided government have been mixed. After studying federal lawmaking from 1946 to 1990, David R. Mayhew concluded that divided governments are as likely to enact "major statutes" as united governments.[82] In his December 13 speech to the Texas legislature claiming victory, Bush indicated that he would seek bipartisan legislation on issues that both he and Gore had addressed in the campaign, such as education and prescription drugs for senior citizens. Political scientists Paul J. Quirk and Bruce Nesmith, although cautious in their argument, suggest that on "autonomy issues"—that is, issues such as foreign aid and entitlement reform in which public opinion conflicts with elite conceptions of the public interest—a divided government may act more responsibly than a united government, in which the incumbent party would have to bear the entire burden of political blame for taking principled but unpopular actions.[83]

In at least two areas of fundamental importance to a constitutional system, however, the effects of divided government are corrosive. One is democratic accountability. Voters need to know who is responsible for what the government is doing if they are to render an effective judgment on Election Day. Yet divided government confuses the matter by allowing both the Republican and the Democratic Parties to evade responsibility, each blaming the other and the branch of government that it controls for whatever is wrong in Washington. During the 1980s and early 1990s, Republican presidents and Democratic Congresses did little more than point accusatory fingers at each other as the annual federal budget deficit quintupled from less than $60 billion to nearly $300 billion. The voters, not knowing which party to believe, believed neither. Serious deficit reduction came only in 1993, the first year since 1980 that the same party controlled both the presidency and Congress.

The other clearly corrosive effect of divided government is on the federal judiciary, which has become a political football in the partisan battle between presidents and Senates of different parties. From 1900 to 1968, during the era of united government, only three of forty-five Supreme Court nominations (7 percent) were rejected by the Senate. Two of these rejections came in 1968, a year of de facto divided government, because the Republicans firmly expected to win control of the presidency but not the Senate in that year's elections. Since 1969, four of seventeen Supreme Court nominations (24 percent) have been rejected, including four of twelve (33 percent) of those made when the president and Senate were of different parties. Even worse, as political scientist John Anthony Maltese has shown, the "selling of Supreme Court nominees" has recently become indistinguishable from overtly (and appropriately) partisan battles about public policy.[84] An equally partisan approach—rejection by inaction—characterized the Republican Senate's response to many of Clinton's nominations to fill vacancies on the district and circuit courts. Consequently, the legitimacy of the courts, dependent as it is on public trust in the courts' nonpartisanship, has been seriously called into question.

The courts' legitimacy will be in special jeopardy during Bush's term. The Supreme Court has seldom been more closely divided between liberal and conservative justices than it is now. Fully one-third of the Court's cases during its 1999–2000 term, for example, were decided by a vote of 5–4. The Court's 5–4 decision in *Bush v. Gore,* which effectively ended the 2000 presidential election, was more controversial still. All five justices who voted in Bush's favor were conservative Nixon, Reagan, or Bush appointees, provoking Justice John Paul Stevens, joined by Clinton's two appointees, Justices Stephen Breyer and Ruth Bader Ginsburg, to charge that the Court's decision "can only lend credence to the most cynical appraisal of the work of judges throughout the land."[85] Complicating matters further, no vacancy has occurred on the Supreme Court since 1994, the longest stretch without a vacancy since 1870. (On average, a vacancy occurs every two years.) Four justices will be in their seventies or eighties by the end of Bush's term: liberals Stevens (84) and Ginsburg (71) and conservatives William Rehnquist (79) and Sandra Day O'Connor (74). The prospect of several vacancies occurring seems great. The prospect that the confirmation battles to fill these vacancies will be bruisingly partisan seems even greater.

Conclusion

The elections of 2000 will surely be remembered for their extraordinary elements. Yet the ordinary and enduring aspects of modern American politics that the elections manifested are of more lasting importance. This chapter has looked at several such elements, paying particular attention to the general election campaign for president between Bush and Gore. The vice presidency's modern political status as the prime stepping-stone to a presidential candidacy helps to account both for Gore's success in getting nominated and for his failure to be elected. Bush's nomination was shown to be emblematic of the unifying national party conventions that characterize contemporary politics. The prominence of the Nader and Buchanan candidacies manifests the political system's growing openness to third parties. Other aspects of the 2000 elections—the now-institutionalized presidential and vice-presidential debates, the all-too-familiar low voter turnout, the varying political effects of the electoral college, and the persistence of divided government in reality if not in form—also embody the ordinary politics of the contemporary era.

Not every aspect of modern American politics has been charted in this chapter. Some are treated in the chapters that follow. In Chapter 4, for example, Daniel Wirls explores the deepening lines of cleavage in the nation's voting behavior. Matthew Robert Kerbel describes in Chapter 5 the misdirected coverage of election campaigns that the mass media now routinely offer. In Chapter 6, Richard J. Ellis explores the causes and consequences of the recent emphasis on voter initiatives in state politics. Paul J. Quirk and Sean C. Matheson, writing about the presidency in Chapter 7, rue the public's shrinking concern about suitable presidential qualifications. Gary C. Jacobson suggests in Chapter 8 that congressional elections have reached a virtual stalemate. Even Chapter 9, which explores the almost unique "postelection election," treats the legal battle between Bush and Gore as the latest manifestation of another enduring aspect of modern American politics: the use of "politics by other means," especially legal means, to wage political combat.

Notes

1. Michael Nelson, "Constitutional Aspects of the Elections," in *The Elections of 1988,* ed. Michael Nelson (Washington, D.C.: CQ Press, 1989), 192.
2. The history of the vice presidency that follows is drawn from Sidney M. Milkis and Michael Nelson, *The American Presidency: Origins and Development, 1776–1998* (Washington, D.C.: CQ Press, 1999), chap. 15; Michael Nelson, *A Heartbeat Away* (Washington, D.C.: Brookings, 1988); and Michael Nelson, "Is There a Curse of the Vice Presidency?" *American Prospect,* July 31, 2000, 20–24.
3. See, for example, Robert K. Murray and Tim H. Blessing, "The Presidential Performance Study: A Progress Report," *Journal of American History* 70 (December 1983): 535–555.
4. Ibid.
5. Nelson, *Heartbeat Away,* 91.
6. Bob Woodward, *The Agenda: Inside the Clinton White House* (New York: Simon and Schuster, 1993), 281.
7. Nelson, "Is There a Curse of the Vice Presidency?"
8. George Sirgiovanni, "The 'Van Buren Jinx': Vice Presidents Need Not Beware," *Presidential Studies Quarterly* 18 (winter 1988): 61–76.
9. Bill Turque, *Inventing Al Gore* (Boston: Houghton Mifflin, 2000), 356.
10. Ibid., 361.
11. "Transcript of Debate between Vice President Gore and Governor Bush," *New York Times,* October 4, 2000.
12. Michael Nelson, "Evaluating the Presidency," in *The Presidency and the Political System,* 6th ed., ed. Michael Nelson (Washington, D.C.: CQ Press, 2000), 3–28.
13. Voter News Service "Exit Polls," online at http://www.cnn.com/ELECTION/2000/results/index.epolls.html.
14. Jules Witcover, *Crapshoot: Rolling the Dice on the Vice Presidency* (New York: Crown, 1992), 138.
15. Nelson, "Constitutional Aspects of the Elections," 190.
16. David E. Sanger, "After 'Next Best Thing,' Clinton Carefully Praises Gore," *New York Times,* November 4, 2000.
17. Robert G. Kaiser, "Academics Say It's Elementary: Gore Wins," *Washington Post,* August 31, 2000. "It's not even going to be close," said Michael Lewis-Beck of the University of Iowa as early as May. Robert G. Kaiser, "Is This Any Way to Pick a Winner?" *Washington Post,* May 26, 2000. After the election, the political scientists ascribed the inaccuracy of their predictions to Gore's inept campaign, the Clinton scandals, and Ralph Nader's candidacy. Robert G. Kaiser, "Political Scientists Offer Mea Culpas for Predicting Gore Win," *Washington Post,* February 9, 2001.
18. Voter News Service "Exit Polls."
19. Michael Duffy, "What It Took," *Time,* November 20, 2000, 130.
20. Thomas M. DeFrank, "I'm My Own Man, Says Al," *New York Daily News,* August 18, 2000.

21. David S. Broder, "Gore's Clinton Problem," *Washington Post* National Weekly Edition, October 30, 2000, 4.
22. Michael Kinsley, "The Art of Finger-Pointing," *Slate,* October 30, 2000, online at http://slate.msn.com/00-10-30/readme.asp.
23. "What a Long, Strange Trip," *Newsweek,* November 20, 2000, 126.
24. Voter News Service "Exit Polls."
25. Ibid.
26. Gary C. Jacobson, *The 2000 Elections and Beyond* (Washington, D.C.: CQ Press, 2001), 26.
27. Martin P. Wattenberg, *The Rise of Candidate-Centered Politics: Presidential Elections in the 1980s* (Cambridge: Harvard University Press, 1991), chap. 3.
28. Stephen J. Wayne, *The Road to the White House 2000: The Politics of Presidential Elections* (Boston: Bedford/St. Martin's, 2000), 156.
29. Ibid., 178.
30. Michael Nelson, "Who Vies for President?" in *Presidential Selection,* ed. Alexander Heard and Michael Nelson (Durham: Duke University Press, 1987), 120–154.
31. Only eleven of the fifty state governors' terms end in the presidential election year.
32. Bush wrote the foreword for Marvin S. Olasky, *Compassionate Conservatism: What It Is, What It Does, and How It Can Transform America* (New York: Free Press, 2000).
33. Thomas M. DeFrank, " 'It Won't Be Long Now,' Bush Vows to Lead GOPers to Victory," *New York Daily News,* August 4, 2000.
34. Voter News Service "Exit Polls."
35. Ibid.
36. In this chapter, the term *third-party candidates* also includes independent candidates. The distinction is nicely drawn in Steven J. Rosenstone, Roy L. Behr, and Edward H. Lazarus, *Third Parties in America,* 2d ed. (Princeton: Princeton University Press, 1996), 48, 81.
37. Maurice Duverger, *Political Parties: Their Organization and Activity in the Modern World,* trans. Barbara North and Robert North (New York: Wiley, 1963).
38. John H. Aldrich and Thomas Weko, "The Presidency and the Election Campaign: Framing the Choice in 1992," in *The Presidency and the Political System,* 4th ed., ed. Michael Nelson (Washington, D.C.: CQ Press, 1995), 255.
39. Erwin C. Hargrove and Michael Nelson, *Presidents, Politics, and Policy* (Baltimore: Johns Hopkins University Press, 1984), 161.
40. Paul R. Abramson, John H. Aldrich, and David W. Rohde, *Change and Continuity in the 1996 and 1998 Elections* (Washington, D.C.: CQ Press, 1999), 291.
41. Rhodes Cook, "Third Parties Push to Present a Respectable Alternative," *Congressional Quarterly Weekly Report,* July 13, 1996, 1986.
42. See, for example, Sidney M. Milkis, "The New Deal, the Modern Presidency, and Divided Government," in *Divided Government: Change, Uncertainty, and the Constitutional Order,* ed. Peter F. Galderisi (Lanham, Md.: Rowman and Littlefield, 1996), 135–171.
43. Voter News Service "Exit Polls."
44. Thirty percent said they would not have voted at all. Peter Slevin, "A Defiant Nader Stands Up to Criticism," *Washington Post,* November 9, 2000.
45. Peter Slevin, "Defections Threaten Nader's 5% Vote Goal," *Washington Post,* November 8, 2000; and "For Nader, Little Momentum but Lots of Political Impact," *Washington Post,* October 23, 2000.
46. Most of the historical material in this section is from Nelson, *Heartbeat Away.*
47. Milkis and Nelson, *American Presidency,* 404.

48. A partial exception is Franklin D. Roosevelt's third-term vice president, Henry A. Wallace, who was elected in 1940 and dropped from the ticket in 1944.

49. Michael Nelson, "Choosing the Vice President," *PS: Political Science and Politics* 21 (fall 1988): 858–868.

50. Nelson, "Constitutional Aspects of the Elections," 190.

51. Gore balanced the ticket in subtle ways—for example, as a stable family man and as a Vietnam veteran.

52. David Von Drehle, " 'First, Do No Harm' Rule," *Washington Post* National Weekly Edition, July 31, 2000, 9.

53. Because the Republican Party dominated the nation's statehouses—in 2000, they had thirty governors and the Democrats had twenty, including only one governor from a large state—Gore had few governors from whom to choose.

54. Duffy, "What It Took," 136.

55. Bob Woodward, *Shadow: Five Presidents and the Legacy of Watergate* (New York: Simon and Schuster, 1999), 454.

56. Voters News Service "Exit Polls."

57. Actually there were three reasons, if one includes Congress's temporary suspension of Section 315 of the Federal Communications Act, the so-called equal-time rule. In 1976 and 1983, the Federal Communications Commission reinterpreted Section 315 in ways that effectively eliminated it as a legal barrier to televised debates.

58. Sidney Kraus, *Televised Presidential Debates and Public Policy* (Hillsdale, N.J.: Lawrence Earlbaum Associates, 1988).

59. James Fallows, "An Acquired Taste," *Atlantic Monthly*, July 2000, 33–53.

60. "What a Long, Strange Trip," 109.

61. Raymond E. Wolfinger and Steven J. Rosenstone, *Who Votes?* (New Haven: Yale University Press, 1980), 18.

62. An excellent discussion of the literature on voter turnout may be found in Abramson, Aldrich, and Rohde, *Change and Continuity in the 1996 and 1998 Elections*, chap. 4.

63. Richard Lacayo, "Is This Any Way to Vote?" *Time*, November 27, 2000, 54–56.

64. *Bush v. Gore*, 69 U.S.L.W. 4029 (2000).

65. Steven J. Rosenstone and John Mark Hansen, *Mobilization, Participation, and Democracy in America* (New York: Macmillan, 1993).

66. Ibid., 130–131; and Abramson, Aldrich, and Rohde, *Change and Continuity in the 1992 Elections*, 117–120.

67. Richard Morin and Claudia Deane, "As Turnout Falls, Apathy Emerges as Driving Force," *Washington Post*, November 4, 2000.

68. See my discussion of this matter in Nelson, "Constitutional Aspects of the Elections," 192–195.

69. Quoted in "Power of Geography Taking Root," *USA Today*, November 7, 1996, 43.

70. Thomas B. Edsall, "Electoral Leanings Now Favor Democrats," *Washington Post*, September 18, 2000.

71. Michael Nelson, "College for Duncesisms," *American Prospect*, December 4, 2000, 14–15.

72. The remaining three states that Gore carried by at least 400,000 votes were Illinois (569,628 votes), Massachusetts (733,269 votes), and New Jersey (493,654 votes).

73. Nelson, "College for Dunces."

74. Andrew Cain, "Gore Will Accept Popular Vote," *Washington Times*, November 9, 2000.

75. For evidence to support this argument, see Morris P. Fiorina, *Divided Government* (Boston: Allyn and Bacon, 1996), chap. 5. For an argument that the voters

do not create divided government intentionally, see John R. Petrocik and Joseph Doherty, "The Road to Divided Government: Paved without Intention," in *Divided Government: Change, Uncertainty, and the Constitutional Order,* ed. Peter F. Galderisi (Lanham, Md.: Rowman and Littlefield, 1996).

76. Samuel Kernell and Gary C. Jacobson, *The Logic of American Politics* (Washington, D.C.: CQ Press, 2000), 412.
77. Fiorina, *Divided Government,* 72–91.
78. Gary C. Jacobson, *The Electoral Origins of Divided Government* (Boulder, Colo.: Westview Press, 1990), chap. 6.
79. Nelson, "Constitutional Aspects of the Elections," 195–201.
80. Gary C. Jacobson, "The 105th Congress: Unprecedented and Unsurprising," in *The Elections of 1996,* ed. Michael Nelson (Washington, D.C.: CQ Press, 1997), 143–166.
81. Gary C. Jacobson, *The Politics of Congressional Elections,* 5th ed. (New York: Longman, 2001), 259.
82. David R. Mayhew, *Divided We Govern: Party Control, Lawmaking, and Investigations, 1946–1990* (New Haven: Yale University Press, 1991). For a different view, see Sean Kelly, "Divided We Govern? A Reassessment," *Polity* 25 (1993): 475–488.
83. Paul J. Quirk and Bruce Nesmith, "Divided Government and Policymaking: Negotiating the Laws," in *The Presidency and the Political System,* 6th ed., ed. Michael Nelson (Washington, D.C.: CQ Press, 2000), 570–594.
84. John Anthony Maltese, *The Selling of Supreme Court Nominees* (Baltimore: Johns Hopkins University Press, 1995).
85. *Bush v. Gore.*

4

Voting Behavior: The Balance of Power in American Politics

Daniel Wirls

T he historic and controversial outcome of the presidential contest was clearly the most memorable feature of the American elections of 2000. The election was preceded by the tightest race in recent history, with a large number of undecided or unenthusiastic voters and the two leading candidates neck and neck in the polls until the last moment.[1] No one, however, predicted what followed. The razor-thin margins in both the popular vote and electoral vote made history, as did the divergence between the two. The major party division of the popular vote was the closest since the Kennedy-Nixon race of 1960. The electoral college vote, which almost always inflates the winner's margin of victory relative to the popular vote, also resisted tradition and ended up closer than in any election since the disputed contest in 1876. The presidential election overshadowed the results of the congressional elections, which produced partisan divisions in the House and Senate as close as any since the 72d Congress during Herbert Hoover's presidency, with the 107th Senate evenly divided: fifty Democrats and fifty Republicans.

Although the elections of 2000 were unique in their closeness, they accurately reflected consistent trends in American voting behavior. During the past two decades the two parties have fought their way toward a singular balance of power at the national level. It is altogether fitting that the first election of the new century expressed that equilibrium in historic fashion. This chapter places voting behavior in the 2000 elections in historical context by focusing on several important aspects of the vote that have helped to shape the balance of power between the parties during this period and that are likely to be significant in the future.[2]

The Changing Electorate: Evolution of the Balance of Power

History making as they were, the 2000 elections did not portend a new direction in American politics. The voters followed familiar patterns. Since the 1970s the Republicans have made significant though fluctuating gains at all levels—state, congressional, and presidential. But the public has swung back and forth in various ways by, for example, defeating an incumbent Republican president in 1992, electing a Republican Congress in 1994,

Figure 4-1   Ideological Self-Identification, 1973–1998

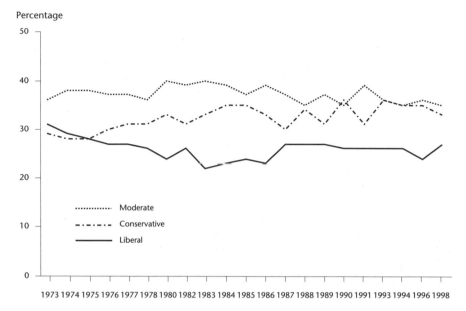

Source: General Social Survey, NORC, from Harold W. Stanley and Richard G. Niemi, *Vital Statistics in American Politics, 1999–2000* (CQ Press, 2000).

reelecting a damaged Democratic president in 1996, and eroding the Republican congressional majority in 1998. As a result, the nation has gone through nearly every permutation of united and divided party government. This is an era characterized by order and chaos—order in the overall Republican gains and chaos in the fluctuations from election to election.

For much of the past two decades, analysts have sifted electoral results for indications of a political realignment—that is, for the emergence of a clear majority party. Ronald Reagan's victory in 1980 touched off this speculation, but the persistence of Democratic majorities in Congress caused it to be replaced by musings on the nature of divided government.[3] Bill Clinton's victory in 1992, complete with a Congress controlled by Democrats, launched a new round of thinking about the revival of the Democratic Party. This notion was dispatched by the truly historic congressional elections of 1994, which produced the first bicameral control of Congress by the Republicans since 1953, during the Eisenhower administration. After Clinton's reelection in 1996, the rest of the decade, much like the late 1980s, revived theories that divided government was the norm.[4]

The continuity and chaos of recent years are consistent with a process of "secular realignment." Secular realignment, a concept developed in the 1950s by political scientist V. O. Key, refers to gradual changes in one or more of a wide variety of demographic, economic, and cultural aspects of American society that then produce significant political changes, especially in

Figure 4-2   Partisan Identification, 1952–1998

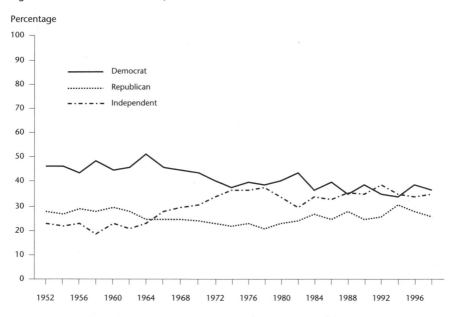

Percentage

Source: National Election Study from Harold W. Stanley and Richard G. Niemi, *Vital Statistics in American Politics, 1999–2000* (CQ Press, 2000).

the partisan and ideological preferences of voters.[5] In the 1980s John Petrocik and other analysts resurrected the concept of secular realignment to explain the current era, emphasizing that secular realignment need not produce a new majority party.[6] Petrocik concentrated on the role of the South— once solidly Democratic, now strongly Republican—in producing a significant change in the regional and ideological composition of the two parties' electoral bases. Political trends in the 1990s strengthened this view of secular change, as has the work of other scholars who argue that an ideological realignment of sorts has taken place, with an overall tilt in a conservative and Republican direction, but not strong enough to produce a clear majority party.[7]

Several trends characterize this secular realignment. Ideologically, the American public grew more conservative during the last quarter century. But this trend seems to have stalled and stabilized, with a modest advantage in favor of conservatives (Figure 4-1). Since the mid-1970s the Republicans have made significant inroads on the Democratic advantage in partisan identification (Figure 4-2).[8] But during this period more than a third of the public has identified itself as independent with remarkable consistency.[9] The rise of independents has been accompanied by the decline of voter turnout in elections. Thus, although the Democrats have lost ground to the Republicans, both parties have experienced an erosion of their base in favor of both independents and nonparticipants. Finally, this era has been characterized by a high level of split-ticket voting—voters casting ballots for different parties for different offices in the same election—which in turn has made divided government a common occurrence at the state and national level.[10]

Some political scientists see the fragmentation of the electorate as balanced by other trends in partisanship that, at first, seem paradoxical by comparison. Especially with the significant change in the South from a stronghold of Democratic (albeit conservative Democratic) support to an increasingly reliable source of Republican strength, each of the two parties has become more ideologically homogenous: liberal Democrats, conservative Republicans. This trend is especially evident in Congress.[11] With the disappearance of conservative southern Democrats, the two congressional parties have become more clearly differentiated from each other by several measures of partisanship. With the increasing differentiation, the relationship between partisanship and mass voting behavior appears to be growing on a nationwide level in both presidential and congressional elections.[12]

The two parties have achieved a notable degree of parity as a result of these and other trends. But they find themselves fighting over a smaller electorate, which, despite becoming more Republican and conservative than in the past, is by most evidence relatively flexible and even fickle in its partisan loyalties. How did the elections of 2000 mirror or deviate from the patterns that form this partisan balance?

The Disappearing Electorate: Nonvoters

The elections of 2000 were a dramatic reminder that one of the striking characteristics of the current balance of power era is the shrunken universe of voters. Efforts to reverse the decline, including the national "motor-voter" law and a host of measures taken by the states to make registration and voting easier, have not yielded significant dividends. Despite reportedly sharp increases in turnout in some states and among some demographic groups, the overall turnout rate of 50.7 percent in 2000 only marginally exceeded the modern low of 49 percent in 1996 (Figure 4-3). Competitive races for statewide offices, Ralph Nader's campaign, and a variety of conspicuous get-out-the-vote efforts appeared to boost turnout in some states, but were largely offset by lassitude and disaffection elsewhere.[13] Overall, the election indicated how intractable the turnout problem seems to be, even though the short-term (and probably evanescent) effect of the presidential controversy was to remind voters that every vote can make a difference.[14]

Nonvoting seems so persistent that it has become, as one pair of authors put it, the "dinosaur in the living room," the big problem that no one really wants to talk about.[15] In this case, however, there is plenty of talk about nonvoting—but much of it is perfunctory: people don't vote, there's nothing we can do about it, so let's move on. Certainly the two parties have adopted that attitude even as they send forth the faithful to register voters;

Figure 4-3   Voter Turnout in Presidential Elections, 1960–2000

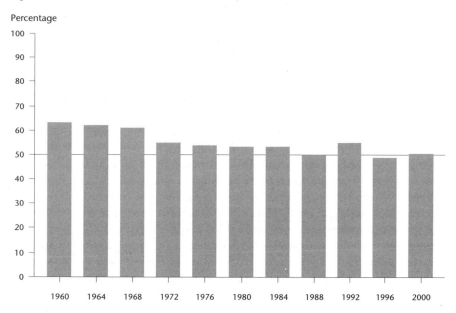

Sources: United States Census and *Washington Post,* November 9, 2000.

likewise the news media, which bemoan civic sloth but also embrace and reinforce this reality by restricting their election polls to "likely voters." Although substantial in size, this particular dinosaur is not easily character-ized—some see it as a carnivore eating away at the heart of democracy; oth-ers see it as a benign, if rather large, herbivore.[16] Nonvoting is sometimes simplistically portrayed as either the fundamental manifestation of a disaf-fected public or the rational choice of largely contented citizens who have better things to do. The reality is that it is a bit of both and even more com-plicated than that.[17] Whether satisfied or not, however, these nonvoters have been shown by some polls to be, when forced to choose between major party candidates, little different in their candidate preferences from their voting counterparts.[18]

Nevertheless, Bill Clinton's relatively exciting 1992 contest against George Bush and Ross Perot showed that the right circumstances, candi-dates, and campaign can get more voters to the polls, if only temporarily. Realignments and the creation of new partisan majorities are sometimes associated with increases in turnout through the mobilization of new vot-ers.[19] At least intuitively, therefore, it is hard to imagine fundamentally alter-ing the current balance of power between the two parties in a shrunken world of participants. But the connection between nonvoting and the balance of power is more direct than that because of generational differences in vot-ing participation and behavior.

The Aging Electorate:
Absent Youth and the Older Voter

In an election dominated by three issues—Medicare, Social Security, and tax cuts—it perhaps comes as no surprise that younger voters turned out in relatively small percentages. Voters under age thirty constituted 17 percent of all voters in the 2000 Voter News Service (VNS) exit polls, even though they make up nearly 22 percent of the voting-age population.[20] This phenomenon is not new: it is in fact one of the signal trends in American political participation of the last twenty years. The electorate is getting older. One reason is that the population as a whole is getting older, but more important is the contrast between the high and relatively consistent rates of participation by older voters and the deteriorating levels of voting by young adults. Although they make up nearly 13 percent of the population eligible to vote, eighteen- to twenty-four-year-olds constituted only 7.6 percent of the electorate in 1996 because their turnout rate was only 32.4 percent (Figure 4-4). In contrast, Americans sixty-five and older—16.5 percent of the voting age population—constituted more than 20 percent of the electorate by turning out at 67 percent. Moreover, this problem has been growing. According to census data, turnout among young adults has deteriorated at a faster rate than turnout in the electorate as a whole and accounts for much of the overall decline in participation in recent decades.[21]

Figure 4-4   The Aging Electorate, 1972–1996

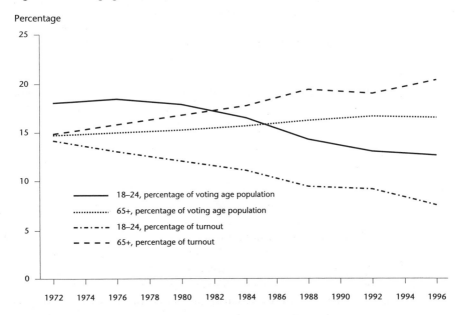

Percentage

18–24, percentage of voting age population
65+, percentage of voting age population
18–24, percentage of turnout
65+, percentage of turnout

Source: United States Census.

Although the generation difference in turnout is dramatic, it has a subtle effect on electoral outcomes. In some cases, young and old vote alike. In 2000, according to VNS exit polls, voters age sixty and older divided 51 percent to 47 percent in favor of Al Gore, making them the most Democratic age group. Young voters (eighteen to twenty-nine) split 48 percent to 46 percent in favor of Gore (and 5 percent for Nader), with everyone between young adults and senior citizens dividing 49 percent to 48 percent for George W. Bush. In 2000, at least, the voting behavior of the young and the old was not so different. The difference in turnout rates between them affects the campaigns, however, and that in turn probably affects elections. Here, the problem of distinguishing cause and effect arises, but the following seems a rather plausible hypothesis. In a world in which politicians adjust their campaigns to appeal to likely—that is, older—voters, younger voters are neglected. They stay away from the polls, confirming politicians in the wisdom of their strategy. Those young adults who do vote must choose between candidates whose campaigns mute potential intergenerational differences in voting behavior.

One of the initial projections based on voting and opinion data from the early 1980s was that Ronald Reagan and the apparent triumph of conservative values would produce a new generation of more conservative younger voters. This hypothesis was indicated by increases in both Republican self-identification and Republican voting among young adults. But just as the Reagan Revolution faltered and limped along in the form of divided government, generational recruitment into the Republican Party stalled. In 2000 the political patterns of the generations fully reflected the fluctuating balance of power that characterizes the era. Instead of augmenting the ranks of one or both of the major parties, young adults have been the largest source of growth for self-identified "independents." Even though their political beliefs would seem to put them squarely in one camp or the other, they do not identify strongly enough with either party to claim a loyalty. In 1999, for example, a Gallup survey found that 41 percent of eighteen- to twenty-nine-year-olds identified themselves as politically independent, compared with 37, 38, and 34 percent for the three older age groups.[22] The loyalties of younger voters who do identify with a political party are similar to those of other age groups.

Older voters, while retaining a stronger sense of partisan identity than the young, are almost evenly divided between Republicans and Democrats. The natural conservatism of older voters on many issues, which would tend to move them in the direction of the GOP, is balanced by their commitment to programs—Social Security, Medicare, Medicaid—that the Democrats have agreed never to cut and that have been among the major issues in recent elections. Because older voters are so evenly divided, their large turnout at the polls contributes heavily to the parity between the parties.

Conversely, the turnout factor may have hindered a sharper partisan realignment of American politics. The younger generation, which grew up in a more Republican and conservative era and is relatively independent and politically malleable, does not vote in large numbers. The potential political effect of generational change has been muted by intergenerational differences in participation. And if today's young adults are the citizens most alienated from and least engaged by politics, then the mobilization of the next generation of voters, by either party, is unlikely at best.

The Gendered Electorate: Women versus Men

Since 1980 no political cleavage among the voters has been more thoroughly investigated and discussed than the "gender gap"—the partisan and other political differences between women and men. Although small by comparison with many classic social divisions, the gender gap's persistence has intrigued analysts.[23] It was the most widely discussed aspect of public opinion in the elections of 1996.[24] And the gender gap played a prominent role in the elections of 2000. Both presidential campaigns took it seriously: Gore pressed to increase his advantage among women, and Bush sought to stem the hemorrhage of potential support among female voters. Both candidates went so far as to appear on *Oprah*, the highly popular women-centered talk show.

The gender gap in the elections of 2000 followed its familiar pattern, with women providing majority support to the Democratic candidate and

Figure 4-5   The Gender Gap in Presidential Elections, 1976–2000

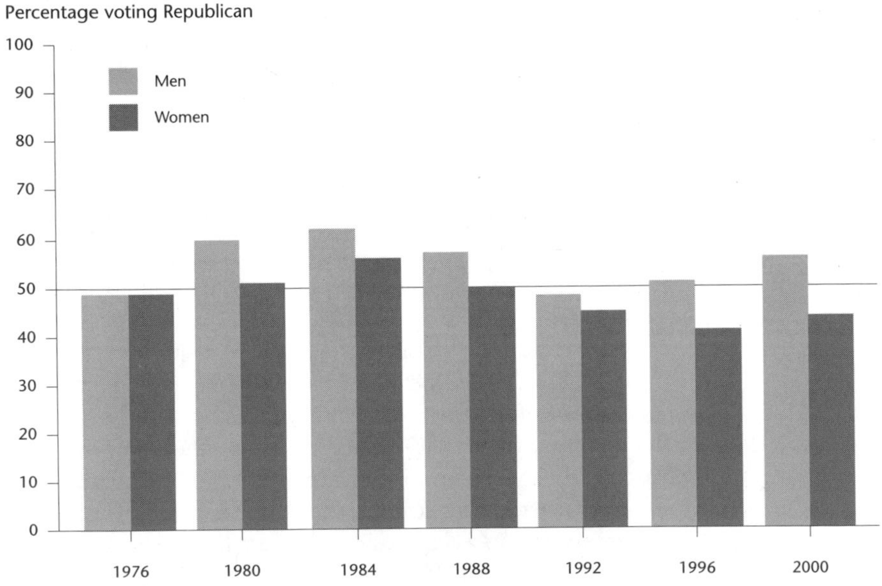

Percentage voting Republican

Sources: New York Times/CBS News polls, VNS exit surveys.

Note: Columns equal percentage of the two-party vote.

men providing majority support to the Republican. The gap was significant: in the major party vote, 56 percent of women supported Gore and nearly 56 percent of men voted for Bush (Figure 4-5). Among *white* men and women, the two-party gender gap was the same relative size, but, as in the recent past, both sexes gave majority support to the Republican candidate (just under 63 percent for men and just under 51 percent for women).

The gender gap reflects the combination of chaos and order that has defined this political era. The chaos is in the swings back and forth from the putative "year of the woman" in 1992, to the year of the "angry white male" in 1994, to the year of the "soccer mom" in 1996, with the gender gap seeming to alternate between being an advantage for Democrats in one election and for Republicans in the next.[25] The order is in the underlying reality that the gender gap mirrors the contemporary era's overall shift toward the Republicans within a highly competitive balance of power. During the past two decades, white men in particular have drifted, somewhat erratically, toward the Republican Party in both their partisan identification and their voting behavior, with white women changing their loyalties and behaviors less significantly or, according to some data, insignificantly.[26] Regardless of the exact nature of the relative motion, the gap between women and men, especially among whites, has reinforced the balance of power between Republicans and Democrats.

The size and consistency of the gender gap beg for an explanation. Is sex a causal variable, or are its effects artifacts of underlying social and economic factors? Although the gender gap cuts across social and economic divisions, such as income, education, and race, it is still misleading to talk about women and men as opposing political camps waging an eternal "battle of the sexes"—and not only because the differences are often rather small. The differences do cut across various social and demographic divisions, and underlying psychological differences in men and women seem to play a role in the gender gap. Nevertheless, a more material, rational choice explanation lies in the systematic differences between men and women's relationship to government and the economy. The persistent gender gap on many issues and in voting behavior is consistent with the lack of security women face relative to men. This difference can be found in all age brackets and for a variety of circumstances. Women rely more than men on the kind of security that activist government provides as a mediator between the market and the individual, whether that security comes in the form of civil rights protection against sexual discrimination in the workplace, actual employment in government, or retirement on a fixed income.[27] Although this relationship does not explain all politically relevant gender differences, it certainly fits the size, consistency, and breadth of the gender gap, in an era when the Republican Party and Democratic Party have diverged in their commitments to the welfare state and regulatory intervention in markets.

The presidential contest of 2000 did nothing to contradict this view of the gender gap. One indication in the available data was the consistent finding throughout the campaign and election of much higher support for Gore among single voters, with unmarried women overwhelmingly for Gore and unmarried men more evenly divided.[28] The exit polls also showed that working women divided 58 percent to 39 percent in favor of Gore. Again, although several factors could be at work here, these data are consistent with the rational choice explanation of the gender gap, with working and unmarried women more supportive of the services and protections provided by a liberal and activist government.[29]

In an era of close elections and uncertain coalitions, the gender gap can mean the difference between winning and losing, and both parties have to consider the risks of alienating either sex. The breadth of the gender gap's reach across socioeconomic and demographic categories (and issues) complicates partisan calculations. Turnout differences between the sexes further magnify the gap's political influence and impact. Partly because of generational factors (there are more older women than older men), women constitute a significantly higher percentage of the electorate than do men.[30] The political conversion of white men has been one of the strongest forces behind the improved political fortunes of conservatism and the Republican Party. The effect of that force is blunted, however, when the single largest demographic component of the electorate is significantly less inclined in that direction or even pulls the other way.

The Geographic Electorate: Where You Stand Depends on Where You Sit

Although electoral geography always plays a role in American elections, in 2000 Americans got a civics lesson in its importance, at least as concerns the electoral college. But the postelection emphasis on the perilously close vote in several states, especially Florida, obscured the larger patterns at work in the nation's electoral geography that have characterized the balance of power between the parties.

What is notable about the electoral vote maps in recent presidential elections is how precisely the regions have switched their allegiances since the late 1800s, which was the last period during which discrepancies occurred between the popular and electoral votes for president, and the other period characterized by the frequency of divided partisan control of the national government. (For the 2000 map see page 63.) The once Solid South of the Democratic Party has been replaced by an increasingly solid Republican South. The Northeast, once a bastion of the Republican Party, now forms the most consistent source of Democratic support. This transformation has been in the making for several decades, and the elections of 2000 showed its importance clearly. The East (meaning the combination of New England and the Mid-Atlantic states) gave solid popular and electoral majorities to Gore, while Bush easily carried the South. The two regions were mirror images of one another in the popular vote (Figure 4-6a). This North-South divide was

Figure 4-6a   2000 Presidential Popular Vote by Region

Percentage

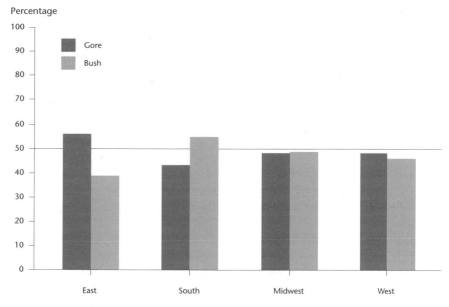

Source: http://www.cnn.com/ELECTION/2000/results, November 16, 2000.

Figure 4-6b   2000 Presidential Electoral Vote by Region

Percentage

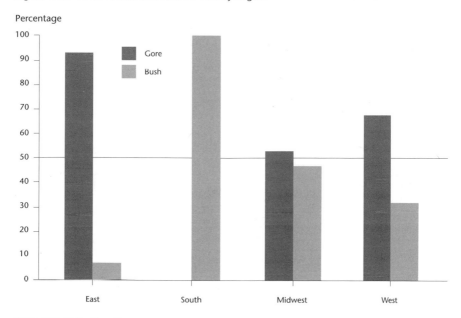

Source: Compiled by the author.

even sharper in the electoral college, with 93 percent of the electoral votes from the East going to Gore and 100 percent of the South's electoral votes going to Bush (Figure 4-6b). Gore received 44 percent of his total electoral votes from the East; Bush got 60 percent of his from the South.

As for the Midwest and West, what the VNS definition of regions disguises is the important distinction between the Pacific West (more Democratic) and the Plains and Mountain states (solidly Republican). Gore's victories in the three Pacific Coast states, California, Oregon, and Washington, provided him with seventy-two electoral votes; Bush's domination of the Plains and Mountain West states (he won twelve of fifteen) gave him sixty-three electoral votes.[31] Adding these partisan strongholds together, Gore got 73 percent of his electoral votes from states in the Northeast and on the Pacific Coast, while Bush gained 83 percent of his from the South and Plains/Mountain West. This same regional pattern of partisan support is evident in recent congressional elections as well. The historically close outcomes in 2000 can obscure the substantial geographic divisions at work in American elections.

Another important aspect of partisan geography in recent elections is the sharp contrast between the two parties' strength in cities, suburbs, and rural areas (Figure 4-7). Democrats depend heavily on city dwellers, who represented 29 percent of the electorate in exit polls. Republicans depend just as heavily on rural voters, who constituted a nearly equal 28 percent. The suburbs, although they tilted toward Bush, represented a closely divided 43 percent of the electorate. The Democrats especially rely on the urban population centers of the Northeast (Boston, New York, Philadelphia, Baltimore, and Washington) and the West Coast (Los Angeles, San Francisco–San Jose, and Seattle) to counteract the Republican strength in much of the rest of the country.[32] This urban-rural divide also reflects important racial and cultural divisions that have a strong geographic component. For example, African Americans, who make up a significant share of the voters in many major cities,[33] gave 90 percent of their nationwide vote to Gore. One might also surmise that the urban-suburban-rural split mirrors other differences in residential patterns, with, for example, more unmarried and nonreligious voters living in the cities. Unmarried voters (57 percent for Gore) and those who seldom attend religious services (54 percent for Gore) were important components of the Democratic vote. Married voters (53 percent for Bush) and those who attend religious services weekly (57 percent for Bush) showed their support for Republicans.[34]

Americans might be an increasingly homogenous society in patterns of material and cultural consumption, a seemingly inexorable process in the information age and era of globalization, but, in important ways, where we stand politically still depends on where we sit (and—because the cause and effect relationship is not unidirectional in this case—vice versa). The elections of 2000 reminded us that social, economic, and cultural divisions are alive and well in the nation's electorate.

Figure 4-7   2000 Presidential Vote by Residential Setting

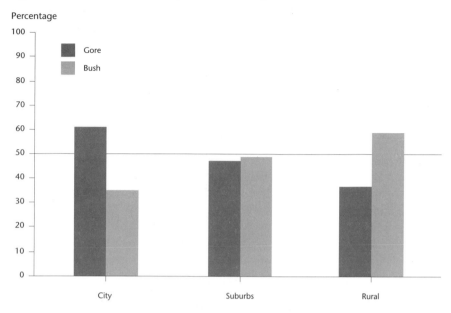

Percentage

Source: http://www.cnn.com/ELECTION/2000/results, November 16, 2000.

Conclusion: A Balance of Power or Impotence?

Although one easily can be excused, especially during campaigns such as the one in 2000, for seeing few substantive differences between the parties, somehow, when decision time comes in the voting booth, Americans split into consistent and often starkly divided socioeconomic, racial, and cultural camps as far as the two parties are concerned. There may be a balance of power, and there may be many Americans in the flexible and fickle middle, but there is also a division between rather different groups with markedly dissimilar visions of the American future. Despite the relative moderation of both presidential candidates and their general avoidance of culturally divisive issues, the voters for the major parties nevertheless formed two fairly distinct and familiar camps, with a predominantly white, rural, and religious Republican constituency at odds with a more secular, urban, and racially diverse Democratic core.

The forces and divisions discussed in this chapter have shaped the partisan balance of power that characterizes the contemporary era. This partisan parity is both a cause and an effect of the decisions of voters (and nonvoters): that is, just as the balance is to some extent a function of voters' preferences, these preferences have been shaped by the behavior of the two parties. Both voters and politicians have contributed to the balance of power in mutually reinforcing ways. For example, attempts to upset the balance

have provided only a temporary partisan advantage, which was then rudely checked by the voters in the next election. Clinton's united Democratic government during his first two years in office was blown apart by the historic Republican sweep in the midterm elections of 1994. The congressional Republicans' attempt to run the country on the basis of a radically conservative agenda was in turn dealt a severe blow by Clinton's reelection in 1996. It is hardly far-fetched to see the 2000 campaign and its results as the synthesis of these shifting forces. Both parties have learned to walk the electoral tightrope in a way that keeps their core constituencies in place while fighting for control of the somewhat nebulous center. What neither party has divined, and what circumstances seem not to offer, is a way to upset the balance of power and emerge as the clear majority party. The United States may never again have elections as close as the elections of 2000, but the kind of divided, blame-game government such elections tend to produce seems quite likely to persist.

Notes

1. Frank Newport, "Popular Vote in Presidential Race Too Close to Call," *Gallup News Service,* November 7, 2000, http://www.gallup.com/poll/releases/pr001107.asp; Richard L. Berke, "Voters All Tepid and Bothered about Candidates," *New York Times,* October 11, 2000, A27; and Janet Elder, "Latest Surveys Reflect an Even Race and a Limited Supply of Enthusiasm," *New York Times,* October 11, 2000, A27.
2. This chapter does not attempt to cover every important aspect of voting behavior in 2000. A glance at Table 2-1 on page 64 reveals several significant divisions between the two parties that will not be discussed here, including the remarkably linear relationship between income and voting.
3. Everett Carll Ladd, "The 1988 Elections: Continuation of the Post–New Deal System," *Political Science Quarterly* 104 (spring 1989): 1–18; and Ladd, "Like Waiting for Godot: The Uselessness of Realignment for Understanding Change in Contemporary American Politics," *Polity* 22 (spring 1990): 511–525; James L. Sundquist, "Needed: A Political Theory for the New Era of Coalition Government in the United States," *Political Science Quarterly* 103 (winter 1988/1989): 613–635; Benjamin Ginsberg and Martin Shefter, *Politics by Other Means: The Declining Importance of Elections in America* (New York: Basic Books, 1990); Byron E. Shafer, ed., *The End of Realignment? Interpreting American Electoral Eras* (Madison: University of Wisconsin Press, 1991); Morris P. Fiorina, "An Era of Divided Government," *Political Science Quarterly* (fall 1992): 387–410.
4. Everett Carll Ladd, "1996 Vote: The 'No Majority' Realignment Continues," *Political Science Quarterly* 112 (spring 1997): 1–28.
5. V. O. Key, "Secular Realignment and the Party System," *Journal of Politics* 21 (May 1959): 198–210.
6. John R. Petrocik, "Realignment: New Party Coalitions and the Nationalization of the South," *Journal of Politics* 49 (May 1987): 347–375. See also Edward G. Carmines and James A. Stimson, "Issue Evolution, Population Replacement, and Normal Partisan Change," *American Political Science Review* 75 (March 1981): 107–118; and John G. Geer, "Critical Realignments and the Public Opinion Poll," *Journal of Politics* 53 (May 1991): 434–453.
7. Alan I. Abramowitz and Kyle L. Saunders, "Ideological Realignment in the U.S. Electorate," *Journal of Politics* 60 (August 1998): 634–652.

8. More evidence on this point can be found in ibid.
9. A convincing explanation for this phenomenon is offered by Edward G. Carmines, John P. McIver, and James A. Stimson, in "Unrealized Partisanship: A Theory of Dealignment," *Journal of Politics* 49 (May 1987): 376–400.
10. Fiorina, "Era of Divided Government."
11. Keith T. Poole and Howard Rosenthal, *Congress: A Political-Economic History of Roll Call Voting* (New York: Oxford, 1997).
12. Larry M. Bartels, "Partisanship and Voting Behavior, 1952–1996" *American Journal of Political Science* 44 (January 2000): 35–50. Bartels makes clear, however, that his analysis does not measure the "consistency or variability of partisan effects over time (and across electoral levels)" (p. 39). In "Ideological Realignment in the U.S. Electorate," Abramowitz and Saunders offer evidence of a greater consistency in the relationship between ideology and voting from 1978 to 1994 (p. 644).
13. Susan Schmidt and John Mintz, "Voter Turnout Up Only Slightly Despite Big Drive," *Washington Post,* November 9, 2000, A35.
14. For example, see Rick Bragg, "Florida, Awaiting Retally, Learns the Power of One," *New York Times,* November 9, 2000, B6.
15. Rob Richie and Steven Hill, "The Dinosaur in the Living Room," November 11, 1997, http://www.igc.apc.org/cvd/op_eds/oped_971111.htm, October 12, 2000.
16. For example, see Robert Kuttner, "Why Americans Don't Vote—and Why They Should," and Charles Krauthammer, "In Praise of Low Voter Turnout," both reprinted in *Perspectives on American Government,* ed. William Lasser (Lexington, Mass.: D. C. Heath, 1992), 205–212.
17. Jack C. Doppelt and Ellen Shearer, *Nonvoters: America's No-Shows* (Thousand Oaks, Calif.: Sage Publications, 1999).
18. For example, see E. J. Dionne Jr., "If Nonvoters Had Voted: Same Winner, but Bigger," *New York Times,* November 21, 1988.
19. For perspectives on how mobilization and conversion affected both the New Deal realignments and the contemporary secular changes in the party system, see Kristi Anderson, *The Creation of a Democratic Majority, 1928–1936* (Chicago: University of Chicago Press, 1979); Robert S. Erikson and Kent L. Tedin, "The 1928–1936 Partisan Realignment: The Case for the Conversion Hypothesis," *American Political Science Review* 75 (December 1981): 951–962; Edward G. Carmines and James A. Stimson, "Issue Evolution, Population Replacement, and Normal Partisan Change," *American Political Science Review* 75 (March 1981): 107–118; Edward G. Carmines, John P. McIver, and James A. Stimson, "Unrealized Partisanship: A Theory of Dealignment," *Journal of Politics* 49 (May 1987): 376–400.
20. Unless otherwise noted, exit poll data used in text and figures are from the Voter News Service exit polls for the 2000 elections, as reported by CNN on their Web site, http://www.cnn.com/ELECTION/2000/results/, November 16, 2000. The VNS national exit poll consisted of 13,130 respondents.
21. "The Aging of the Electorate," *Los Angeles Times,* January 13, 2000: A7. See also Federal Election Commission, http://www.fec.gov/pages/agedemog.htm.
22. Lydia Saad, "Independents Rank as Largest U.S. Political Group," http://www.gallup.com/poll/releases/pr990409c.asp. Another Gallup poll from 1999 showed a much greater gap, with 52 percent of younger adults claiming to be independents; see Harold W. Stanley and Richard G. Niemi, *Vital Statistics on American Politics, 1999–2000* (Washington, D.C.: CQ Press, 2000), 115.
23. Richard A. Selzer, Jody Newman, and Melissa Voorhees Leighton, *Sex as a Political Variable: Women as Candidates and Voters in U.S. Elections* (Boulder: L. P. Rienner, 1997).
24. Kathleen A. Frankovic, "Why the Gender Gap Became News in 1996," *PS: Political Science and Politics* 32 (March 1999): 20–22.

25. Susan J. Carroll, "The Disempowerment of the Gender Gap: Soccer Moms and the 1996 Elections," *PS: Political Science and Politics* 32 (March 1999): 7–12.
26. Karen M. Kaufmann and John R. Petrocik, "The Changing Politics of American Men: Understanding the Sources of the Gender Gap," *American Journal of Political Science* 43 (July 1999): 864–887; Daniel Wirls, "The Gender Gap in American Elections: Lingering Illusions and Political Realities," in *Do Elections Matter?* 2d ed., ed. Benjamin Ginsberg and Alan Stone (Armonk, N.Y.: M. E. Sharpe, 1991), 117–133; and Wirls, "Reinterpreting the Gender Gap," *Public Opinion Quarterly* 50 (fall 1986): 316–330.
27. Frances Fox Piven, "Women and the State: Ideology, Power, and the Welfare State," in *Gender and the Life Course,* ed. Alice S. Rossi (New York: Aldine Pub. Co, 1985); Steven P. Erie and Martin Rein, "Women and the Welfare State," in *The Politics of the Gender Gap: The Social Construction of Political Influence,* ed. Carol Mueller (Newbury Park, Calif.: Sage Publications, 1988); and Kristi Andersen, "The Gender Gap and Experiences with the Welfare State," *PS: Political Science and Politics* 32 (March 1999): 17–19.
28. For example, Katharine Q. Seelye, "Marital Status Is Shaping Women's Leanings, Surveys Find," *New York Times,* September 9, 2000, 19.
29. Another line of explanation of the gender gap, and one that can complement the welfare state–rational choice perspective, is that the gender gap can be ascribed to greater liberal feminist values among certain strata of women, including working and unmarried women.
30. In 1996, according to census data, 55.5 percent of women and 52.8 percent of men reported voting, which translated into a numerical difference of 56.1 million female voters versus 48.9 million male voters. This gap has been growing steadily since the 1960s. Data available through the Center for American Women and Politics.
31. The fifteen are: Arizona, Colorado, Idaho, Iowa, Kansas, Minnesota, Missouri, Montana, Nebraska, Nevada, New Mexico, North Dakota, South Dakota, Utah, and Wyoming.
32. Another visual demonstration of this is evident in the map of the presidential popular vote by county. See *New York Times,* November 9, 2000, B1.
33. According to census data, 55 percent of black Americans live in central metropolitan areas versus 22 percent of non-Hispanic whites. See http://www.census.gov/population/socdemo/race/black/tabs99/tab16.txt, November 16, 2000.
34. Those who regularly attend services and those who rarely do each made up 28 percent of the electorate in the exit polling. There was an even more dramatic split between the 14 percent of voters who attend services more often than weekly (63 percent voted for Bush) and the 14 percent who never attend (61 percent voted for Gore).

5

The Media:
Old Frames in a Time of Transition

Matthew Robert Kerbel

The *Saturday Night Live* skit depicted ABC's Ted Koppel, NBC's Tom Brokaw, and CNN's Bernard Shaw lamenting the sorry state of the presidential election after John McCain, the only colorful candidate in the running, had been leveraged out of the Republican field. A dreadful reality was sinking in—there would be months upon months of face time for George W. Bush and Al Gore. For newsmen accustomed to reducing political coverage to the idiosyncrasies of character, this was a nightmare: how do you cover politics as personality when neither candidate has one?

The SNL skit resonated with what a lot of journalists were saying about the major party standard-bearers. Following the swift resolution of the primary campaign, long before the remarkable turn of events of November 7, journalists found themselves saddled with two candidates who were the most uninteresting pair to survive the frenzied primary selection process in twelve years. They were a decidedly undynamic duo: two sons of privilege; two insiders trying to be regular guys; prolific fund-raisers ostensibly opposed to prolific fund-raising. Poll-driven, focus-group-using, handler-dependent politicians trying to look spontaneous, fresh, and original. Two interchangeable parts. Mawkish and dull. Bush and Gore. Gush and Bore.

But *Saturday Night Live* was skewering more than these two national politicians. Against the sorry backdrop of the 2000 contest, the Brokaw character implores his colleagues to forget the ratings and use this opportunity to do something reminiscent of the days of real journalism: to ignore personalities and instead dig deep into the issues in order to produce responsible, meaningful coverage. After a brief comedic pause, all three characters dismiss this crazy idea with a wave of the head. Forget the ratings? What a joke.

Of course it's a joke. What's interesting is that people were laughing. The fact that it's funny when a national anchor suggests that he's ready to cover a campaign responsibly says much about public expectations of the press going into the 2000 election. The audience appreciated the parody because they were fully aware of how thoroughly correspondents can embrace distasteful reporting techniques in their slavish quest to gain good audience ratings. In an era when journalists are held in slightly lower regard than used car dealers, it's easy to make a joke about campaign coverage at Tom Brokaw's expense.

These two characteristics of political reporting—the tedium journalists experienced covering a campaign that was far too long and much too scripted, and their need to hold an audience at all costs anyway—constitute the main parameters of the journalist's experience during much of campaign 2000. They shaped a long video and paper trail of stories stretching over a year and a half, which, broadly speaking, seem familiar to anyone acquainted with presidential contests from the recent past. The character of the political combatants gets a lot of attention, although without the connect-the-dots follow-through necessary to draw well-rounded conclusions about how they might perform in office. The strategic twists and turns of the campaign is an ongoing theme, although a rationale is never offered for why it is important for readers and viewers to know so much about it. The otherwise private ruminations of reporters on the trail and the influence of the media on the political process are offered as a peculiar substitute for news about the campaign itself. Issue stands are commonly discussed as tactical positions taken by candidates for political gain rather than as meaningful suggestions. Although during the 2000 general election period policy discussion was more prevalent than it has been in recent years, over the long sweep of the campaign, issue coverage was an ad hoc backdrop to a story line relevant to those who wished to become political handlers rather than informed voters.

Choices and Constraints

This is not a new story. The names and issues may be different, but in content and tone, the Y2K version of political reporting mirrored its undistinguished cousin, the 1996 election. Four years ago, I characterized election coverage this way:

> For reporters, election coverage was approached as if the only purpose of the electoral process was to pick a winner. Speeches were covered more for their political relevance than for content. Policy proposals were portrayed as tactical elements of a broad electoral strategy. And in a self-referential gesture that bordered on the absurd, reporters made themselves the object of their own news as they covered how effectively the media were covering how well the candidates were playing the political game.[1]

That coverage of the 2000 election largely held to this pattern suggests that the reporters, editors, and producers responsible for generating it made similar choices about what constitutes election news. If news coverage is a constructed entity stemming from the conscious and unconscious choices of the people who create it,[2] political news in 2000 can be understood as the product of a decision-making process that has not evolved appreciably in recent years.

An election may be about numerous things, including but not limited to horserace benchmarks, strategy, character, and reporters' self-references. It could be about how political actors plan to deal with an overriding issue or issues. It could be an opportunity to sort among competing visions of the future, for examining the past performance of candidates to determine how each might act as president,[3] or for selecting among different ideological positions. When these latter perspectives are minimized or reduced to slogans by campaign coverage, as they were during much of the 2000 race, one of two things is going on. Either the campaign is not producing news from these perspectives, or the people responsible for turning words and action into stories do not have the means, the understanding, or the desire to address the election in a serious manner. The similarities in coverage from election to election, joined with an understanding of how news people make choices, point to the latter explanation.

There actually were moments in the 2000 campaign—particularly during the McCain surge and in the days before November 7—that produced discussions among the candidates of substantive concerns, including tax cuts, environmental issues, and reforms of the campaign finance, Social Security, and education systems. Accordingly, news stories about these matters in newspapers, periodicals, and occasionally on television probed beyond rhetorical chatter about "trusting the people." At times, especially in the campaign's final weeks, attention was given by the media to broad philosophical differences between Bush and his support of limited government and Gore's belief in the positive role of federal action. In this regard, the media acted responsibly, departing from their long-standing fascination with character and contest.

But over the course of the election, stories like these constituted mere moments; usually, issue discussions assumed a horserace perspective as the story of the electoral competition unfolded. In the story lines that dominated so much general election coverage, issue positions were regarded as tactical devices used by candidates to win the support of key demographic groups. This story line made it difficult to distinguish rhetoric from record, or to imagine how either candidate would govern.

Massaging issue positions into horserace stories was one manifestation of the process of framing the news, in which context is offered to make sense of otherwise disparate facts.[4] Framing is by definition a process through which choices are made to select and eliminate material for stories and subsequently place story elements in a thematic context in order to communicate news to the audience. Gatekeepers—producers, editors, and reporters—make choices about news content while constrained by such things as corporate financial pressures, the need to hold viewers' interest with colorful, conflict-laden story lines, and the demands of good video on television. These constraints are compounded on the campaign trail by the judgment-distorting demands of endless whirlwind travel side-by-side with political operatives for each candidate, who relentlessly pitch their version of events to a skeptical and exhausted press corps.[5] If news reports are somehow produced amid this confusion, so is the widely held belief among the gatekeepers that what they are doing is simply reporting the news that's out there. In other words, they believe they are not making choices at all.

But the fingerprints of the gatekeepers are all over their work. In their most self-absorbed state, reporters even find news in the confusion of their own lives. Periodically, campaign coverage is reduced to little more than a description of why it is difficult to cover a campaign, as in this *Los Angeles Times* article which mirrored similar stories appearing in other reputable print and broadcast media:

> Take the chaos of a circus, the conversation of C-SPAN and the silliness of World Wide Wrestling. Throw in a ringmaster who enjoys discussing things like the Antiballistic Missile Treaty, a particularly unruly herd of reporters and lots of lost luggage. This, pretty much, is the world of presidential campaign travel. A typical day involves moving more than 100 people, including the candidate, his staff, dozens of reporters and security through stops in as many as six states per day. . . . But for all its complexity, the punishing demands of campaign travel are probably lost on voters.[6]

It likely never occurred to the reporter who penned these lines that voters may not want or need to know about the behind-the-scenes logistics that occupy his day. In the same vein, it may be too much to ask reporters living in a fast-forward world to recognize how they make decisions that affect the news product. But this does not relieve them of their news judgments or make the news produced by their judgments disappear. The constraints on news personnel that produce horserace-oriented, strategy-centered, self-referential coverage of the campaign are real. So are the results of these constraints, which include a diminished role for news stories that present the election in a useful context for readers and viewers who might wish to use them to make informed political decisions. Reporters' choices, whether or not they perceive them as such, limit voters' options for understanding the election. The limitations that shape their choices, real as they are, become the reader's burden. Their constraints become our constraints.

Tune Out, Turn Off, Drop Out

It should not be surprising that in 2000, notwithstanding the remarkable November finish, the public mirrored the boredom felt by journalists saddled with a campaign longer than the NBA season. At Harvard, the Joan Shorenstein Center on the Press, Politics, and Public Policy tracked the relationship between political coverage and citizen response through the ominously named "Vanishing Voter Project." Among the Center's findings was the discouraging fact that "we did not record even a single week when Americans claimed to be more excited than bored by the campaign. The New Hampshire primary produced the highest excitement level: 31% of our respondents claimed it had been an exciting week in the campaign. Yet 42% said it had been boring. In our [April 14, 2000] poll, those who claimed the week was boring far exceeded (69%–5%) those who found it exciting."[7]

Because people were disengaged, they were not learning about the campaign. Worse yet, after months of political coverage people began forgetting whatever they did learn during those brief moments, like during the New Hampshire primary, when they were somewhat less uninterested. The Shorenstein Center data suggest that knowledge of the main candidates' major issue positions peaked during the early primaries (if a knowledge level in the low 20% range can qualify as a peak); after Super Tuesday, knowledge levels began a gradual summer-long descent toward oblivion.[8]

These patterns of public political awareness and interest correlate closely with the amount of attention the campaign received in the press, which in turn tracks closely with the volume of horserace coverage. As usual, the primary elections from Iowa through Super Tuesday received a lot of press attention. Once the two nomination races were settled, however, media and public attention turned elsewhere. Of course, Topic A during these high-coverage periods was the nomination race itself, abundantly framed in the language of horserace, strategy, and self-reference. So, even during those moments when people were learning, the information they were getting was more suited to fulfilling a career as a political reporter than to developing an appreciation of what the candidates were about.

This makes the relative lack of information about the campaign something of a good news, bad news joke. The good news is that, given the weak content of coverage, the amount of press attention devoted to the 2000 campaign was sharply less than it had been four years ago. The Center for Media and Public Affairs tracked campaign coverage on the three major network evening news shows and found that during the primary season, they collectively ran 576 stories about the election over fifteen and a half hours of prime news time. During the comparable period in 1996, they had aired 737 stories over twenty-two and three-quarters hours.[9]

This is also the bad news. If the rapid resolution of the nomination contests predictably leads to a drop-off in coverage, news elites could have used this opportunity to offer coverage of a more issue-oriented nature. To a small extent, they did. The Shorenstein study found that during the politically slow period immediately prior to the Iowa caucuses, news about issue positions and candidates' records was relatively more prominent. But this constituted a larger portion of a much smaller news hole, which by virtue of its meager presence did little to spark the notice of readers and viewers.[10] A similar phenomenon occurred in 1992, when issue discussions surfaced during brief lulls in that year's longer and more contentious primary contest.[11] The result was the same in both cases: the cues to the audience to pay attention to political news came when the media agenda was least informative, and vice versa.

Getting It Wrong

An optimist might say that in 2000, the press continued to serve up a high fat diet, but at least it did so in smaller portions than in the past. This appraisal dismisses as a lost opportunity the failure to sustain a high level of issue coverage during the slow phases of the campaign, but it respects the normative argument that less horserace, strategy, and self-referential coverage is preferable to more.

Still, after a close look at the content of the horserace/strategy/self-referential coverage that constituted so much news during Campaign 2000, it's hard to avoid noticing a related dilemma that confounds even this rosy interpretation. As in recent past races, time-tested analytical models for assessing political viability were employed by journalists to frame candidates as strategic actors. Only this time, the models didn't apply quite so well. Something was fundamentally different about the 2000 contest and, as is the case with most unexpected changes, it came into focus only in hindsight. By no fault of their own, at just about every important juncture in the race, reporters got it wrong.

In the summer of 1999, when Republicans were clamoring to see how many candidates could fit onto a primary ballot and potential Democratic challengers to Al Gore were just as rapidly peeling away, the old-fashioned political model predicted that the Republican candidates would engage in a long, damaging fight to winnow their number while Gore pranced to victory at his convention on the strength of a strong economy. Then George W. Bush entered the contest and sucked most of the money away from the rest of the field, and the story shifted to how Bush's formidable financial assets would help him in the primaries. But that speculation initially missed the important fact that those assets were already helping him do what it usually took the primaries to do, namely to clear out the field.

Meanwhile, Bill Bradley's lone challenge to the vice president was labeled "quixotic"—until the mighty Gore campaign "unexpectedly" stumbled and the vice president suddenly had a fight on his hands. So it wasn't going to be the Republicans who were going to have a divisive battle after all—it was going to be Gore versus Bradley. But—wait—the Bradley Moment had barely materialized when a "new" Al Gore ended the big challenge before New Hampshire voted. And—wait again—the Bush organization that so effectively vanquished most Republican comers without suffering through a real ballot was suddenly and unexpectedly upended in New Hampshire by a second-tier challenger who had initially been given little initial chance of success, John McCain. The possibility of Bush's potential demise then became the tantalizing story until Super Tuesday, when the pundits recognized that, of course, Bush had always been too strong to lose the race.

At which point everyone settled in for a long, hot summer.

Following the Republican Convention, with Bush buoyed by a double-digit lead in opinion polls, reporters incorrectly speculated that the task facing the Gore camp might be too formidable. Then came the Democratic Convention, the fabled Al and Tipper kiss, and the rousing acceptance speech that bounced the Democratic nominee into the lead. Reporters began saying that no candidate who was ahead on Labor Day had lost a presidential election for twenty years, and in Gore's case, he would simply have to maintain his lead through three debates, a forum that should play to his strength. But when that didn't happen, and Gore lost his advantage during the debates, the analysis shifted again. With Bush slightly ahead for several weeks leading up to the election, reporters began to speak of a likely Bush victory following a close vote, or even of the possibility that Bush could win the popular vote but lose the Electoral College. No one imagined the scenario that started to take shape on election night: a popular vote defeat, but an electoral vote victory for Bush.

Throughout the late summer and early fall, pundits and journalists speculated about which previous election best modeled this one. All of their observations turned out to be incorrect. First it was supposed to be 1988, when an incumbent vice president came from way behind to dominate the fall campaign. When that didn't happen, it was thought to be 1960, an even contest between a vice president who didn't excite voters and a challenger they were unsure about. Then, as Bush appeared to hold a steady lead during the final weeks, it was thought perhaps to be 1980, when the voters made a late break for the challenger. At no point did anyone speculate that 2000 might actually be 1876.

So the conventional wisdom—and the horserace story—kept changing as outdated incorrect analyses yielded to newer incorrect analyses. In September, it was said that Bush could not be elected president without winning Florida, but Gore could. By early November, it was said that Gore could not be elected president without winning Florida, but Bush could. On an election night when no one was elected, each man carried Florida at some point, only to see it taken away by network anchors who, to the end, could not seem to figure out what was happening.

It could be argued that if reporters were going to continue to frame politics in horserace terms, there was a useful story to be told about changes in the campaign process in 2000. Whereas voters in an odd assortment of unrepresentative states once winnowed the primary field, the ability to raise big money performed that function in this election as never before. This says something new and important about political choice, and certainly reporters took notice. But, in keeping with past tendencies, they told the story in strategic terms. News reports tended to be about what candidates had to do to keep up financially and politically, rather than about the significance of the effort. Once again, this is a story of interest to political handlers and their clients, not to mention political reporters, but one with limited reach to general audiences.

Let's take a closer look at the content of news reports during the arduous 2000 campaign. Although not intended to be a systematic or comprehensive discussion of major news coverage, this account traces important contours of press reporting as it appeared in noteworthy print and broadcast media.[12] The story naturally divides itself into four phases, all of them closely correlated with changes in the political situation. In 1999 and the first weeks of 2000, reporters covered what came to be known as the "money primary," in which the field of candidates grew and dissipated in proportion to the candidates' ability to raise funds. The "voting primary" was the brief (compared to recent years) second phase, which culminated with a whimper on Super Tuesday when the two early frontrunners, having outlasted everyone else, became the "likely nominees" of their parties. The end of the second phase ushered in a longer-than-usual "silly season," during which the lack of relevant political benchmarks left reporters scrambling for something to write about other than who would likely win the vice-presidential sweepstakes. Perhaps because the silly season began so early, reporters switched to full combat mode during the late-summer conventions, starting the fourth and final phase of coverage more than a month ahead of the traditional Labor Day general election kick-off—and keeping it going long after election day had passed.

The Money Primary

On October 3, the *Washington Post* speculated that the last week of September would be seen as "the most significant week to date in the campaign" because it would mark for Al Gore "a fresh start after a summer of missteps."[13] The question is, in what *year* did this story run? If you correctly said 1999, you have grasped the true significance of the task facing journalists who just as readily could have filed the same story twelve months later. During a campaign that had "significant weeks" fully thirteen months before election day—a contest that saw Gore periodically blundering and recovering—political news rhythms were established early and went on indefinitely.

Traditionally, reporters would rely on the regular benchmarks of primaries and caucuses during the early months of a campaign as ready pegs on which to hang political reports. They could do so back in the days when the early months of a campaign occurred during the same year as the election itself. The year 1999, unevenly divisible by four, supplied only one of these benchmarks: a nonbinding, free-for-all, midsummer Iowa straw poll that in past years had received cursory attention commensurate with its insignificance. Predictably, the event was inflated beyond recognition during the 2000 campaign. Even so, it simply provided reporters with relief for a few news cycles.

In a manner befitting the entire campaign, the Iowa straw poll was approached self-referentially by reporters who, with little to talk about, were as fascinated with the empty way they were building up the event as they were with the political stakes. This *Los Angeles Times* excerpt takes television coverage to task for devoting attention to visually enticing, meaningless photo opportunities:

> I clicked on the PBS "NewsHour.". . . There on my living room TV was Elizabeth Dole patting a pig. Why wasn't this former transportation secretary talking about fixing our federal highway system? Pat

Buchanan then was shown petting a dog. And George W. Bush was flipping flapjacks. Or were they burgers? Whatever. Since when does fast-food dexterity qualify one for a job in the Oval Office? It's no wonder only 15% of Americans recently polled by the Pew Research Center said they were paying "very close attention" to the 2000 presidential campaign.[14]

Similar laments about the quality of campaign coverage were offered in campaign coverage for more than a year in different venues. Take, for instance, the bizarre way ABC News covered the New Hampshire kick-off of the Bush campaign. In a report that all but admitted the absence of news in the traditional sense of the word, Dean Reynolds called the Bush appearance "truly remarkable." Why? Because it attracted so many reporters: "Here is the governor of Texas, who acknowledges talking about issues in only the broadest of terms with no specifics. But a huge press corps is hanging on his every word, and no one seems to know why."[15] Reynolds acknowledged that Bush had held a press conference, but all he told us about it was that "he made little news," leaving us to conclude that it was the *fact* of the press conference—indeed, the fact that the press conference drew so much press attention—that warranted coverage in prime time.

Traditionally, a story about a candidate's inaugural campaign event would be about the candidate. In the ABC story, the press was the story's subject and its main source, to the point that a news photographer was interviewed for his reaction to the way the press flocked to Bush. As for the candidate, he was nowhere to be found. Reynolds told us as much:

> You'll have to trust me but—that is the governor back there. I can't see him. Most of the voters here can't see him, because he's surrounded by the press. There are at least ten TV stations here from Texas alone and journalists from all over the world. As many as forty cameras are recording everything down to the boots he wore in Iowa or the street shoes he changed to in New Hampshire.[16]

In a similar vein, consider how the *Los Angeles Times* reported the story of Republican Gary Bauer's alleged extramarital affair, which came to light in September 1999. Acknowledging that Bauer's candidacy was of little political significance, self-consciously admitting that he could barely get coverage for his substantive policy addresses, and conceding that the public had little appetite for political scandal, the *Times* made clear that the presence of reporters themselves made the Bauer nonevent newsworthy:

> Gary Bauer summoned the media to a small hotel conference room Wednesday to announce what he had not done. But the real news was the wall-to-wall press throng that showed up to listen. Most Americans have probably never heard of Gary Bauer, a Republican White House wannabe, let alone the allegations he vociferously denied. Still, it was standing room only for 45 minutes of question-and-denial, as 50 journalists—including eight TV crews—chronicled the latest turn of Washington's Wheel of Scandal. Just last week, when Bauer deliv-

ered a 15–page address about his views on U.S.-China policy, a measly five print reporters and three local TV crews showed up and the event garnered scarcely a line in most newspapers. But advance word that Bauer would deny a rumored affair with a young aide drew a relative mob, once more demonstrating the media's seemingly insatiable hunger for naughty nuggets—regardless of the public's seemingly well-sated appetite.[17]

Throughout the early months of the campaign, stories also abounded about the character of the horserace and which candidates were favored to advance. These were typically followed by stories about how the press had gotten it all wrong.

The horserace coverage started as early as April 1999, with stories noting that the campaign had surprisingly "developed earlier and more distinctly" than most observers had anticipated, and predicting that the Republicans in particular were "headed for a bruising, ideological contest, driven by long-standing divisions and a debate over how to make up the ground lost in the past two elections."[18] On the Democratic side, the early conventional wisdom that Gore would face only token opposition from Bradley yielded by May 1999 to the new assumption that Bradley's "strength as a challenger is now a given" because he was "paving his road to the nomination with doubts about the vice president."[19]

But matters didn't quite work out this way. In the months ahead, Bradley's advantages would dissipate against an overhauled Gore campaign that for much of 1999 had looked to reporters to be top-heavy and indecisive. And, over the course of the summer, the ideological debate in the Republican party was short-circuited by Bush's ability to suffocate most of his challengers with his fund-raising prowess.

Indeed, something novel was happening. The winnowing process was almost entirely complete before the first primary votes were cast, with fund-raising rather than vote-getting determining which candidates would get to carry on. By the time horserace reporting caught up to what was happening, it had already been accomplished, and the coverage reflected the sense of astonishment from reporters who had been caught off guard. Said the *Washington Post* in early November 1999, "The campaign of 2000 continues to surprise. Operating on a timetable never before seen, the Republican race already has taken on the shape of a contest that usually occurs after the Iowa caucuses and the New Hampshire primary. In a race in which the voters have yet to be heard from, the once-large field has been cut in half."[20]

Enter John McCain, and the next twist. A single-digit contender for much of the summer of 1999, McCain was rarely mentioned as a serious candidate when the Republican field included Elizabeth Dole, Dan Quayle, Lamar Alexander, and Steve Forbes. But when the first three fell victim to the Bush money machine and when Forbes proved unsuccessful in his efforts to reinvent himself as a social conservative, McCain appeared, apparently from nowhere, to become the main challenger to the Texas governor before any primary votes were recorded.

Few if any reporters had predicted this scenario, and it left them struggling to explain how it had happened. Typically, the explanations included things that appeared obvious only in the rearview mirror of hindsight: McCain's "best-selling memoir of his days in a North Vietnamese prison camp; a maverick's appeal to independents and voters disenchanted with the system; a direct style in a year when 'authenticity' has become a buzzword for what voters want."[21] Part of McCain's success, of course, was that he ran an effective low-budget campaign during the months when money determined most candidates' viability, making him the last credible challenger standing after all of his better-known rivals had fallen away. But even after reporters came to this conclusion, the McCain phenomenon remained difficult for them to figure out, and would continue to bedevil them throughout the primary season.

Horserace coverage continued to reflect reporters' doubts and acknowledge their inaccuracies. In the autumn before the primary season, the *Los Angeles Times* reflected that

> Not long ago, back when George W. Bush was a mere governor and not a Goliath, experts had the Republican presidential race all figured out. With no clear front-runner, the pundits declared the GOP nomination up for grabs and forecast the most wide-open contest in decades. They couldn't have been more wrong. Less than three months after first planting his cowboy boots on the campaign trail, Texas Gov. Bush is running so far ahead of the pack that many analysts are ready to proclaim the race over—before a single vote is cast.[22]

And why not "proclaim the race is over," considering that Bush was now consuming media attention as effectively as he dominated fund-raising. "In the race for the 2000 Republican presidential nomination," said the *Times*, "Gov. George W. Bush's lopsided share of press coverage may have already rendered next year's GOP primaries all but meaningless, according to a host of media observers and news executives."[23]

Or maybe not. "Who's to say," the *Times* acknowledged, "the know-it-alls aren't wrong again?"[24]

The Voting Primary

Three months after this disclaimer appeared in print, the know-it-alls indeed confessed to having inadvertently buried the horserace lead. Bush the political marvel had slipped so badly by the eve of the Iowa caucuses that he was being compared to the hapless Dan Quayle. Questions about Bush's intellect and his preparedness for office began to pop up in places where just weeks before reporters had wondered aloud if they were giving the Texas governor a free ride. In time-tested fashion, falling poll ratings were explained in terms of previously unnoticed but potentially lethal character flaws. To "many" of the unmentioned mentioners in the press, "Bush came across . . . as uncertain, propped up by rehearsed responses and a series of stilted talking points."[25] In other words, reporters now were saying Bush had an image problem. In the self-referential world of media politics, there is no greater political liability.

As the primary season began for real and news coverage increased on a wave of horserace interest, incorrect predictions and analyses abounded, along with stories lamenting incorrect predictions and analyses. If readers and viewers learned little about what was going on in the campaign, at least they gained insight into the thought processes of political reporters.

In early January 2000, it appeared reasonable to assume that "the presidential front-runners in both parties are being tugged away from the political center in a way that may create headaches for them if they meet in November."[26] There was no way to know then that Gore would dispatch Bradley without moving too far to the left or that Bush would spend the spring reestablishing his centrist credentials.

By February, the talk was about what to make of the size of McCain's New Hampshire victory. The consensus opinion: who knows?

> Pollsters who failed to predict the size of John McCain's victory in Tuesday's New Hampshire primary—and the narrowness of Bill Bradley's defeat—are not hanging their heads, but they are scratching them. "We're all saying, 'What the hell happened?'" said Andy Smith, director of the University of New Hampshire's Survey Center.[27]

> Bush's crushing defeat in New Hampshire was not supposed to happen to a candidate with $70 million and the support of 27 Republican governors, 37 senators and 175 members of the House. But the voters seemed unimpressed with all those institutional trappings.[28]

> New Hampshire has always been useful less for picking winners—ask almost-Presidents Buchanan, Tsongas and Hart—than for chastening losers, stripping them bare, exposing the phonies, humbling the pundits, rewarding the pirates and generally leaving the impression that the voters might actually have some role to play in deciding who gets to be President. Even so, no one was prepared for what happened to American politics last week.[29]

Expressions of confusion multiplied as the McCain phenomenon spilled over into the Michigan primary in late February, puzzling journalists who obligingly wrote about their confusion. The press wanted to know who the McCain voters were and what they represented. But they couldn't seem to find the answers to these questions:

> Just what vein McCain has tapped remains in dispute. Is it a reaction against President Clinton and the character scandals that have marred his seven years in office? Is it the reawakening of the Ross Perot movement from its earliest days in 1992? Is it a rejection of Bush as the anointed candidate of the GOP hierarchy? Or is it mostly people who simply want to cast a positive vote for a former war hero?[30]

Those with long memories will recall that George W. Bush spent the better part of last year promising that he would be the one to restore honor and dignity to the office, so help him God. And he was the sunny conservative who was flirting with all those minivan moms and flinging open the G.O.P. primaries so that moderate voters could help him fend off threats from Steve Forbes and the rest of the pack. So how is it that the candidate whose stake as the front runner was based on his war chest, his invincibility and his proven crossover appeal now finds himself running out of cash and scrambling for the attention of those same swing voters?[31]

In the end, questions about the basis of McCain's support were not answered so much as dropped from consideration by the fast-moving tide of political events. Within weeks, McCain would disappear from electoral contention after Bush's superior war chest and organization helped him win enough Super Tuesday contests to secure the nomination. The competitive portion of the primary season had come and gone with greater rapidity than ever before. Something different had happened in 2000—reporters knew this much and said so—but it had happened so quickly and unexpectedly that it was hard to know exactly what it all meant.

For journalists inclined toward analyzing the horserace, the long stretch between March and the August conventions could have provided an opportunity to sort out and explain the changes in the electorate that they had witnessed during the primary phase. Doing so would have added a novel, educational wrinkle to horserace coverage. But it was not to be. Instead, in classic fashion, reporters trained their attention on the next benchmark five months away. They began to settle into the bland possibilities of a Bush–Gore contest, content to spend those months speculating on whom the two nominees-to-be would select as their running mates. The silly season had begun.

The Silly Season

Perhaps because the competitive phase of the primary season ended so early and so abruptly, there was an overabundance of stories with leads like this:

Republican presidential aspirant Sen. John McCain said Sunday that he would "under no circumstances" accept a vice presidential slot under current front-runner George W. Bush.[32]

Then again, this particular version of the vice presidential sweepstakes watch appeared *before* the primaries began, in December 1999. Think of it as foreshadowing.

The empty spring and summer months between Super Tuesday and the Republican Convention brought a daily diet of stories that portrayed Gore and Bush thinking about running mates, vetting resumes from potential running mates, and timing the announcement of running mates to win maximum media attention. There were stories about running mates who could deliver a state, running mates who could attract voters from a demographic group, running mates who would surprise, running mates who would be conventional choices. There were biographies of potential female running mates, Hispanic running mates, African American running mates, and Catholic running mates. Stories featured Colin Powell's lack of interest in being a running mate and Energy Secretary Bill Richardson's declining fortunes as a potential running mate. So much was written about Pennsylvania Governor Tom Ridge during the summer that it became hard not to imagine him arranging the furniture in the vice presidential mansion.

Electoral maps showed the states where running mates could help or hurt the two tickets. Stories discussed how positions on abortion among possible Republican running mates could affect George W. Bush's standing with moderate swing voters and religious conservatives. Running mate choices were put forward as tests of character and as maps of the cognitive processes of the nominees-in-waiting. Dark-horse running mate choices were discussed, rejected, and sometimes discussed again. Pundits chimed in with their (largely incorrect) predictions about what Gore and Bush would do. It seemed as if every name in official Washington was circulated as a possible running mate at some point, except for Dick Cheney, who escaped all speculation, and Joseph Lieberman, who was not taken seriously by pundits. And, every so often, reporters would find a political scientist to say that, historically, the choice of a running mate makes little difference in the outcome of an election.

What else was there to talk about during this long political interlude? To reporters, March through July was a time when Gore and Bush were making very little news.

In truth, over a period of weeks in the spring of 2000, Gore and Bush outlined their positions on education, crime, Social Security, prescription drug benefits for the elderly, abortion, and a host of other substantive items. With the horserace in neutral, it would have been an ideal time for reporters to turn their analytical minds to describing and analyzing these positions. And they did—to a degree. Attentive news consumers could find stories about the details of the major candidates' positions, particularly in print media. But, thematically, reporters' issue coverage during this period tended to be more political than programmatic.

Reporters generally framed the Bush and Gore proposals, not in terms of the likely consequences of implementing their proposals or whether their promises were consistent with their political records, but rather in terms of how their proclamations positioned the candidates for the fall campaign. Often, policy statements were trivialized as mere weapons in a war of strategic positioning and image manipulation.

"Many political observers say this election has already presented the American public with more serious policy initiatives covering a broader range of issues than any presidential campaign they can recall," marveled the

Los Angeles Times. But, instead of addressing the details, this article, like many others, told the reader how such a "wonkfest" served the political interests of the candidates:

> The civic-minded may see nothing but goodness in this clash of ideas. But each candidate has tactical reasons for trying to out-wonk the other. For Bush, it is part of a strategy to seize the political center by redefining the Republican approach to various issues including some, such as education, that have long been the province of Democrats. For Gore, a famous policy grind, the emphasis on issues is a way to challenge Bush's depth and keep the race from turning into a personality contest, which would likely favor the more easygoing governor. For both, it's a way to woo a public increasingly skeptical of sweeping pronouncements or simple solutions.[33]

Substance as campaign style. It's a frame that began in the silly season and continued through election day as reporters looked for ways to organize information about the candidates' policy proclamations into familiar themes. To be sure, some stories addressed the particulars of the policy proposals articulated by the candidates, taking their proposals at face value and framing them in terms of what the candidate said he hoped to do. But policy-as-strategy was the overarching theme from March through November. This frame turned issue stories into horserace stories, sometimes with touches of media self-reference, as in this *Time* magazine discussion of policy as political theater:

> It made for great TV. There was Maxine Waters, an outspoken member of the Congressional Black Caucus, live on CNN defending the Clinton Administration's efforts to return Elian Gonzalez to his father in Cuba. Suddenly, on air, Waters learned that Al Gore had come out in support of the Cuban exiles who are trying to keep Elian in Miami. Waters exploded, saying she would "rethink" her endorsement of the Vice President. The next morning, Gore phoned Waters to make peace.[34]

The article continues with a discussion of the "perils of ethnic politics,"[35] explaining that Gore's pronouncement had nothing to do with policy or principle and everything to do with making a play for the Hispanic vote in south Florida. Could there be a connection between stories like this and the *Los Angeles Times*'s observation that the public is "increasingly skeptical of sweeping pronouncements or simple solutions" from politicians? The prominence of the policy-as-strategy frame makes the question a reasonable one.

Strategically, a candidate may take a position in order to, say, generate the appearance of integrity. The press will then dutifully report the political rationale behind the effort, inviting the public to regard the politician as manipulative and without integrity. Readers are told that a Democratic National Committee commercial about Al Gore's proposal to reform managed health care is "the latest piece in a mosaic being assembled by Gore's

media consultants, one that would portray the vice president as a principled
person intent on advocating consumers' interests." [36] Perhaps George W.
Bush holds a principled position on abortion. It's hard to know when
reporters frame the matter in terms of his political self-interest, when we are
told that "for all the success George W. Bush has had straddling the center,
there is one place he ventures at his political peril: challenging the Republican Party's unwavering stand against abortion. If the Texas governor chooses a running mate who supports abortion rights, . . . he would risk an enormous backlash—a mutiny, even—within the GOP." [37]

And what of politicians who offer details about how they would handle
issues of import to the electorate? Perhaps they seek to have a governing
mandate should they win the election. Conceivably, they imagine voters
would benefit from knowing where they stand. Maybe they even believe
some of the things they're saying. Or, to hear *Time* magazine tell it, they may
just be tacticians—and bad ones, at that:

> By revealing some of his thoughts on Social Security reform, Bush suc-
> cumbed to the journalists and voters who clamor for specificity. For
> the Texas Governor, who has been caricatured as an intellectual light-
> weight, there's a special imperative to provide detail. It's seen as proof
> of gravitas. But specificity kills. Just ask Bill Bradley. He was running
> strong until he laid out a detailed health plan. Gore cherry-picked the
> details and used them to paint the former Senator as both a spendthrift
> crazy and a Medicaid-destroying ogre. [38]

It's difficult to appraise which journalists were clamoring for specific policy details, considering how rapidly the particulars were buried under strategic coverage. The strategic frame is perfectly valid, of course, and the analyses
presented in these excerpts and countless others like them are apt. But the
strategic frame poses a dilemma for the voter who turns to news reports for
information about Bush's proposal for Social Security reform or Gore's plan
to reform managed care. It's impossible to assess the attractiveness and viability of these ideas within the framework of strategic coverage. The public is
denied an opportunity to assess what the candidates would do in office when
they are fed a diet of why they are talking about what they would do.

Compounding matters is the tendency for issue-as-strategy analysis to
put forward—correctly at times, but cynically—the most self-serving reasons
for politicians to take positions on issues. Emphasizing political motives
instructs the public on political tactics they may not need to know about and
probably do not understand in the same manner as the professionals who
report them, while casting politicians in the most self-serving light. Such an
emphasis also precludes the possibility that politicians, whose pursuit of high
office demands that they be self-serving, could also have principles and
beliefs. This important nuance is lost when strategy overtakes policy stories.

The dilemma was detailed in typically self-referential fashion by the *Los
Angeles Times*. But, instructively, the writer overlooked or could not see the
role her profession plays in advancing a condition she regards as ironic:

It is one of the strange ironies of politics: Candidates expound on issues and people assume they are angling for votes. Politicians try harder, only to have people believe them less—even when they are speaking from the heart. Rarely does a candidate emerge with that trait that neither charm nor money can buy: the assumption that one wholly means what one says.[39]

Ironic, indeed.

Denouement

Press coverage of the 2000 campaign didn't get any better during the frenzied race to the finish. In the final months of the marathon, with the contest close and defying all predictions, reporters began to frame just about everything in terms of the horserace and electoral strategy. As the race cascaded unpredictably through September and October, crashing with full momentum past the November 7 finish line, there was something almost out of control about the way everything—issues, character, media self-references, and nonevents—became fodder for the story of who would be the ultimate winner. Surely the horserace deserved great attention in an election that turned out to be one of the closest in history, but as the undecided voters waffled between Bush and Gore, news coverage of those final weeks did very little to help them make meaningful decisions.

During the fall campaign, the most valuable time for reporters to clarify the policy differences between the candidates, issue coverage diverted attention away from the details by framing the issue story in strategic political terms. Although this coverage followed the pattern established earlier in the year, it was in the end even more concentrated and relentless.

For example, voters learned that Gore was trying to "seize the initiative" on Social Security reform to "turn up the heat on Bush,"[40] who in turn was talking about tax relief in order to make "inroads with middle-class voters" as part of a "strategy that aides said would put Bush on the offensive."[41] Gore took on "managed-care companies, other health insurers, drug companies and oil companies" as "a way to sully the image of Bush" and "appeal to [the] middle-income, middle-of-the-road voters who are likely to decide the election."[42] Bush released a document called "Blueprint for the Middle Class," a compilation of policy proposals, in an effort "to project a take-charge image and wrest control of the debate."[43] Gore "appears to have lost confidence in his gun control agenda" because "Bush, despite his opposition to ostensibly popular new gun control measures, generally runs even or ahead of Gore when voters are asked who can best handle the gun issue."[44]

But what of the substance of Gore's Social Security, health care, and gun control proposals, or of Bush's tax plan? At the very time when many people were starting to pay close attention, the media's predominant thematic message was that the details of policy weren't important enough to consider, a message rendered all the more cynical by the suggestion that the effort to win votes at all costs was the reason the candidates fabricated these proposals in the first place. Stories that placed the political motivation for a candidate's behavior ahead of his philosophical or programmatic concerns underscored the point:

> Women of America, beware: George W. Bush wants your vote, and on Monday he went straight to the maternity ward to get it.[45]

> Many Republicans outside the Bush camp believe Gore is highly vulnerable on the big-spending issue and have urged the Republican nominee to pursue this line of attack.[46]

> In retiree-heavy Florida, Gore tore into his rival's Social Security proposal, which would allow younger workers to invest a small percentage of their Social Security payroll taxes into secure stocks. His choice of Florida for the address was intended to knock a variety of birds off a single branch with one projectile.[47]

As went the issue coverage, so went the coverage of every other thematic element of the campaign. Reporters scrutinized the nonissues and miniscandals that popped up along the way for their strategic ramifications. Was it a big strategic blunder when Bush and Cheney chatted like frat boys into an open mike, using an off-color epithet to describe a senior reporter? Did the Bush campaign miscalculate by dragging out the negotiations for holding campaign debates? What about the flap over how a videotape of the Texas governor rehearsing for the debates ended up in the vice president's camp, or the last-minute revelation of Bush's DUI arrest in 1976? Both of the latter two incidents were picked apart for their strategic implications:

> In a presidential race where rats infested a Republican commercial and Vice President Gore's dog was drawn into a debate over the price of prescriptions, both campaigns suddenly are in the grip of a mole hunt [over the rehearsal videotape]. Even many of the central participants confess they are unsure which side is the victim and which is the perpetrator. Another possibility is that an impulsive action by a random outsider is being painted as a grand conspiracy in an effort to score political yardage.[48]

> As the Bush campaign dealt with a barrage of inquiries about the [DUI] arrest, strategists in both parties tried to weigh any possible impact on the still-close presidential race. Several strategists said that, while the report of the arrest drew attention to a problem in Bush's past, it did not tell voters something fundamentally new about Bush because he has already confessed to having a problem with alcohol. But they said if the long-hidden arrest raised new questions about Bush's candor, credibility or trustworthiness—all traits he has stressed this fall—the political fallout could be damaging.[49]

And if perceptions of the candidate's character could become a strategic matter as the result of a scandalous story, so was it considered by reporters to be a critical element of the horserace:

> In this final week of the closest presidential campaign in a generation, the candidates' demeanors have become as crucial a part of their message as their stands on prescription drugs or any other issue. Gore is trying to show how hard he would work in office, jetting from the West Coast to Florida overnight tonight, and promising to hold weekly—yes, weekly—town-meeting-style forums as president. And Bush seems to be working to create a bandwagon effect, campaigning deep in Democratic territory.[50]

Even media self-references were framed in terms of the strategic imperatives of the campaign during the final weeks. Reporters assessed how and where the campaigns were buying television time, commented on the way they were being "spun" by campaign operatives in order to gain strategic advantages, and evaluated how reporters' own commentaries after each debate helped to position the candidates in the horserace.[51] Such commentary had assessed how the candidates appeared rather than the substance of what they said. Essentially, it addressed the questions raised in the *Los Angeles Times* prior to the first debate.

> Bush may be easygoing and friendly, but does the Texas governor have the heft to fill the president's Oval Office chair? Vice President Gore may be smart and experienced, but is he grounded in a set of principles that go beyond the tactical maneuvers needed to win the White House?[52]

These are legitimate questions, but the post-debate analysis tended to address them using television's standards of assessment, the standards of effective body language and well delivered sound bites. Standards of this kind lead reporters to question whether Gore stood too close to Bush, or whether Bush properly pronounced the names of foreign leaders.

Absent from most of the post-debate analysis was any meaningful discussion of the content of the candidates' answers. Substantive analysis would have compelled journalists to ask different questions, such as whether the programs each candidate offered were internally consistent, whether their claims were practical, and whether their charges were accurate. Instead, post-debate television viewers were treated to focus groups of undecided voters who never could make up their minds, interspersed with expert commentary that praised Governor Bush for rising above press-generated performance expectations by accurately pronouncing East Timor or that noted how Vice President Gore had the more complex and therefore the more difficult political case to make with voters. It is not impossible to imagine that these two things—public indecision and strategic debate analysis—may somehow be related.

Can We Do Better?

Press coverage of the 2000 presidential election was an odd juxtaposition of worn-out horserace themes and dramatic changes in the political process. Yes, the campaign went on way too long, and, yes, for tedious stretches it lacked compelling drama and engaging personalities. But, for a press corps bent on telling the story of the strategic machinations of the political process, this campaign rewrote the script on the nomination process more dramatically than any since Jimmy Carter's 1976 campaign showed how obscurity could be an asset in the game of momentum and expectations. Why, then, were reporters so frustrated by what they had to work with?

Partly, the answer lies in the tendency for people—even pundits—not to recognize what's happening until well after the fact. The amount of coverage reporters devoted to explaining their previous inaccuracies in coverage attests to how far behind the curve most of them were in detecting and explaining what was happening in the horserace. Only in hindsight is it clear that the 2000 election, like none before it, produced an early conclusion to the horserace, ushering in an interminably long silly season dominated by less than fascinating political personalities, followed by an agonizingly close fall campaign that refused to conform to conventional wisdom. If it was unfair to expect reporters to recognize these differences, it was perhaps not unreasonable to expect them to address more relevant and compelling matters, rather than to force existing frameworks for political reporting onto a fluid and volatile process. This is especially true of frameworks that turned issue positions into tactical posturing, overemphasized the media's role in presidential selection, and fixed on minute turns in political strategy.

Together, these frames placed the emphasis on the now familiar strategic machinations of an all-too-long campaign, highlighting minutia and missing important novelties such as the meaning of the McCain phenomenon and the revolution in presidential selection-by-fund-raising. Instead, the public again was subjected to horserace-centered coverage of questionable value for generating interest in the campaign, much less for informing voters on matters of substance.

For once, it could have been different, because campaign 2000 raised important questions about the direction of the political process and the contours of political discourse. By simply modifying rather than relinquishing the frames they use to structure their coverage, reporters could have had their horserace and produced edifying reports, too. Without delving into the issues coverage that reformers advocate and political reporters resist, reporters could have used the horserace as a forum for generating a serious discussion of why the public is dissatisfied with politics rather than producing coverage that contributes to the problem.

As they evaluate their work in the aftermath of the election, reporters might remember why people were laughing at the *Saturday Night Live* skit—that is, why the public was laughing at them. And they might be wise to consider the self-referential but on-target analysis of Howard Rosenberg who, after Super Tuesday, wrote in the *Los Angeles Times* that coverage of the primaries had lacked a certain thoughtfulness. "Missing," he said, "was a thoughtful discussion of ideas, as if this country's future would be shaped by the candidate's slogans and Tuesday exit polls instead of their vision." Contending that no one would confuse all-news cable coverage with Rodin's "The Thinker," he continued:

> They have perfected and polished to a high gloss, in fact, the art of reporting about nothing. And even more stunningly, doing it in-depth. The . . . nadir was an MSNBC segment putting under a microscope Bush's rebounding late-night appearance with Jay Leno on NBC-TV following his flop [the previous week] with David Letterman on CBS-TV. "Was he funnier this time around with Leno than he was with Letterman?" a political humorist was asked. That this stroking of chins over something so trivial actually went on for several minutes confirmed how adept these news channels have become at holding their noses and shoveling You Know What into the great pit they are required to fill every day.[53]

If you're looking for a good explanation of why public interest in and knowledge of politics grew more brittle as the campaign season stretched to infinity, you may not have to look much further than this.

Postscript: An Internet Future?

As the third night of the Republican National Convention was winding down, Cokie Roberts sat on the small ABCNews.com set in the huge air-conditioned press tent outside the convention arena. There, she chatted on line with visitors to the network's website. When she was finished, she was approached by an MTV "V.J." who jumped on stage to interview her for a segment of that network's "Choose or Lose" election coverage. Several hundred feet away, down what was labeled "Internet Alley," young staff for Foxnews.com wrote interactive reports to supplement the more traditional coverage on their upstart cable network. The old media was staring at its future on that steamy Philadelphia night. And nobody was quite certain what they were seeing.

Back in the convention hall, where a band of luxury boxes had been converted into towering stage sets for the likes of Dan Rather and Bernard Shaw, a modest booth bearing the name "Pseudo" sat astride the more familiar corporate logos of media giants. From that perch, one of the largest Internet TV networks carried what it billed as gavel-to-gavel "unconventional" convention coverage. Seven panoramic cameras throughout the convention hall sent streaming video to users who, through controls on the pseudo.com home page, could act as their own directors and display pictures on their computers from the perspectives they wanted to see. Guests like *Newsweek*'s Eleanor Clift, Michigan Senator Spencer Abraham, and other mainstream journalists and politicians sat in the Pseudo booth overlooking the podium as electronic "E.J.'s" buffered questions sent by users through electronic messaging. Behind them, multipierced Pseudo staffers, most of them too young to legally rent a car, took in the show. And in the system's chat room, hundreds of users, many in the typically apolitical under-twenty-five demographic, talked politics over the web with other like-minded users.

Unlike the big-time journalists, many of these young people wanted to talk about political issues.

People numbered in mere hundreds are hardly measurable in the world of mass media. But these are the early days of the Wild West. Rough and raw, backed by corporate dollars and a braintrust with its roots in traditional network television, the new medium takes its glitzy seat alongside the old ones. Four years from now, it may even give jaded political reporters something imaginative to think about.

Notes

1. Matthew Robert Kerbel, "The Media: Viewing the Campaign through a Strategic Haze," in *The Elections of 1996,* ed. Michael Nelson (Washington, D.C.: CQ Press, 1997), 82.
2. See, for instance, Gaye Tuchman, *Making News* (New York: Free Press, 1978); Mark Fishman, *Manufacturing the News* (Austin: University of Texas Press, 1978); Michael Schudson, *Discovering the News* (New York: Basic Books, 1978).
3. This follows the retrospective voting tradition. See Morris Fiorina, *Retrospective Voting in American National Elections* (New Haven: Yale University Press, 1981).
4. The seminal work on framing is Erving Goffman's *Frame Analysis: An Essay on the Organization of Experience* (Cambridge: Harvard University Press, 1974). But a huge literature has developed in recent years which applies framing to news production. Although scholars may vary in their definition of frame analysis, the existence of framing is broadly accepted as a device used by producers, editors, and reporters for making news. For a good overview, see Robert M. Entman, "Framing: Toward Clarification of a Fractured Paradigm," in *Journal of Communication* 43 (autumn 1993): 51–58.
5. See Matthew Robert Kerbel, *Edited for Television: CNN, ABC and American Presidential Elections* (Boulder: Westview Press, 1998).
6. T. Christian Miller, "For a Campaign in Motion, the Idea Is 'Have Chaos, Will Travel,'" *Los Angeles Times,* May 21, 2000.
7. "Public Involvement and the 2000 Nominating Campaign: Implications for Electoral Reform." Presented at the National Press Club, Washington, D.C., April 27, 2000, 3.
8. Ibid.
9. Report of the Center for Media and Public Affairs, Washington, D.C., March 24, 2000.
10. "Public Involvement and the 2000 Nominating Campaign: Implications for Electoral Reform," 7.
11. Kerbel, *Edited for Television.*
12. Among the media prominently discussed here are the *Washington Post,* the *Los Angeles Times, Time,* and ABC News.

13. Dan Balz, "Gore's Moves Intensify 'Preseason,'" *Washington Post,* October 3, 1999, A1.
14. George Skelton, "Why the Media Makes Hay out of Iowa Straw Poll," *Los Angeles Times,* August 19, 1999.
15. *ABC World News Tonight,* June 14, 1999.
16. Ibid.
17. Geraldine Baum and Mark Z. Barabak, "The Media Swarm to Bauer for a Political Nonevent," *Los Angeles Times,* September 30, 1999.
18. Dan Balz, "Starting Early and Urgently," *Washington Post,* April 4, 1999, A1.
19. Dan Balz, "Bradley on a Fast Break," *Washington Post,* May 2, 1999, A1.
20. Dan Balz, "McCain's Rise Alters Dynamics of Race," *Washington Post,* November 6, 1999, A1.
21. Ibid.
22. Mark Z. Barabak, "News Analysis," *Los Angeles Times,* September 12, 1999.
23. Josh Getlin, "Bush Coverage: Straight News or Media Coronation?" *Los Angeles Times,* October 22, 1999.
24. Mark Z. Barabak, "News Analysis."
25. Mark Z. Barabak, "Bush's Winning Glow Dims after Poor Debate Reviews," *Los Angeles Times,* December 9, 1999.
26. Ronald Brownstein, "Challengers Dragging both Gore and Bush Away from Center," *Los Angeles Times,* January 11, 2000.
27. Massie Ritsch, "Pollsters Study Outcome They Didn't See Coming," *Los Angeles Times,* February 4, 2000.
28. Dan Balz, "S.C. to Test McCain's Appeal, Bush's Mettle," *Washington Post,* February 6, 2000, A1.
29. Nancy Gibbs, "McCain's Moment," *Time,* February 7, 2000.
30. Dan Balz, "McCain's Surge Shakes GOP, Puzzles Analysts," *Washington Post,* February 27, 2000, A1.
31. Nancy Gibbs, "Who Are McCain's Forces?" *Time,* February 28, 2000.
32. "Number Two Spot Ruled Out by McCain," *Los Angeles Times,* December 6, 1999.
33. Mark Z. Barabak, "White House Race Is Styled by Substance," *Los Angeles Times,* May 30, 2000.
34. Matthew Cooper and John Dickerson, "The Perils of Ethnic Politics," *Time,* April 3, 2000.
35. Ibid.
36. Jeff Leeds, "Ad Touts Gore Health Plan in an Indirect Swipe at Bush," *Los Angeles Times,* June 20, 2000.
37. Mark Z. Barabak, "Bush Faces Tough Choices in Taking a Stand on Abortion," *Los Angeles Times,* June 11, 2000.
38. James Carney, "The Dangers of Being Specific," *Time,* May 8, 2000.
39. Cathleen Decker, "A Sincere Distrust of Politicians," *Los Angeles Times,* June 11, 2000.
40. Edward Walsh and Ceci Connolly, "Gore Hits Bush on Social Security," *Washington Post,* November 4, 2000.
41. Dan Balz, "Bush Begins to Stress Differences with Gore," *Washington Post,* September 19, 2000.
42. Mike Allen, "With Trustbuster Echoes, Gore Goes after Big Business," *Washington Post,* September 19, 2000.
43. Frank Bruni, "Bush Campaign Turns Attention to Middle Class," *New York Times,* September 17, 2000.
44. Ronald Brownstein, "NRA, Unions Fight for Blue-Collar Voters," *Los Angeles Times,* October 22, 2000.

45. Maria L. LaGanga, "Bush Tries to Woo Female Voters, Middle Class Away from Rival Gore," *Los Angeles Times,* September 19, 2000.
46. CNN, September 27, 2000.
47. Ibid., November 2, 2000.
48. Mike Allen, "Message Takes a Back Seat to the 'Mole,'" *Washington Post,* September 28, 2000.
49. Mike Allen and Dan Balz, "Bush Seeks to Minimize DUI Fallout," *Washington Post,* November 4, 2000.
50. Mike Allen, "Style Counts, Strategists Say," *Washington Post,* November 1, 2000.
51. See, for instance, Howard Fineman, "Hidden Factors in Campaign 2000," *MSNBC News,* October 5, 2000; and Mike Ferullo, "Fewer Jabs, But Plenty of 'Spin' after Second Presidential Debate," CNN, October 12, 2000.
52. Mark Z. Barabak and Cathleen Decker, "Outcome of Election May Turn on Debates," *Los Angeles Times,* October 1, 2000.
53. Howard Rosenberg, "Coverage Misses Its Political Opportunity," *Los Angeles Times,* March 8, 2000.

6

The States: Direct Democracy

Richard J. Ellis

Elections between candidates have been a staple of American democracy for more than two centuries. They are the primary means by which citizens ensure that public officials remain not only reasonably well behaved but also responsive to their policy concerns. In countries where competitive elections are absent, political leaders generally have little need to pay close attention to the concerns of the citizenry. But while choosing policymakers through competitive elections would be regarded as a great democratic advance in many parts of the world, in the United States growing numbers of people dismiss representative democracy as at best a pale reflection of true democratic principles. Internet enthusiasts claim that the technology of the twenty-first century makes possible a truer form of democracy in which citizens can involve themselves directly in the making of public policy rather than relying on the judgment of elected officials or the lobbying of organized interest groups.[1] In an age of electronic communication, representative institutions appear to some to be an archaic holdover from a bygone era. Compared with the prospect of voters directly and instantaneously registering their policy preferences, candidate elections seem a crude and clumsy instrument of popular control, even in the absence of laborious, drawn-out hand counts. And in a nation that is both populist and strongly distrustful of government, this vision of e-democracy has a special resonance. It promises not only unprecedented popular control of public policy but also laws without government.[2]

In much of the United States these visions of direct democracy may still seem futuristic if not fantastic. But in many of the twenty-four states and hundreds of localities that possess the initiative power, the future is now. The initiative process enables citizens to bypass their elected representatives and take issues directly to the people. Voters are given the opportunity not just to express their preference for a candidate or political party but also to pass judgment directly on specific public policy questions. To its defenders, the initiative process is the highest stage of democracy, the closest we have yet come to realizing government of and by the people. To its detractors, direct legislation undermines the deliberation and compromise that lie at the heart of the democratic process.

Although the initiative process in the United States dates back to the early twentieth century, only in the past several decades has it begun to

Table 6-1   Initiative Use per Two-Year Election Cycle, 1950–2000

Decade	Average number of initiatives on ballot	Average number of initiatives passed	Passage rate (in percentage)
1950s	25	9	36
1960s	19	9	45
1970s	35	13	38
1980s	50	22	44
1990s	76	35	46
2000	76	35	46

Source: Compiled by author.

attract widespread national attention and commentary. During the 1950s and 1960s, the initiative process was of generally limited importance (see Table 6-1). About 95 initiatives appeared on state ballots in the 1960s, and fewer than half passed. The number of statewide initiatives nearly doubled in the 1970s, and in the 1980s the number was close to triple what it had been in the 1960s. Statewide initiatives increased yet again during the 1990s, reaching 382, four times the number that had been placed before state voters three decades earlier. More initiatives passed in the 1990s than were passed in the 1950s, 1960s, and 1970s combined.

The 2000 elections continued this general trend toward increased initiative use. In 2000, the number of statewide initiatives (76) was the second highest number in the past half-century, trailing only the 1996–1997 election cycle, which produced a record 103 initiatives. Perhaps initiative use will continue to increase in the twenty-first century, as it has in each of the preceding three decades, but initiative use and passage rates in 2000 were consistent with the patterns from the 1990s, during which the nation averaged 76 initiatives per two-year election cycle and passed 46 percent of them. Although political commentators and initiative activists often attribute initiative use to amorphous public moods, the fact is that initiative use in the past decade, with the exception of the 1996 election, has been quite stable and relatively impervious to swings in public mood or trust in government (see Figure 6-1). Initiative use has become institutionalized, driven less by the demands of the public than by the activists and professionals who supply the initiatives.

Who Plays?

Although use of the initiative process has increased nationally during the past few decades, a great gulf remains between the initiative haves and have-nots. A handful of high-use states experience the effects of direct legislation in a way that is qualitatively different from other initiative states. In the 2000 election, for example, almost 40 percent of the nation's 76 initia-

Figure 6-1 Initiative Use by Election Cycle, 1988–2000

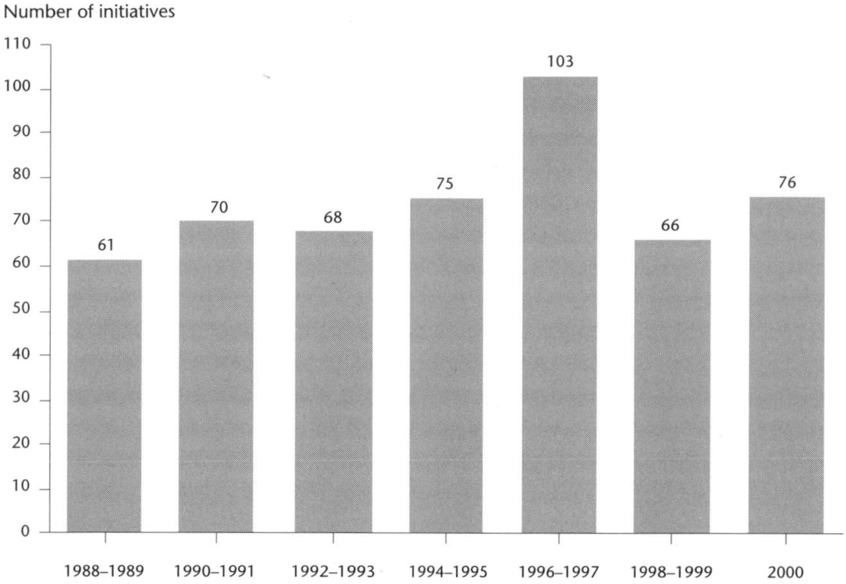

Number of initiatives

Source: Compiled by the author.

tives were in two states: Oregon and California. The comparable number during the preceding two decades, although somewhat smaller, is still 30 percent. Moreover, the next three heaviest initiative users during the past decade—Colorado, Washington, and Arizona—account for nearly an additional 25 percent of the statewide initiatives in 2000. The remaining 37 percent of initiatives were distributed among the other nineteen initiative states, seven of which did not have a single initiative in 2000. The states that made more frequent use of the initiative process during the 1980s and 1990s tended to be the same states that generated more initiatives in the 2000 election, and the states that rarely used the initiative during the 1980s and 1990s were generally the same states that did not use the process in 2000.[3] (See Table 6-2.)

Why do some states consistently make minimal use of the initiative process, while other states rely on it heavily? The voters' mood or confidence in government has little to do with it. Citizens in Oregon or California are no more alienated from government or distrustful of politicians than are voters in Idaho or Ohio. Nor is legislative performance the answer. Legislatures in Washington or Colorado are not consistently more ineffective than legislatures in Wyoming or Oklahoma.

Part of the answer is that legal procedures for qualifying initiatives differ substantially from state to state. In Wyoming, for example, which has had only seven initiatives in thirty years, petitioners must gather signatures

Table 6-2 Initiative Use by State, 1980–2000

State	Average per two-year election cycle in the 1980s and 1990s	Number in 2000
California	10.5	12
Oregon	8.8	18
Colorado	5.2	6
Washington	4.2	6
Arizona	3.3	6
Montana	3.2	1
North Dakota	3.0	0
Massachusetts	2.7	6
South Dakota	2.3	3
Maine	2.3	3
Nevada	2.1	2
Alaska	2.1	2
Missouri	1.9	2
Arkansas	1.6	2
Ohio	1.5	0
Michigan	1.4	2
Nebraska	1.3	2
Florida	1.3	1
Idaho	1.3	0
Oklahoma	1.2	0
Utah	0.9	0
Mississippi	0.7	0
Wyoming	0.7	0
Illinois	0.1	0

Source: Compiled by the author.

equal to at least 15 percent of the total number of votes cast in the preceding general election. In California and Colorado, petitioners need only 5 percent to qualify a statutory initiative. Also important is the presence or absence of a geographic requirement that requires signatures to be gathered in a certain number of counties or legislative districts across the state. None of the top six initiative-producing states in the 1980s and 1990s had a geographic requirement. In contrast, all but two of the states ranking in the bottom half of initiative use have some form of geographic requirement.

A few states are initiative states in name only. In Illinois, for example, initiatives can be used only to amend the section of the state constitution relating to the structures and procedures of the legislature. In Mississippi, the only state to adopt the initiative process in the past two decades, the obstacles placed in the way of initiative proponents are enormous. In addition to a 12 percent signature threshold and a strict geographic requirement mandating that one-fifth of the petition signatures must come from each of the state's five congressional districts, Mississippi also requires that the majority in favor of an initiative must be at least 40 percent of the number of all voters who went to the polls in that election. Moreover, every initiative that has revenue implications must identify the amount and source of revenue required to implement it, and if the initiative reduces revenues or reallocates funding, it must specify which programs will be affected. Finally, Mississippi prohibits initiatives that would change the initiative process itself or that would alter either the state's Bill of Rights or its constitutional right-to-work guarantee.[4]

Procedural hurdles and legal restrictions account for much of the differences among states in initiative use, but they also leave much unexplained. On paper it is easier to qualify an initiative in South Dakota than in Oregon, yet Oregonians have used the initiative process more than six times as often as South Dakotans. In California, petitioners have only 150 days to gather signatures for initiative petitions. This circulation period is among the most restrictive in the nation, yet California typically has far more initiatives on the ballot than other states, including states that allow petitioners several years to gather signatures. Nor can signature requirements explain why Arizona, which has a relatively high requirement (10 percent for statutory initiatives and 15 percent for constitutional initiatives), has seen far more initiatives than many states with much lower signature thresholds.

Signature requirements clearly matter, but these anomalies suggest that other factors also make a difference. What separates states that are heavy initiative users from those that are not is less a matter of legal requirements or procedural hurdles than the existence of networks of experienced initiative activists and professionals who are skilled at using the initiative process to serve their political ends. One-third of Oregon's eighteen initiatives in 2000 were placed on the ballot by one activist, Bill Sizemore. Since 1993, Sizemore has been the head of Oregon Taxpayers United (OTU), and since 1997 he has also run his own signature-gathering firm, I&R Petition Services, which enables him to make it his business not only to introduce initiatives but also to qualify them for the ballot. Initiatives are Sizemore's life and livelihood.[5]

Sizemore, however, is only the most prominent of a dense network of initiative activists in Oregon. Measure 9, which unsuccessfully tried to ban the teaching of homosexuality in schools, was placed on the 2000 ballot by the same person (Lon Mabon) and organization (Oregon Citizens Alliance) that qualified three antigay initiatives in the late 1980s and early 1990s and came close to qualifying several more in the mid- and late-1990s. Measure 8, which would have placed a lid on state spending, was sponsored by Don McIntyre, one of the fathers of Oregon's landmark 1990 property tax limitation initiative. Coordinating the signature drive for Measure 8 was Ruth Bendl, who in the mid-1990s worked in a similar capacity for Loren Parks, the financial archangel of conservative initiatives in Oregon, including many of Sizemore's. Together with Parks, Bendl played a pivotal role in qualifying nearly half of the sixteen initiatives on the 1996 ballot, as well as several on the 1994 ballot. Bendl had been active in the Oregon initiative wars since the early 1980s, when she, along with McIntyre, worked on a 1982 property tax limitation initiative, one of a string of four such initiatives to fail at the ballot box in the 1980s.

On the left, Lloyd Marbet has been a fixture of Oregon initiative politics since the mid-1980s, when he led three separate initiative campaigns to close the Trojan Nuclear Power Plant and several more to clean up radioactive wastes. In 2000, he spearheaded a popular referendum that repealed a law allowing Portland General Electric to earn profits from the mothballed Trojan plant.[6] Many of these veteran initiative activists on the right and the left came together in 2000 to promote Measure 96, which would have prohibited the legislature from enacting or referring to the voters any law that would make the initiative process more difficult to use.

Neighboring Washington State boasts a burgeoning network of initiative activists, the most visible of whom is Tim Eyman, author of two of the six initiatives on the 2000 Washington ballot. One of them (I-722) limited property tax increases and nullified recent tax and fee increases; the other (I-745) would have required that 90 percent of state and local transportation funds be spent on roads. Eyman burst onto the public stage in 1999 with the passage of I-695, which required public votes on all increases in state and local taxes and fees, slashed motor vehicle taxes, and left state and local governments scrambling to make up a $600 million loss in annual revenue. Eyman's first taste of initiative politics came in 1995, when he collected signatures for a petition to force a vote on a proposed new stadium for Seattle's baseball team. He enjoyed the experience so much that in 1996 he introduced an anti–affirmative action initiative modeled on California's Proposition 209. The latter effort faltered until Eyman handed control of the initiative over to John Carlson, a prominent conservative talk show host (and later the 2000 Republican gubernatorial nominee). Carlson, a veteran of several high-profile state initiative campaigns, steered the initiative to victory.

Eyman then turned his attention to the unpopular motor vehicle excise tax. In many ways, I-695 was a textbook citizen's measure. The signatures were raised entirely by volunteers, the campaign was run on a shoestring budget, and contributions came overwhelmingly from small contributors upset by high motor vehicle taxes. During the I-695 campaign Eyman cultivated his image as an ordinary citizen outraged by an unjust tax and anxious to return to his mail-order watch business. But within a month of his triumph in the 1999 election, he announced the formation of a political action committee, "Permanent Offense," whose objective was to defend I-695 in court and to push two new initiatives, "Chapters 2 and 3" of what he promised would be an ongoing effort to change state government. As an initiative novice in 1997, Eyman had scoffed at pouring money "down a rat hole" to a professional signature-gathering firm; in 2000, however, he hired the premier initiative consultant in the state, Shirley Bockwinkel, to run a paid signature campaign to qualify I-722 and I-745 for the ballot. Bockwinkel is herself a veteran of initiative politics—she was the chief proponent of the state's term limits initiative in 1992, and she brought the legal suit that ended the state's ban on paying signature-gatherers on a per-signature basis.[7]

Persistence and a flair for populist self-dramatization are also characteristics of Colorado's most notorious initiative activist, Douglas Bruce. Since 1988, Coloradans have been confronted with a Bruce-sponsored initiative in every election but one; the 1998 respite was the result of the Colorado Supreme Court's repeated refusal to title Bruce's initiatives because they violated the single-subject rule for ballot measures that had been approved by the state's voters in 1994. Bruce's early initiative efforts had been relatively amateurish and ineffective, but in 1992 he stunned the political establishment by qualifying and passing the Taxpayers Bill of Rights (TABOR), which required voter approval for most state and local tax increases and placed strict limits on the rate of increase in state and local government spending and taxing. In 2000, Bruce was back again with the mother of all tax cuts, Amendment 21, which proposed to cut taxes on, among other things, cars, telephone service, heating, electricity, television, real estate, and income. The initiative proposed to reduce each tax by $25 the first year and an additional $25 each year thereafter until, at some point, the taxes presumably would disappear altogether. Experts estimated that the measure, if passed, would reduce state revenue by $1 billion in the first thirty months. Although early polls showed the measure ahead, Bruce's sweeping initiative eventually crumbled under an avalanche of criticism from across the political spectrum.

In California, some of the most successful initiative activists have been politicians. Indeed, during the past three decades, about one-third of California's initiatives have been sponsored by elected officials or candidates for elected office. Almost all the major Democratic and Republican candidates for statewide office during the past decade have sponsored state initiatives; the list includes John Van de Kamp, Tom Campbell, Bill Jones, Ron Unz, Dianne Feinstein, Michael Huffington, and Pete Wilson. Governor Wilson was by far the most frequent initiative user in California during the 1990s, spearheading at least seven high-profile initiatives. These included a tough-on-crime measure in 1990; welfare reform in 1992; "Three Strikes and You're Out" and a crackdown on illegal immigrants in 1994; an anti–affirmative action measure in 1996; and education reform and anti-union measures in 1998. As his second term as governor came to a close in 1998, Wilson unveiled another initiative, the "Gang Violence and Juvenile Crime Prevention Act." A compilation of bills the legislature had previously defeated, it included an expansion of prosecutorial discretion to try juveniles as adults, harsher punishment for gang-related crimes, authorization of wiretaps on gang activities, establishment of a registration system for gang members comparable to the system used for sex offenders, and a scaling back of the confidentiality of juvenile court records. One of the political aims of the juvenile justice initiative was to help Wilson position himself for another run for the presidency in 2000. The measure, it was hoped, would help the term-limited governor remain in the public spotlight and activate the immense political and fund-raising apparatus needed to launch a presidential campaign. In 1998, Wilson raised almost $750,000 for Proposition 21, but after he left office and abandoned the idea of a presidential candidacy, the river of contributions slowed to a trickle. Although Proposition 21 failed to advance Wilson's presidential ambitions, it did succeed with voters, who easily approved the measure in the 2000 primary election.[8]

Three of the other eleven California initiatives in 2000 were also spearheaded by politicians or aspiring politicians.[9] Proposition 22, which limited marriage to a man and a woman, was written by Republican state senator Pete Knight, and Proposition 39, which succeeded in lowering the majority required to pass school bond measures from two-thirds to 55 percent, was led by Gov. Gray Davis. Proposition 25, an ambitious campaign finance reform measure, was authored by Ron Unz, a wealthy Silicon Valley entrepreneur whose involvement in statewide politics had begun with his 1994 effort to unseat Wilson as governor. Unz followed his surprisingly strong showing against Wilson by tearing a page from the governor's book and coauthoring Proposition 227, a controversial measure to abolish bilingual education. (In 2000, Unz financed the qualification of a similar initiative in Arizona.) After Proposition 227 passed resoundingly in 1998, Unz looked for a way to hitch his ambition for political office to another popular initiative. Together with Tony Miller, a former acting secretary of state, Unz wrote and financed Proposition 25, which among other things would have restricted contributions to candidate campaigns, banned political fund-raising in non-election years, established a system of voluntary spending limits in candidate campaigns, and allowed for the use of taxpayer money to partially fund initiative campaigns. The effect of the measure would have been to make it easier for wealthy individuals like Unz to qualify initiatives and to run for office against well-financed incumbents. One month after submitting the signatures for the initiative, Unz formally announced his candidacy for the U.S. Senate. His campaign plan was to win an "easy primary" during which he would focus on passing Proposition 25, then ride to victory in November on the measure's popularity. But Unz's fond hope for an easy primary was shattered by Rep. Tom Campbell's decision to throw his hat into the Republican ring. Support for Unz among Republican leaders evaporated, and within eight weeks he pulled out of the race to focus on his initiative, which was overwhelmingly defeated in the 2000 primary election.[10]

Although the politician as initiative activist has flourished most in California, other initiative states have also witnessed a growth in the involvement of politicians in recent years. Of the eighteen initiatives on the Oregon ballot in 2000, for example, four listed incumbent politicians as chief petitioners. A Democratic state legislator led the effort to qualify and pass Measure 94, which would have repealed a mandatory minimum sentencing law enacted by initiative in 1994. The chief sponsor of that 1994 initiative, ironically, was also a legislator. The governor, too, seized the initiative in 2000 by writing and promoting a measure that directs the legislature to provide schools with enough money to meet the state's education goals. Measure 1 represents the first time in modern memory that a sitting Oregon governor has authored an initiative.

A sitting governor also got into the initiative act for the first time in Massachusetts, where Republican governor Paul Cellucci successfully promoted Question 4, an initiative that rolled back the income tax rate to 5 percent and returned an estimated $1.2 billion to taxpayers. Unable to persuade the Democratic-controlled legislature to enact his proposal, Cellucci ostentatiously crashed a Taxation Committee hearing in the spring of 1999 and threatened to lead a petition drive to place the tax cut on the ballot in 2000. The legislature agreed to reduce the rate from 5.95 to 5.75 percent, but nothing short of capitulation to Cellucci's demand could halt the governor's petition drive. In such cases the initiative is less a means by which citizens can circumvent unresponsive politicians than it is an additional weapon in the ongoing battle among politicians.[11]

Special interest groups, like politicians, have become adept at using the initiative in states where it has become a routine part of the political process. The 2000 election was no exception. In Arizona, Proposition 106, which would have deregulated local telephone service in areas where there was competition between service providers, was brought to the voters by the telecommunications giant Qwest at a cost of about $2 million. In California, at least four of twelve initiatives were spearheaded by the same sort of interest groups that are typically active in the legislative process. Proposition 35, for instance, was placed on the ballot by the trade association of private engineers. After a decade of legislative wrangling and judicial jockeying with the public employee union that represents state transportation engineers, the private engineers took their long-standing dispute to the people and won the right to bid on public works projects. Proposition 37 was brought to the voters by a coalition of business groups. It would have required that fees imposed by government on businesses to offset the environmental or health impacts of their products be subject either to a vote of the people or approval by two-thirds of the legislature. Although publicly led by the California Chamber of Commerce, more than 90 percent of the financial backing for the proposition came from alcohol, tobacco, and oil interests—principally Philip Morris, R. J. Reynolds, the Wine Institute, the National Distilled Spirits Council, Anheuser-Busch, BP Amoco, and Standard Oil.

Gambling interests in Maine were behind Question 3, which would have allowed video lottery machines at racetracks. As a sweetener for voters, 40 percent of the profits were designated for property tax relief. Gambling interests also sponsored Arkansas's Amendment 5, which would have authorized casino gambling in the state and established a state lottery, and Measure 1 in South Dakota, which changed the bet limit in Deadwood casinos from $5 to $100. An initiative in Washington State (I-732) that gave annual cost-of-living adjustments to teachers was placed on the ballot by a teachers' union. Two measures in Oregon were sponsored by Oregonians in Action, a property rights group funded by agricultural interests. One of these measures would have made it easier for interest groups to challenge administrative rules, and the other requires payment to landowners if a government regulation reduced their property values. Each of these many interest groups, when not sponsoring (or fighting) initiatives, can readily be found roaming the halls of their respective state legislatures.

Most initiatives emerge primarily from the internal political dynamics of a state, but there is also an increasingly large number for which the primary impetus and funding source come from outside the state, particularly in states that lack strong initiative traditions. During the 1990s, the best example of this phenomenon was the term limits campaign, which, although self-styled as a grassroots movement, was largely organized and funded by U.S. Term Limits, an interest group headquartered in Washington, D.C. The lone term limits measure on the November 2000 ballot was in Nebraska, where there have been only ten initiatives since 1992—four of them term limits measures. (The first three passed, then were invalidated by the courts.) As in the earlier term limits campaigns of 1992, 1994, and 1996, nearly all of the money raised to qualify and pass the Nebraska measure came from out-of-state groups. In 2000, 90 percent of the money raised came from Americans for Sound Public Policy in Washington, D.C. Most of the remaining 10 percent came from U.S. Term Limits and other out-of-state organizations. The opposition, Nebraskans Against Outside Influence, was outspent 4 to 1.[12]

Utah is another state that uses the initiative process infrequently. Only three initiatives qualified for the ballot in the 1990s, none of them after 1994. The last initiative to have passed in Utah had been the 1976 Freedom from Compulsory Fluoridation and Medication Act. In 2000, however, two initiatives appeared on the ballot and both passed. Neither reflected a newfound enthusiasm for direct democracy among Utah's citizenry or the emergence within the state of an organizational infrastructure of initiative activism. Rather, both were placed on the ballot by out-of-state organizations with the money to hire out-of-state signature-gathering firms.

U.S. English, based in Washington, D.C., employed a professional signature-gathering firm to qualify Initiative A, which establishes English as Utah's official language for government business. Since its founding in 1983, U.S. English has helped get official language laws passed in more than twenty states, and Utah was just one more stop in the group's push to make English the nation's official language. A trio of out-of-state billionaires—George Soros, Peter Lewis, and John Sperling—paid about $3 a signature to qualify Initiative B, which makes it more difficult for law enforcement officials to seize and sell assets connected to criminal activity. Initiative B is a carefully calculated part of the billionaires' national campaign to combat the excesses of the nation's drug war. During the previous five years, that campaign led to the qualification and passage of measures legalizing the medical use of marijuana in Alaska, Arizona, California, Colorado, Oregon, Maine, Nevada, Washington, and the District of Columbia.[13] Utah was one of three states selected by Soros and his allies to offer asset-forfeiture initiatives in 2000; the others were Massachusetts and Oregon. In addition, Soros and company funded the qualification of a measure in California requiring that nonviolent drug offenders receive treatment instead of imprisonment.

Another national interest group that has used the initiative process frequently in recent years is the Humane Society, which has launched approximately a dozen statewide initiatives since 1994 to restrict the hunting and trapping of animals. In 2000, the Humane Society financed the qualification of initiatives in Washington (I-713) and Oregon (Measure 97) that banned the use of animal traps for commercial purposes. However, unlike Soros's Americans for Medical Rights, U.S. Term Limits, and U.S. English, which invariably have relied on paid signature-gatherers to qualify initiatives for the ballot, the Humane Society often uses only volunteer signature-gatherers. Washington's I-713 and Oregon's Measure 97 were among a tiny handful of initiatives in 2000 that relied entirely on volunteer signature-gatherers.[14] For the overwhelming majority of issues and interests, playing the initiative game means paying people to gather signatures.

Who Won?

The purpose of drawing attention to the prominence of well-funded and well-organized interest groups in the contemporary initiative process is not to contribute to the historically naive, modern-day jeremiad about the "capture" of the initiative process by special interests. The language of capture suggests that there was a time in the past when the initiative process was not dominated by special interest groups. No such golden age ever existed. Writing in the late 1930s, for example, political scientists V. O. Key and Winston Crouch found that most "initiated measures, like legislative bills, originate with some interest group which has found the existing law unsatisfactory and seeks to secure more favorable legal rules."[15] The modern jeremiad also ignores the clear evidence that money is no guarantee of victory at the ballot box, a political science truism that was reaffirmed in the 2000 elections.

Among the big spending initiatives to lose in 2000 were California's Proposition 38, a school voucher measure that was financed largely by Tim Draper, a Silicon Valley entrepreneur who spent more than $23 million of his own money (the campaign spent nearly $31 million altogether), only to see the initiative garner less than 30 percent of the vote. The same fate afflicted school vouchers in Michigan, even though the provoucher campaign spent nearly $13 million, including $4.5 million from the founders of Amway and $2 million from Wal-Mart heir John Walton. Of course, it helped the antivoucher cause that the opposition was also financially well endowed. In California, opponents of school vouchers matched Draper dollar for dollar.

Their $31 million included about $26 million from the California Teachers Association. In Michigan the opposition fared less well, but it still raised more than $5 million, almost all of which came from the Michigan Education Association and the National Education Association.

The limitations of money were perhaps most dramatically on display in Washington State, where a charter school initiative lost, albeit narrowly, despite more than $3 million in support from Microsoft's cofounder Paul Allen; this amount easily dwarfed the opposition's less than $5,000. Despite outspending the opposition by 600 to 1 and blanketing the state with television ads, Allen and his allies failed to persuade the electorate to adopt charter schools.[16] In California, proponents of the effort to classify regulatory taxes as fees requiring either a public vote of approval or a two-thirds vote of the legislature raised $2.5 million (twenty times the amount raised by the opposition) yet still lost the election narrowly. Lopsided spending by proponents also went for naught in Arkansas, where the Arkansas Casino Corporation contributed $440,000 to support an initiative that would have given the company exclusive right to operate the only casino in each of six counties. Well over 90 percent of the money came from Bob Buchholz, the principal stockholder in Arkansas Casino's parent firm, Natural State Resorts. Although opponents were outspent by about 6 to 1, voters saw through the measure, which tried to deflect attention from the corporation's self-interest by also establishing a state lottery to fund college tuition costs and authorizing bingo and raffles for charitable purposes.[17]

Perhaps the most ironic result of all the 2000 initiative campaigns was the defeat of campaign finance reform measures in Oregon and Missouri, neither of which received more than 40 percent of the vote despite substantially outspending the opposition. Modeled on the system pioneered by Maine in 1996 and subsequently adopted by Arizona and Massachusetts in 1998, the initiatives proposed to provide public financing to state candidates who gathered a specified number of $5 contributions from individual supporters.[18] In Oregon, the proponents of Measure 6 outspent the opponents by about 6 to 1, with most of their three-quarters of a million dollar war chest coming from out-of-state donors. The largest contribution came from Public Campaign, of Washington, D.C., which contributed more than $225,000. Public Campaign gave even more to the Missouri campaign, contributing nearly $400,000 in the months after the measure qualified for the ballot. Opponents of the campaign finance reform measure found it easier to raise money in Missouri than in Oregon, largely because the Missouri measure planned to pay for public financing of candidates with an increase in corporate taxes. But even in Missouri, proponents outspent the opposition by about 3 to 1. Asked about the irony of a campaign finance reform measure spending huge amounts of money, the spokesman for Missouri Voters for Fair Elections explained, "We have to raise a lot of money. If we don't, we will lose." This campaign, he added, is "the fund-raising campaign to end fund-raising campaigns."[19]

Although massively outspending one's opponents could not guarantee victory, it certainly helped a number of initiatives, most notably California's Proposition 39. In the primary election, California voters had narrowly rejected Proposition 26, which would have eliminated the supermajority requirement in local school bond elections. Despite spending $23 million, more than ten times what the opposition spent, proponents saw their measure fail by a 51–49 margin. Proposition 26's backers immediately regrouped and qualified Proposition 39, a more moderate version of the initiative that lowered the supermajority from two-thirds to 55 percent. Proposition 39 faced an uphill battle: a poll conducted in June showed support at only 45 percent, and another survey by the Public Policy Institute of California found only 35 percent favorably disposed to revisiting the voters' decision in the March primary.[20] In a departure from the normal pattern of initiative politics in which an initiative starts strong in the polls and then loses steam as voters learn more about it, Proposition 39, thanks in large part to a $30 million campaign, was able to win a 53–47 victory. This sum, which included $6 million from Menlo Park venture capitalists John and Ann Doerr, dwarfed the $5 million raised by opponents. But the decisive difference between the two outcomes was probably not the money spent (the opposition was heavily outspent in both elections) or the substance of the two initiatives but the fact that the turnout in the primary election was smaller and more conservative. Had the spending been reversed, however, and the opponents raised $30 million, it is highly likely that Proposition 39 would have been defeated, particularly since only 40 percent of likely voters had even heard of it a month before the November election.

The capacity to outspend opponents has been an important part of the success of George Soros, whose millions helped buy him five more victories in 2000 in his personal fight against the federal war on drugs. In 1996 and 1998, Soros focused on legalizing the medical use of marijuana, an issue on which he has lost only once, in Washington in 1997. In 2000, he shifted his attention to forfeiture of assets and rehabilitation of drug offenders rather than incarceration. In all of these elections, Soros and his billionaire allies, Peter Lewis and John Sperling, have dwarfed the spending of their opponents. In California in 1996, for example, the $1.25 million they contributed to their medical marijuana initiative was about 40 times what the opposition spent. In Oregon in 1998, the three billionaires outspent their opponents by 50 to 1, about $750,000 to $15,000. Their spending on the asset forfeiture initiatives in Utah and Oregon in 2000 was similarly lopsided. In Oregon, they spent more than $400,000 compared with about $5,000 for the opposition, and in Utah they contributed about half a million dollars to Utahns for Property Protection, while the opposition raised next to nothing. In California, they each poured another $1 million into the campaign for their drug treatment measure, outspending the measure's opponents by better than 8 to 1. But their lone setback in Massachusetts is a reminder of the limits of money. Despite pouring nearly $2 million into the campaign for an initiative that combined the asset forfei-

ture features of the Oregon and Utah measures with the drug treatment features of the California measure, Soros and company were unable to overcome
the vigorous, albeit poorly funded, opposition of district attorneys and police
chiefs across the state. Although outspent by more than 50 to 1, the opposition prevailed, a result that surprised many. Gratified opponents like Attorney
General Thomas Reilly declared that the voters of Massachusetts had sent a
clear message to the out-of-state billionaires that they were not going to be
allowed "to buy a law."[21]

David sometimes beats Goliath, but a more reliable way to defeat a
financial giant in initiative politics is to call in another financial giant. Qwest's
effort to use the Arizona initiative process to change the rules of the regulatory game to its advantage was thwarted when AT&T and Cox Communications, two Qwest competitors, stepped in with more than $2 million to
finance an October advertising blitz that effectively buried the initiative.
Ahead by nearly 2 to 1 in some September polls, the measure sank below 20
percent in the final vote.[22] The power of money to change voters' minds
about an initiative was probably most strikingly affirmed in Colorado, where
a state record $6 million advertising campaign financed by developers,
builders, and real estate interests turned voters against Amendment 24,
which would have forced cities and counties to place growth plans on the
ballot before proceeding with development. A poll taken shortly after the initiative qualified found nearly 80 percent favoring it, but after the $6 million
onslaught of television and radio ads warning that the measure was too
extreme and would drive up housing prices, Colorado's voters ended up
rejecting it decisively.[23] Precisely the same electoral dynamic occurred with
Arizona's Proposition 202, which would have required cities and counties to
adopt growth-management plans to limit urban sprawl. A poll conducted
several months before the election showed four times as many voters supporting the measure as opposing it, but that support wilted in the face of a
furious $4 million advertising campaign funded by real estate and construc-
tion interests.[24]

Observing the fate of the antigrowth initiatives in Arizona and Colorado, some may be tempted to bewail the power of money and interest
groups to thwart citizen initiatives. But those same critics would probably
find things a great deal worse if special interests had not been mobilized to
help kill a host of other initiatives. In Colorado, Douglas Bruce's radical tax
cut was defeated with the aid of a nearly $2 million war chest that opponents
used to alert voters to the crippling service cuts that would be required if
Bruce's plan passed. Generous contributions from a host of special interests,
including real estate developers, government employee unions, and big business, helped opponents outspend Bruce, who drew out of his own deep pockets 90 percent of the approximately half-million dollars raised in favor of
Proposition 21. An initiative that began in the summer with two-thirds of
Coloradans expressing approval ended on election day with two-thirds voting against it.[25]

The value of special interest money in counteracting some of the worst tendencies of the initiative process was most conspicuous in Oregon, where spending by unions and businesses helped to defeat the Sizemore initiative machine. Two of his measures were designed to restrict the role of labor unions in the political process, and these provoked nearly $5 million in opposition spending by unions. As one union spokesman explained, "If you've got alluring ballot titles like Bill Sizemore has got on Measures 92 and 98, it takes a significant amount of money to educate voters."[26] By outspending Sizemore by about 500 to 1, the unions were able to flood the airwaves with ads and beat back both measures. Sizemore also offered two sweeping tax measures: one made federal income taxes fully deductible on state tax returns and the other (the Taxpayer Protection Initiative) required voter approval of most taxes and fees. The tax deduction initiative, attractively packaged as a prohibition against double taxation, was the jewel in the Sizemore crown, the one on which he lavished the most time and attention during the campaign. A poll conducted in mid-September suggested that it was also the initiative that had the best chance to pass, with 54 percent of respondents approving of the measure and only 41 percent opposing it. But on election day, Measure 91 was defeated by a 55–45 margin, thanks in large part to the $2.8 million raised by a coalition of businesses and labor unions. Teacher unions raised $1.25 million to bury another Sizemore initiative (Measure 95) that would have rigidly tied teacher pay to student performance.[27]

Far from corrupting the initiative process, special interest groups play a vital role in helping voters become aware of an initiative's deleterious effects, which are often obscured by attractive ballot titles or arcane technical language. It is when powerful interest groups mobilize against an initiative and spend large sums of money on television and radio advertisements that voters have the best chance of hearing opposing arguments and making a reasonably informed decision. Draconian term limits and three-strikes initiatives skated through during the 1990s in part because of the lack of powerful interest groups on the opposite side that were willing to spend money to educate voters about the unintended consequences of these proposals. If money is often crucial to intelligent, well-informed voting, then rather than longing for the end of interest group politics, Americans should be thankful that the same pluralist logic of the mobilization and counter-mobilization of interests that holds true in the legislative arena also generally prevails in initiative politics.[28] Special interest groups are sometimes all that stand between the people and an initiative process that is monopolized by full-time initiative activists and individuals with deep pockets.

How Did the Voters Fare?

Although money well spent can often help sow healthy voter skepticism about the wisdom of a seductive-sounding ballot title, a ballot crowded with issues can make it hard for even the most financially well-endowed opponents to gain the electorate's attention. European-style referendums, in which a nation's attention is turned to a single great question, are quite unlike the American experience, in which voters confront ballots crowded with questions. Merely counting the number of initiatives does not begin to capture the task voters face in many states. In Arizona, for example, voters not only had to make up their mind about six diverse and controversial initiatives, but they also had to decide upon another eight measures referred by the legislature. A few of these referrals were relatively uncontroversial, but a number involved contentious proposals that provoked substantial opposition spending. These included proposals to hike the sales tax to fund education (it passed), to require that hunting and wildlife ballot measures receive a two-thirds vote (it lost), and to place a cap on the percentage of state land that can be set aside for conservation (it also lost). In Oregon, voters had to decide the fate not only of eighteen initiatives but also of one popular referendum and seven legislative referrals, four of which were closely contested. And that doesn't count local measures. Voters in Salem, Oregon, for example, had the daunting task of voting upon not only twenty-six statewide measures but also thirteen annexations (including several parcels of land smaller than an acre) and three tax and bond measures that had been referred by the city council.[29]

Unlike in candidate elections, in which voters are often guided by party labels, voters in initiative elections must rely to a greater extent upon the mass media for information. As long as the number of ballot measures is relatively small, voters have a reasonable chance to become aware of who is for a measure and who is against it and of some of the likely consequences if the measure were to pass. The problem with a crowded ballot is that certain issues inevitably hog the limelight, leaving others struggling to gain public attention. In Oregon, which in 2000 had by far the most crowded ballot in the nation, one of the chief ballot hogs was Measure 9, which would have prohibited public schools, including community colleges, from promoting or sanctioning homosexual or bisexual behavior. Between Labor Day and election day, nearly 30 percent of the measure-related letters to the editor in the state's leading newspaper, the *Oregonian,* were devoted to Measure 9. Add Measure 94, the effort to repeal mandatory minimum sentences for violent offenders, and one has accounted for almost half of the letters to the editor. Throw in Sizemore's prohibition on double taxation (Measure 91), and the number exceeds 60 percent. In contrast, sixteen (62 percent) of the twenty-six measures accounted for only about 13 percent of the letters to the editor. News coverage of these sixteen measures was similarly thin. Only two measures that received significant public and press scrutiny (and opposition spending) passed: one of these was a gun-control initiative and the other (Measure 7) was an extraordinary initiative that requires government to compensate a landowner if a government regulation reduces the value of the owner's land.

Measure 7 deserves particularly close scrutiny because it provides a window into the darker side of direct democracy—it is a bracing reminder that although voters generally do quite well sorting the wheat from the chaff, at times they fail miserably. Proponents packaged the measure in the alluring rhetoric of fairness and property rights. Because government cannot take property for public use without compensating the owner, surely it is fair, they argued, that government should compensate an owner when it enacts regulations that lower property values. On first glance, this seems a matter of simple justice. If a zoning rule, building code, safety ordinance, or environmental regulation is enacted for the good of the whole, then everyone should shoulder the financial burden, not just the individual whose land is affected. Only on closer inspection do the many problems with this idea emerge. To begin with, there is the administrative nightmare of estimating the financial consequences of every government regulation for individual property owners. Because the measure retroactively applies to every regulation imposed since the current owner purchased the property, it invites claims against almost any zoning law or environmental regulation enacted in the past thirty years. Local governments, already strapped financially, are faced with enacting mammoth tax increases, declaring bankruptcy, or, most likely, not enforcing environmental safeguards or land-use regulations. Not surprisingly, Measure 7 was immediately tied up in the courts, from which it is unlikely to emerge in the immediately foreseeable future.

Why did Oregon's voters approve such a plainly unworkable scheme? The opposition certainly was not short of money. Aided by the generous support of business leaders and environmental organizations, opponents of Measure 7 raised well over $1.5 million to defeat it. Nor did the opposition lack for prominent voices. Every major newspaper in the state unequivocally opposed Measure 7, as did scores of government officials and civic leaders. The voters' pamphlet included thirty arguments against the measure, more than were submitted for all but three other measures. Yet opponents of Measure 7 had difficulty getting politicians and the media to focus on it until the closing days of the election, when a surprising preelection poll found the measure narrowly ahead. The release of the poll spurred a quick round of last-minute editorials and press conferences condemning the measure, but the reaction was too little, too late. The state's popular governor, John Kitzhaber, had spent virtually the entire campaign focusing public attention on the dangers of Sizemore's tax cuts. The *Oregonian,* too, had helped to focus voters' attention on the tax measures by taking the unprecedented step of running a ten-part editorial opposing them. The handful of stories that the state's major newspapers ran on Measure 7 was dwarfed by the avalanche of news coverage aimed at the tax initiatives and at other controversial initiatives like the ban on promoting homosexuality in schools and the repeal of mandatory minimum sentencing. Had Measure 7 been the only initiative on the ballot, there is little doubt that it would have been defeated because voters would have been made aware of the harmful consequences of the measure. Even with a crowded ballot, if the state's governor and media had focused on Measure 7, it would almost certainly have been defeated.[30]

Voters in initiative elections do not suddenly become political junkies, a new breed of democratic person, engaged by and fluent in the complexities of public policy. Instead, initiative voters like citizens everywhere are interested primarily in earning a living and raising a family. Politics is a sideshow for most people. When the media spotlight fails to illuminate a particular measure—its substance and consequences as well as its proponents and opponents—many voters rely on the wording of the ballot title to make a judgment. The vital importance of ballot titles in initiative elections explains why courts during the past decade have become increasingly involved in the ballot-titling process. In Oregon, where this trend has advanced furthest, more than one-fifth of the Supreme Court's opinions between 1998 and 2000 related to initiative ballot titles.[31]

The critical importance of ballot titles belies the argument often made by defenders of the initiative process that it does not really matter who places a measure on the ballot, or where the money comes from, because it is the citizens of the state who decide whether to vote yes or no. As long as voters have the final say, so the argument goes, no initiative can become law unless it represents the will of the people.[32] The trouble with this argument is that it ignores the enormous power that is bestowed upon the individuals or organizations that frame each issue. As anyone familiar with polling knows, public opinion on many issues is extraordinarily sensitive to how questions are worded. Ask people whether they support spending for "the poor" and their responses will be far more favorable than if they are asked about spending on "welfare." Similarly, people have a much more negative reaction to the term "preferential treatment" than to "affirmative action." Large majorities agree that a terminally ill person should be helped by a physician to "die with dignity," but many fewer people support "physician-assisted suicide" for a terminally ill person. The answer an initiative gets depends in large part on its ballot title.

Even when voters see through a seductive ballot title to the substance of the measure, there remain good reasons to worry about who is placing the issue on the ballot. Those who write initiatives control the ballot's political menu and thereby limit voters' choices. Voters may prefer a particular initiative to the status quo, but if they are given a wider range of options they may rank that initiative near the bottom of their preferences. Given a choice between A and Not-A, the voters may choose A, but given a choice between A and B they may prefer B. Take term limits, for example. During the 1990s, voters in many states approved strict term limits laws with lifetime bans. Faced with the choice between no term limits and very restrictive term limits, voters generally favored term limits. But would voters have made the same decision if they had been offered a choice between a term limits measure with a lifetime ban and a term limits measure that allowed legislators to return to office after a specified number of years? The power to control the choices on the ballot carries with it the power to shape the outcome of the election.

A further reason that voters' approval of an initiative cannot erase concerns about who sponsored it is that by itself passage reveals nothing about the issue's salience to voters. In 1996, for example, affirmative action ranked near the bottom of the list of issues that most concerned Californians. Although citizens passed the anti–affirmative action Proposition 209, they expressed far greater concern about jobs, education, the environment, and taxes.[33] In 2000, as in other recent elections, antitax initiatives dominated state ballots, appearing in Alaska, California, Colorado, Massachusetts, Oregon, South Dakota, and Washington,[34] even though polls consistently showed that voters were far less concerned with reducing taxes than with improving the quality of government services.[35] Candidates for office tend to be much more responsive to the issues that matter most to voters than are initiative advocates, for whom there is little incentive to select issues that are important to voters. Unlike initiative activists, candidates must seek out issues that are not only popular but that matter to ordinary voters.

The diminished salience of tax issues to voters was reflected in the defeat of a number of antitax initiatives in 2000, including Alaska's Measure 4 (which would have capped property taxes), California's Proposition 37, Colorado's Amendment 21, and Measures 91 and 93 in Oregon. But the presence of these initiatives on the ballot forced political officials and interest groups to play defense on the question of taxes. Thus, even when they lose the electoral battle, initiative activists may win the political war by controlling the agenda. Although six of Sizemore's initiatives lost, for example, he still managed to dictate Oregon's political agenda by forcing the state's political leaders to react to his agenda rather than to define their own. In the 1998 gubernatorial election, Governor Kitzhaber had unceremoniously trounced candidate Sizemore by a better than 2 to 1 margin, yet within little more than a year Kitzhaber felt compelled to challenge his defeated opponent to a series of debates about Sizemore's $1 billion tax-cut proposal. Moreover, Kitzhaber scaled back his own initiative plans, which included establishing a rainy day fund for schools, so that he could concentrate his campaigning and fundraising efforts on defeating Sizemore's tax proposals. The cost to the state of enacting a reckless antitax measure, Kitzhaber and his allies calculated, outweighed the potential benefit that might be gained by passing his own set of education initiatives.

Labor unions have experienced similar frustrations. They were forced to raise millions of dollars in California and Oregon in 1998, and again in Oregon in 2000, to fight initiatives designed to limit their ability to contribute money to political campaigns.[36] Although all of these measures failed at the ballot box, they succeeded in placing unions on the defensive and diverting valuable resources from candidate elections and from their own agendas.

Labor unions in Oregon gave about $2 million to state legislative candidates in 2000, and that was less than half of what they spent to defeat Sizemore's two antiunion measures (Measures 92 and 98). Partly as a result, the gap in Oregon between labor and business spending on candidate races grew from less than 2 to 1 in 1998 to nearly 3 to 1 in 2000.[37] Moreover, the unions decided not to pursue a number of initiative petitions that they had submitted to the secretary of state, including the Minimum Wage Protection Act of 2000, which among other things would have required that the state's minimum wage be automatically adjusted for inflation. They also dropped the Workplace Safety and Workers' Compensation Fairness Act, which would have made it easier for workers to receive workers' compensation benefits; a Patients' Bill of Rights; and a State Purchases of Products Made with Child Labor Act, prohibiting the state from buying from vendors who employ children under age fourteen. Diverting unions' attention from their own agenda was arguably the primary objective of Sizemore's antiunion initiatives. As one Sizemore assistant exulted after the election, "Imagine the mischief [the unions] could have done in Oregon if they had had that money to spend on something else. . . . They were completely tied up trying to play defense and were not able to play offense."[38] That calculation explains why on election night Sizemore confidently promised that even if voters "don't pass [Measures 92 and 98] this time, we'll be back next time and let the voters vote on it again."

Sizemore's promise underscores the supply-side nature of initiative politics. Voter demand generally bears little or no relationship to the quantity of initiatives on a ballot and often bears only a tenuous relationship to the content of ballot measures. A seasoned initiative supplier like Sizemore will survey the public to pretest the popularity of ballot titles. In some cases he won't be able to obtain a ballot title that can poll 50 percent and thus will drop the idea, at least temporarily. But for most issues a ballot title can be found that will make the idea sound attractive to voters. A journalist who writes "the most provocative proposals for governing the state aren't being offered by elected officials, but by anyone who can capture the public's imagination enough to qualify an initiative for the ballot" betrays a woeful ignorance of the process by which most initiatives reach the ballot.[39] In an era of professional signature-gathering firms, an initiative needs only to capture the sponsor's imagination to qualify for the ballot. There are precious few ideas that a professional signature-gathering firm cannot qualify, given sufficient time and money.[40]

The Future of Direct Democracy

Notwithstanding the myriad problems of initiative politics—the influence of professional signature-gatherers, the poorly worded measures that get dragged through the courts for years,[41] the divisiveness of winner-take-all politics, and the ability of rich individuals and out-of-state lobbies to set a state's agenda—voters generally remain strongly supportive of the initiative process. If surveys are to be believed, a majority of Americans would like to see the initiative process tried at the federal level. Even in the states that have experienced the worst excesses of initiative politics, most citizens remain committed to the initiative process as a means of enhancing democratic control of public policy. To be sure, most people in these states say they would like to see the role of money curbed in initiative politics. They think that there are too many initiatives and that they are frequently badly written, and few believe that their fellow citizens are well informed about the ballot questions on which they are asked to vote. Yet despite these persistent dissatisfactions with how the initiative process operates, voters usually have resisted efforts to make qualifying initiatives or passing them more difficult. In the May 2000 primary, for example, Oregon voters soundly rejected a legislative referral that would have increased the number of signatures needed to qualify an initiative to amend the state constitution. In November 2000, Nebraska voters refused to approve legislative proposals to shorten the circulation period for signature gathering and to require two votes before a constitutional amendment becomes law.[42]

The 2000 election predictably brought renewed calls for initiative reform. Toward the end of the summer, for example, Arizona's Republican governor Jane Hull expressed her dissatisfaction with the quantity and quality of initiatives on the ballot. She proposed that the state take a fresh look at the initiative process and consider making it harder for petitioners to qualify an initiative. Hull's sentiments were echoed at the other end of the country by Maine's Independent governor Angus King. And only days before the November election, California's speaker of the assembly, Democrat Robert Hertzberg, announced the formation of a nonpartisan commission to study and recommend reforms of California's initiative process. If recent history is any guide, little useful or genuine reform will come of these efforts, at least in the states that most need reform.[43] During the 1990s, California established four distinguished commissions charged with reforming the process, but none of them produced significant changes. An Oregon commission in the mid-1990s was similarly unsuccessful in changing the state's initiative process.

Reformers who aim to reduce the number of initiatives on the ballot face two huge obstacles: the courts and American political culture. The reforms that most voters readily endorse—banning paid signature-gatherers and restricting the ability of rich people to purchase a spot on the ballot— have been prohibited by the U.S. Supreme Court as violations of free speech.[44] The reforms that the courts will allow—increasing signature thresholds, adding geographical requirements, and requiring supermajorities—run headlong into deep-seated American skepticism about politicians and a naive American faith in the power of "the people." When legislatures have the audacity to suggest that the number of signatures required to place a proposed constitutional amendment on the ballot should be raised or that a geographic distribution requirement for signatures should be imposed, champions of the initiative have little difficulty portraying these suggestions as fresh examples of an arrogant political class trying to rob the people of their fundamental rights.

Although the states in which the initiative process is currently ensconced are unlikely to see much meaningful reform or reduced initiative use in the foreseeable future, the forecast for representative government is brighter in the rest of the nation. The states that lack the initiative process seem little disposed to adopt it, and enthusiasm for a national initiative process has dimmed since the late 1970s, when the U.S. Senate held public hearings on the subject. Indeed, the populist paradox of the current political era is that although initiative use has increased steadily since the early 1970s, only Mississippi has added the initiative power during this period and the state so diluted it that the process has been almost unusable. This pattern of initiative politics stands in marked contrast with the first two decades of the twentieth century, when frequent use of the initiative power was accompanied by a host of states rushing to enact the initiative and referendum. To be sure, in recent decades some states, including Texas, have seriously considered adopting the initiative, and at least one, Minnesota, came very close to doing so.[45] But if the rapid or at least gradual spread of the initiative appeared likely in the early 1980s, today the prospects appear far less certain.[46] Fears of "Californication" have scared many states away from direct democracy.[47] Groups from across the political spectrum—labor unions as well as businesses, liberals and racial minority groups as much as conservative, rural white constituencies—seem more concerned with what they might lose as a result of direct democracy than with what they might gain. So long as high-use initiative states continue to dramatize the volatile, expensive, polarized, winner-take-all character of direct legislation, resistance to extending the initiative power will remain strong. Critics who fear that direct democracy will spread across the country like a populist cancer are probably as misguided as the enthusiasts who anticipate that the nation will be redeemed by direct democracy's glorious march from sea to shining sea.

Notes

1. See, for example, Dick Morris, *Vote.Com* (Los Angeles: Renaissance Books, 1999).
2. "Laws without Government" is the title of the last chapter in David S. Broder's *Democracy Derailed: Initiative Campaigns and the Power of Money* (New York: Harcourt, 2000).
3. In statistical terms, the correlation is very strong; the Pearson's r correlation coefficient is .90.
4. Philip L. DuBois and Floyd Feeney, *Lawmaking by Initiative: Issues, Options, and Comparisons* (New York: Agathon Press, 1998), 82–83. David B. Magleby, "Direct Legislation in the American States," in *Referendums around the World: The Growing Use of Direct Democracy,* ed. David Butler and Austin Ranney (Washington, D.C.: AEI Press, 1994), 224.

5. A seventh initiative in 2000, Measure 7, was written by OTU but was handed off in the closing stages of the qualification campaign to a property rights group, Oregonians in Action, so that Sizemore could focus on what he considered the organization's most important measures. On election night, as it became clear that OTU's six initiatives were going down to defeat, Sizemore scrambled to associate himself once again with Measure 7, declaring it "our most important measure" and "our most powerful and our favorite measure."

6. The popular referendum enables citizens, by gathering signatures, to force a public vote on legislation enacted by the legislature and signed by the governor. Because the popular referendum adds an additional check to the normal legislative process, it raises qualitatively different issues than the direct initiative, which circumvents the legislative process entirely by enabling citizens to place their own issues on the ballot. The Oregon referendum was one of only two statewide popular referendums in November 2000. The other one was in Alaska, where a new law that would have allowed hunters to use airplanes to hunt wolves was referred to the voters, who resoundingly rejected the legislative action. The popular referendum is used relatively infrequently, largely because petitioners find it easier to repeal a law through the initiative process, in which the number of days allowed for gathering signatures is typically far less restrictive. Often, too, legislatures protect their actions from being overturned by referendum by declaring them to be emergency measures.

7. Laurence M. Cruz, "Eyman Files Initiatives 745 and 722—Latest Chapters in Reform 'Novel,'" Associated Press State and Local Wire, July 7, 2000. Marsha King, "State, Local Preferential-Treatment Programs Targeted," *Seattle Times,* August 4, 1997, A1; *Limit v. Maleng* 874 F. Supp. 1138 (1994).

8. Matt Isaacs, "Why Giant Corporations like PG&E Bankrolled a Juvenile Crime Initiative," *SF Weekly,* January 12, 2000.

9. Proposition 23, which would have created a "none of the above" option for voters in candidate elections, was written and financed by a computer industry entrepreneur who, though he had not himself campaigned for high office, had run his dog for a seat in Congress.

10. Lynda Gledhill, "Unz Bows Out of U.S. Senate Race," *San Francisco Chronicle,* December 1, 1999.

11. Throughout the qualification and electoral campaign for Question 4, the governor worked closely with the veteran antitax activist Barbara Anderson, who two decades earlier had passed a landmark initiative (Proposition 2–1/2) that reduced and limited Massachusetts's property taxes on the model of California's Proposition 13. Anderson's organization, Citizens for Limited Taxation and Government, had tried and failed to qualify a similar tax reduction measure in the preceding election cycle. The alliance between governor and initiative activist made Question 4 unusual; the normal relationship between initiative activists and state governor is adversarial. Plenty of initiative activists have used the visibility gained through the initiative process to run for the state's top office. The founding father of the Oregon initiative, William U'Ren, ran for governor in 1914. Bill Sizemore was the Republican nominee in 1998, as was Washington's John Carlson in 2000. Rarely if ever have these initiative activists been successful in persuading voters to let them lead the state.

12. Kevin O'Hanlon, "Term Limits Group Holds 4-to-1 Money Advantage," Associated Press State and Local Wire, October 30, 2000. Bill Hord, "Outside Cash Backed Term-Limits Effort," *Omaha World Herald,* September 16, 1996, 9SF. Americans for Sound Public Policy was founded by Dane Waters, formerly a field director for U.S. Term Limits and currently head of the Initiative and Referendum Institute.

13. Medical marijuana initiatives appeared on the 2000 ballot in two states: in Nevada, because state law requires that an initiative amendment must be approved in

two successive elections before it becomes valid, and in Colorado, because a decision by the secretary of state to strike the measure from the 1998 ballot for insufficient signatures subsequently was found to be in error, so it was reinstated on the 2000 ballot.

14. Reliance on volunteers does not mean that the costs of qualification are free. The Humane Society gave $125,000 to qualify Measure 97. Approximately half of that sum went to fund-raising for the electoral campaign, and the other half covered the costs of conducting and coordinating the volunteer signature campaign (author's interview with Kelly Peterson of the Yes on 97 campaign, October 2000).

15. V. O. Key Jr. and Winston W. Crouch, *The Initiative and Referendum in California* (Berkeley: University of California Press, 1939), 444.

16. Linda Shaw, "New Faces, Big Money behind Charter-School Vote," *Seattle Times,* October 15, 2000, A1.

17. During the past decade, initiatives to expand gambling have lost far more often than they have won. Only about one in four gambling initiatives passed during the 1990s. But even at those long odds, gambling interests will keep playing because of the potentially huge payoffs if they win, as they did in Colorado in 1990, Missouri in 1994 and 1998, Arizona in 1996, Michigan in 1996, and California in 1998.

18. In Maine, Arizona, and Massachusetts, public campaign financing passed through the initiative process. Vermont, which does not have a statewide initiative, also adopted a similar scheme in 1997.

19. John A. Dvorak, "Report Shows Irony of Big-Money Battle," *Kansas City Star,* October 25, 2000, B1.

20. Ed Mendel, "Prop. 39 Looks like Tough Fight for Davis," *San Diego Union-Tribune,* August 20, 2000, A3. Greg Lucas, "School Vouchers Losing Support; New Field Poll Shows Increasing Doubt on Prop. 39 Too," *San Francisco Chronicle,* October 13, 2000, A26.

21. Tom Farmer, "DAs Tout Question 8 Defeat," *Boston Herald,* November 9, 2000, 36.

22. Max Jarman, "Qwest Hangs Up on Prop. 108," *Arizona Republic,* November 2, 2000, D1.

23. Michele Ames and Todd Hartman, "Growth-Control Amendment Fails: $6 Million Ad Campaign Helps Defeat Initiative, but Supporters Vow to Press On," *Denver Rocky Mountain News,* November 8, 2000, A24.

24. Adam Klawonn, "Who's Funding Initiative Drives?" *Arizona Republic,* November 4, 2000, A23. Kathleen Ingley, "Poll Finds Support for Directing Growth," *Arizona Republic,* July 26, 2000, B5.

25. Mark Obmascik, "Bruce's Tax-cutting Amendment 21 Takes It on the Chin," *Denver Post,* November 8, 2000, A4.

26. Dave Hogan and Steve Mayes, "The Measures: Unions Spend Millions Fighting Sizemore Tax Proposals on Ballot," *Oregonian,* November 3, 2000, A14.

27. All but two of Sizemore's measures were financial orphans. Sizemore did not spend or raise more than a few thousand dollars for any of his initiatives. In the closing weeks of the campaign, Loren Parks, an eccentric millionaire, financed half-million-dollar ad campaigns for two Sizemore initiatives (Measures 91 and 95), but Sizemore had no control over these ad campaigns.

28. See David B. Truman, *The Governmental Process: Political Interests and Public Opinion* (New York: Knopf, 1951); and Frank R. Baumgartner and Beth L. Leech, *Basic Interests: The Importance of Groups in Politics and in Political Science* (Princeton: Princeton University Press, 1998).

29. Legislative referrals, which are often uncontroversial technical changes to the state constitution, typically pass at a substantially higher rate than do citizen ini-

tiatives (in every state but Delaware a constitutional change must be ratified by the people). The 2000 elections were no exception. Whereas fewer than half the initiatives passed, more than 70 percent of legislative referrals were approved. In some states, however, referrals have become more contested in recent years as some state legislatures have learned to use the referral process to circumvent the governor's veto. The partisan use of the legislative referendum is particularly likely to occur when one party controls the legislature and the other party controls the governorship.

30. Measure 91, which began with a better than 2–1 margin in some polls, might have been enacted instead.

31. William A. Lund, "What's in a Name? The Battle over Ballot Titles in Oregon," *Willamette Law Review* (winter 1998): 143–167; and B. Carlton Grew, "Governing by Initiative," *Oregon State Bar Bulletin* (October 2000): 9–18. Perhaps the most consequential judicial involvement was in Florida, where the state supreme court prevented four anti–affirmative action measures from appearing on the 2000 ballot (Jim Saunders, "Court Snuffs Connerly's Anti–Affirmative Action Drive," *Florida Times–Union,* July 14, 2000, B1). The justices ruled that the ballot captions and summaries were misleading and that the initiatives violated the single-subject rule. Although the logic of the court's decision is suspect, it was welcomed both by liberal Democrats, who hoped to preserve affirmative action, and conservative Republicans, who feared that the four initiatives would mobilize the minority vote and thereby damage Republican electoral prospects in 2000 and beyond. Ironically, in keeping these measures off the ballot, the Florida Supreme Court may have cost Al Gore the presidential election.

32. The widely quoted Dane Waters of the Initiative and Referendum Institute, for example, says, "It's really irrelevant who puts it on the ballot, because Oregonians, and only Oregonians, can vote yes or no" ("Outsiders Finance Ballot Measures," Associated Press State and Local Wire, July 30, 2000). See also Patrick B. McGuigan, *The Politics of Direct Democracy in the 1980s: Case Studies in Popular Decision Making* (Washington, D.C.: Free Congress Research and Education Foundation, 1985), 119.

33. Lydia Chavez, *The Color Bind: California's Battle to End Affirmative Action* (Berkeley: University of California Press, 1998), 118, 160.

34. Had it not been for the courts, there would have been two additional antitax initiatives on the ballot, both radical—one in Arizona, the other in Arkansas. Arizona's Taxpayer Protection Act of 2000 was thrown off the ballot in August for violating the single-subject rule. The act would have eliminated the state's income tax over four years, required public votes on new state taxes, and allowed candidates for federal office to include ballot notations next to their name indicating that they pledged to eliminate the federal income tax. Two weeks before the election, the Arkansas Supreme Court (*Kurrus v. Priest,* 2000 Ark. LEXIS 504) struck down Amendment 4, which would have repealed the state sales tax on used goods and required public votes on future tax increases. The ballot title, the court argued, failed to inform voters "of the far-reaching consequences of voting for this measure." In particular, the court assailed the title for not making it clear to voters that "by approving this measure, he or she may risk losing valuable government services." Moreover, the court faulted the ballot title for failing to define clearly what counts as a "tax increase" and what counts as "a regularly scheduled statewide election." As a result, the voter could not know for certain what acts would trigger the voter-approval provision and when those votes would take place. According to the court, "the ultimate issue is whether the voter, while inside the voting booth, is able to reach an intelligent and informed decision for or against the proposal and understands the consequences of his or her vote based on the ballot title." One can agree with the court about the importance of

voters being able to make informed decisions; that is the reason we have campaigns. It is less clear, though, that the decision about whether voters are capable of making informed decisions should be left to judges.

35. In 1980, for example, 62 percent of Americans agreed that Washington "ought to cut taxes even if it means putting off some important things that need to be done." In 1999, only 21 percent agreed with this statement. *Los Angeles Times* polls conducted in 2000 showed that voters by nearly a 3 to 1 margin preferred to use government surpluses for Social Security, Medicare, or debt reduction rather than tax cuts. See Peter G. Gosselin, "Tax Cuts Seen as Spoiler in Boom Times," *Los Angeles Times,* August 26, 2000, A1; Jeff Mapes and Harry Esteve, "Healthy Economy Cools Oregon Tax-Cutting Fever," *Oregonian,* September 24, 2000, A1; and Brent Steel and Robert Sahr, "Oregon Governmental Issues Survey-2000," Program for Governmental Research and Education, Oregon State University, July 2000.

36. The story of the 1998 battle over Proposition 226 (the Paycheck Protection Act) in California is well told by Broder in *Democracy Derailed,* chap. 3 ("Initiative War in Close-Up").

37. Dave Hogan and Steve Suo, "Business Groups Help Drive Campaign Spending into Record Territory," *Oregonian,* October 23, 2000, A1.

38. Becky Miller, quoted in Dave Hogan and Harry Esteve, "Unions Enjoy Election Victories," *Oregonian,* November 12, 2000, B4.

39. Lisa Grace Lednicer, "Ballot Measures Reflect New Era," *Oregonian,* October 1, 2000, A16.

40. Elizabeth Garrett, "Money, Agenda Setting and Direct Democracy," *Texas Law Review* 77 (June 1999): 1845–1890.

41. Between 1960 and 1999, according to Kenneth Miller, about half of successful initiatives have been challenged in court. In California, the number has been closer to two-thirds. More than half the time, an initiative challenged in court is struck down either in whole or in part. See Kenneth P. Miller, "The Role of Courts in the Initiative Process: A Search for Standards" (paper presented at the annual meeting of the American Political Science Association, Atlanta, September 1999); and Kenneth P. Miller, "Judging Ballot Initiatives: A Unique Role for Courts" (paper presented at the annual meeting of the Western Political Science Association, San Jose, Calif., March 2000).

42. Voters have also sometimes shown a healthy skepticism of reforms of the initiative process offered by initiative advocates. Oregon voters in November 2000, for example, overwhelmingly rejected a Sizemore measure that would have forbidden the legislature from referring to the voters or enacting any law that would make it more difficult for citizens to use the initiative and referendum process. In Arizona in 1998, however, voters narrowly approved a citizen initiative that prohibited the legislature from repealing an initiative and required a three-fourths vote to amend one.

43. An irony of initiative reform is that reform seems most likely to occur in the states that need it least. In 1998, for example, Wyoming voters approved a legislative referendum that added a provision requiring petitioners to meet the 15 percent signature threshold in at least two-thirds of the state's counties. Prior to that, Wyoming's geographic distribution requirement had been nominal: petitioners only needed one signature in two-thirds of the counties as long as petitioners gathered 15 percent in the entire state. The 1998 reform was approved even though Wyoming's 15 percent signature requirement was already the highest in any state, and only seven initiatives had qualified for the ballot since the state adopted the initiative and referendum in 1968.

44. *Citizens Against Rent Control v. City of Berkeley,* 454 U.S. 290 (1981); *Meyer v. Grant,* 486 U.S. 414 (1988). See also *Victoria Buckley v. American Constitutional Law Foundation,* 525 U.S. 182 (1999).
45. In 1980, 53 percent of Minnesotans approved a legislative referral proposing a statewide initiative and referendum, but the measure failed because Minnesota law required that a constitutional amendment be approved by a majority of all votes cast, not just a majority of those who voted on a particular issue.
46. See the predictions in McGuigan, *Politics of Direct Democracy,* 114.
47. Bill McAuliffe, "House OKs Bill That Gives Voters Power to Pass Laws at the Polls," *Star-Tribune* (Minneapolis–St. Paul), March 23, 1999, 3B.

7

The Presidency: The Election and the Prospects for Leadership

Paul J. Quirk and Sean C. Matheson

E lections not only choose presidents, they also shape presidencies. What matters about an election is more than whether it installs a Democrat or a Republican, a liberal or a conservative or a moderate, in the Oval Office. The campaigns as well as the outcomes in both the presidential and congressional elections shape presidents' capabilities for leadership, their opportunities and constraints, and their prospects for success. Stated very broadly, how a president is elected tells a great deal about how, and how effectively, he or she will govern.[1]

This chapter looks at three ways that elections shape the presidency, paying special attention to the elections of 2000. First, a presidential election chooses an individual with particular skills, experience, and personality. These traits, or qualifications, affect a president's performance. Some presidents have been poorly suited to the office in important respects. Richard Nixon, for example, was driven by deep-seated anger and suspicion; his aggressive illegality provoked the constitutional crisis of Watergate. Jimmy Carter disdained politicians and often had difficulty dealing with them. Bill Clinton's reckless mendacity led to an impeachment crisis that undermined his effectiveness and nearly ended his presidency.

Second, the rhetoric of the campaign, especially that of the winning presidential candidate, creates commitments that carry weight after the election. These commitments may help to establish a popular mandate for the president's program. But they also may bind the president to an unworkable strategy for governing. After making an emphatically categorical campaign promise in 1988 to oppose new taxes, George Bush was politically devastated by having to reverse his position two years later and tell voters in effect to re-read his lips.

Third, elections measure and ultimately define the support for the president and his or her initiatives. The tenor of debate in both the presidential and congressional elections, the balance of partisan and ideological power in Congress, and the president's margin of victory all affect the support for his agenda and the prospects for effective leadership. When Lyndon B. Johnson won the 1964 presidential election in a landslide and fellow Democrats won lopsided majorities in both the Senate and the House of Representatives, the stage was set for the enactment of an ambitious domestic agenda. In contrast, when Bill Clinton won the presidency with 43 percent of the popular vote in a three-way race in 1992, Senate Republican leader Robert J. Dole warned on election night that his party would stand up for the majority of voters who had not voted for Clinton. The remark foretold the bitter partisan conflicts and limited policy achievements of the Clinton presidency.

In short, elections affect the presidency in three ways: through the *qualifications* the winner brings to the job, the governing *commitments* the successful candidate established in the campaign, and the *support* that accompanies the new president into office. To shed some light on these effects, this chapter first explores each of them in general terms. It then looks closely at the elections of 2000 and examines their implications for the presidency of George W. Bush. The prospects for the Bush presidency are problematic in important respects—and not only because of the questions surrounding the legitimacy of his victory. But the election did give Bush potential advantages and a reasonable chance for a presidency of substantial achievement.

Qualifications

The campaign and election determine what manner of person will occupy the White House. The skills, experience, and personality of the victorious candidate will shape his or her performance in office. Put differently, even if the traditional mythology that anyone can grow up to be president were true, it is certainly not true that anyone—or even any prominent politician—can do the job effectively. The voters should think hard, therefore, about whether a presidential candidate is reasonably qualified for the presidency, and they should think especially hard during the primary elections, when there may be more than one candidate from each party for the voters to choose from.

How well did the election process work in 2000 at selecting for appropriate qualifications? The answer to that question lies in turn in the answers to several other questions: What traits matter in a president? Did the campaign reveal those traits? To the extent that it did so, did the voters pay attention and weigh the candidates' qualifications in their decisions? In the end, how well qualified were the two party nominees and especially the victor, George W. Bush?

Defining Qualifications

There is no simple checklist of qualifications for the job of president that would satisfy all citizens and commentators.[2] In identifying the most important qualifications, the public focuses largely on traits that reflect general cultural values—that is, a preference for people who are honest, strong, open-minded, warm, and caring, and not "power hungry," among other things.[3] Such preferences derive more from what people want in a father, a spouse, or a professional colleague than from a careful look at the specific requirements of the presidency. It is doubtful, for example, that a president should always be strictly honest, or that a president should not have a taste for power. An adequate approach must recognize that there are several kinds of specifically presidential qualifications.[4] The main categories are skills, experience, and personality.[5]

Skills. Several skills are important. First, a president must have a broad strategic sense—that is, the ability to see the big picture and set a viable course for his administration. In doing so, a president must be able to set coherent, attainable policy goals and formulate general plans to achieve them.

Second, a president should have a reasonably strong grasp of the major policy issues in national government and especially in economic and foreign policy, the central arenas for presidential decision making. It is neither necessary nor clearly even desirable that he be a "policy wonk," able to speak knowledgeably about a variety of specific issues. But the president should be sufficiently familiar with the substance of policy debates to avoid simplistic or formulaic thinking and to distinguish balanced, responsible advice from tendentious advocacy.

Third, presidents must be able to work with other policy makers, especially in Congress, and to build coalitions to enact their policies. Doing so requires communication skills and a desire to exercise interpersonal influence.[6] (Remarkably, some presidents, such as Richard Nixon and Jimmy Carter, have had difficulty even asking other officials for their support.) It also requires tactical shrewdness and a refined understanding of the policy-making process, although these skills can be provided largely by the president's staff. Because other policy makers have their own goals and independent sources of power, building coalitions often requires flexibility and a collaborative disposition.

Fourth, a president must be able to speak persuasively to the public. Appealing "over the heads" of Congress and the rest of the Washington establishment is a central technique of modern presidential leadership.[7] As Ronald Reagan demonstrated, the skills required for effective public appeals are much akin to those of acting.

Finally, a president must understand how to manage the White House and the executive branch to obtain the assistance needed to perform all the other tasks of leadership. Devising a broad strategy, making good policy decisions, forming coalitions to adopt policies, and persuading the public are all, in large part, a matter of getting subordinates to work effectively.

It almost goes without saying that exercising these skills requires, ordinarily, a large investment of personal effort. With rare exceptions, such as Calvin Coolidge and Ronald Reagan, presidents have been energetic, if not driven, and have put in long hours on the job. It is hard to know to what extent a president can make up for a less-than-normal personal effort by delegating tasks skillfully. Certainly delegation can help enormously, but a president who relies on delegation too heavily will lose influence, even within his administration.

Experience. In parliamentary systems, the prime minister is prepared for leadership by years of rising through the party ranks, normally including service in the cabinet or shadow cabinet. Indeed, becoming prime minister is often a matter of moving from the side to the head of the table at cabinet meetings. In the United States, however, no comparable training system exists. Success in waging a presidential campaign presumably guarantees some skills in mass communications. But none of the other dimensions of presidential leadership can be taken for granted.[8] Whether presidents have developed the relevant skills depends on their prior careers. Inevitably, most presidents are new to crucial aspects of the job.

Almost all presidents have held one of three positions before becoming president or vice president: member of Congress, governor of a state, or high official in the executive branch, including the cabinet and military. In the twentieth century, only four presidents (William McKinley, Theodore Roosevelt, Franklin D. Roosevelt, and George Bush) held two of these positions, and none held all three.[9] Each position has severe limitations from the standpoint of training presidents. A member of Congress manages a staff roughly the size of a large automobile dealership. Governors, especially of small states, do not participate in national policy making or deal with comparably complex policy processes. Some governors have limited authority under their state constitutions and thus few substantial tasks. Nor do governors manage an economy or make foreign policy. Most executive branch officials have highly specialized responsibilities and only modest exposure to the mass public; in addition, some have little involvement in the legislative process.

Perversely, the only job that provides well-rounded preparation for the presidency *is* the presidency. One other emerging training ground may be the vice presidency, inasmuch as recent presidents have tended increasingly to treat their vice presidents as partners or understudies rather than as rivals.[10] An important consideration in judging presidential candidates, therefore, is what kinds of political and governmental experience they have had and what skills of presidential leadership they have demonstrated.

Personality. Finally, personality or character—fundamental traits that precede specific experience or skills—may be important to presidential performance. But it is hard to say which traits matter. In 1972, political scientist James David Barber proposed a simple typology of psychological character that he claimed could explain important aspects of presidential performance.[11] In one of political science's most celebrated predictions, Barber got Nixon right, using Nixon's "active-negative" personality to predict irrational and self-destructive tendencies before they were dramatically revealed in the Watergate crisis. Unfortunately, as Jeffrey Tulis has pointed out, Barber's scheme also would have warned against Abraham Lincoln, often considered the greatest American president, who was just as clearly an active-negative.[12]

The scandals of the Clinton administration renewed interest in personality, or the "character issue," triggering a variety of psychological studies.[13] Taking a theoretically elaborate psychoanalytic approach, Stanley A. Renshon points to three basic elements of personality: ambition, integrity, and relatedness (relationship abilities). He argues that these elements shape a president's fundamental mental health and especially his interpersonal, cognitive, and characterological skills. These skills in turn combine to determine the president's decision-making and political leadership abilities.[14] After reviewing earlier research on presidential personality and performance, however, psychologist Dean K. Simonton concluded that no single personality type was clearly best suited for the presidency. Instead, various traits have both advantages and disadvantages.[15]

The key to presidential personality may not be finding a candidate of the right personality type but recognizing the dangers of various specific flaws. Barber was convincing in describing extreme, if not pathological, rigidity on the part of Woodrow Wilson[16] (in the controversy over ratifying the League of Nations treaty), Herbert Hoover (in responding to the Great Depression), and Lyndon Johnson (in escalating the Vietnam War), in addition to Nixon's paranoid aggression. Reagan's simplistic, categorical thinking helped to produce the huge budget deficits that dominated American politics in the 1980s and early 1990s.[17] Clinton's lack of self-discipline not only produced the misconduct that ultimately led to his impeachment but also contributed to the chaotic, inconsistent White House decision making that produced numerous gaffes, scandals, and political failures in his first two years as president.[18]

One lesson of all these examples is that presidents can go wrong in many different ways, making it almost impossible for citizens to identify and therefore avoid all potentially harmful personal weaknesses. The American political system will just have to work with flawed presidents. It would seem reasonable, however, to expect the electoral process to filter out candidates who have glaring deficiencies in skills, experience, or personality—for example, a candidate with no experience in building coalitions and no disposition to work with political opponents.

This expectation pertains especially to the nominating process. Leaving aside independent and third-party candidacies, it is the nomination of the major-party candidates that narrows the field of potential presidents from the hundreds or thousands of constitutionally eligible persons who would like to be president to just two. Any ability of the electoral process to filter out unsuitable candidates must operate primarily at this stage. Although the candidates' qualifications should certainly be debated in the general election, for most voters the choice by then will be dominated by party and ideology.

Qualifications and the 2000 Campaign

In the 2000 presidential election, the treatment of Democrat Al Gore's and Republican George W. Bush's qualifications for office was in important respects disappointing. To a great extent, the general election contest zeroed in on the qualifications of the candidates rather than on their policies or philosophies of government. One reason for this emphasis was that the candidates, both portraying themselves as moderates, advanced somewhat similar platforms. Another was that weariness with the scandals of the Clinton presidency, so-called "Clinton fatigue," led many Americans to stress the importance of the "character issue." [19] Yet the campaign's discussion of candidate qualifications was superficial and even misleading. It is far from clear that it helped the voters to weigh the attributes that are genuinely significant for presidential performance.

Perversely, the nomination phase of the election provided a minimal test of the candidates' qualifications. The roles of the two leading players in the 2000 campaign were essentially cast within a year of the 1996 elections. A September 1997 Gallup poll showed 49 percent of Democrats lining up behind Al Gore, and George W. Bush was receiving a strong plurality (22 percent) in a crowded Republican field.[20] On the Democratic side, where a sitting two-term vice president who was generally respected in Washington was seeking the presidential nomination, the early Gore lead was largely compatible with a concern for candidate qualifications—although Gore had widely recognized limitations in communicating with the public. Meanwhile, the Republicans were rallying around a candidate whose main advantages were his father's name, an appealing personality, a moderate stance as a "compassionate conservative," and a successful but very short career in Texas politics. Bush was so little known to Americans at this stage of the campaign that pollsters measuring his support found it advisable to remind respondents that he was the son of the former president, not the former president himself.

Each party's establishment and major donors rallied early behind these standard bearers in an effort to avoid divisive primary battles that could weaken their candidate in the general election campaign. Before the first caucus ballot was cast in Iowa, Bush had secured the endorsement of all thirty-one Republican governors and almost every Republican senator and representative, and he had raised a staggering $48 million.[21] In fact, Bush raised so much money that he was able to forgo federal matching funds in the primaries and ultimately set the record for campaign fund-raising with his more than $94 million. One of his Republican rivals, Arizona senator John McCain, raised about half as much ($45 million, about a third of it from federal matching funds), and another rival, magazine publisher Steve Forbes, spent just $48 million ($42 million from his own pocket).[22] Gore enjoyed a similar level of support from his party's establishment, with nearly every Democratic governor, senator, and representative endorsing him before the primary season began. Although Gore raised only about half of what Bush raised ($49 million), it was enough to scare off all but one primary challenger. Former New Jersey senator Bill Bradley nearly kept pace with Gore's fund-raising, bringing in $42 million, but he could not match the vice president's endorsements and organization.

Gore's and Bush's early leads were virtually locked in by a "front-loaded" nominating process that heavily favored front-runners. Although McCain managed a nineteen-point upset win over Bush in the New Hampshire primary, Bush dealt McCain's candidacy a crushing blow by winning the vast majority of Super Tuesday primaries on March 7. The Democratic nomination was even less competitive, with Gore winning every caucus and primary. By March 10, McCain had suspended his campaign, and Bradley had endorsed Gore.

The truncated nomination campaign failed to test either nominee's qualifications for the presidency. McCain's challenge to Bush was based on his own heroism as a prisoner of war, his political "maverick" image, and his support for campaign finance reform. He did not attempt to challenge Bush's experience, capabilities, or qualifications for the office. The media had fun with Bush's frequent mispronunciation and misuse of words, and the late-night comedians seized on them to portray Bush as a dimwit. But serious commentators did not treat the verbal slips as worthy of the voters' attention. That Bush had graduated from Yale University and the Harvard Business School, among other things, militated against questioning his basic intelligence. Gore's lackluster skills addressing the public were, if anything, matched by those of Bradley; in other respects, his credentials for the presidency could not be readily challenged.

The general election campaign, in contrast, centered on personal qualifications more than any other in recent history. But it was not especially revealing of the attributes that were likely to affect either candidate's presidential performance. Instead, the campaign focused on alleged weaknesses that were misleading or dubious, while overlooking or failing to clarify important deficiencies in the candidates.

Overall, the clear loser in the test of personality and qualifications, from the voters' standpoint, was Al Gore. He encountered two kinds of troubles. First, Gore was dogged by questions about his honesty. The Pew Research Center for the People and the Press found that by late October fewer than one-third of poll respondents considered Gore to be honest and truthful, putting Gore eleven percentage points behind Bush on this score.[23] The grounds for the mistrust, however, were far from compelling. For one thing, Gore had been involved in two episodes of questionable fund-raising during the 1996 presidential campaign. Justice Department officials had recommended the appointment of an independent counsel to investigate possible criminal wrongdoing. But Attorney General Janet Reno, who had appointed six independent counsels to investigate President Clinton, First Lady Hillary Rodham Clinton, and various Clinton administration officials, was not persuaded by the preliminary evidence and declined to do so. Although Gore answered questions about these episodes evasively, there was never clear evidence that he knowingly had acted illegally. In any case, comparable violations of the campaign finance laws are (regrettably) quite common and rarely lead to criminal prosecution.

In addition, Gore was described in media reports and by the Bush campaign as having claimed, preposterously, that he had "invented the Internet." But what Gore actually had said was quite different. While reciting some of his accomplishments in the course of an interview with CNN correspondent Wolf Blitzer, Gore said, "During my service in the United States Congress, I took the initiative in creating the Internet." In fact, he had been a leader in Congress in behalf of various policies that promoted the development of the Internet. Instead of an absurd lie, Gore's remark was a fairly routine example of the inflated credit-claiming favored by politicians. Nevertheless, Bush ridiculed Gore for the alleged falsehood during the televised presidential debates. Bush's emphatic statement in the third televised debate that he had supported the HMO (health maintenance organization) reform law in Texas—when in fact he had opposed the measure and only reluctantly allowed it to become law, without his signature—was a far more substantial distortion of the record than Gore's misstated anecdotes.

Second, Gore had trouble presenting himself to the voters in an appealing way. Long criticized as a "wooden" speaker, Gore cast about unsuccessfully for an effective style in the presidential debates. In the first debate, he was aggressive, evidently thinking that it would show leadership if he frequently interrupted and insisted on speaking beyond his time limit. Criticized for that performance, he was agreeable to the point of passivity in the second debate. In the final debate, he switched back to the aggressive style. The abrupt changes in his debate personality overshadowed his imposing knowledge of substantive issues. They also reinforced the doubts about his trustworthiness. The Bush campaign seized on Gore's flip-flopping debate strategy to ask, effectively, "Who is the real Al Gore?"

These problems hurt Gore's campaign significantly even though he had had a squeaky clean, Boy Scout reputation through two decades of nearly scandal-free government service, and even though his frequent awkwardness in public speaking had not hampered his performance as vice president. It is unlikely that either problem foretold serious deficiencies in a Gore presidency.

At the same time, the Bush campaign and the media overlooked aspects of Gore's decision making that were genuinely troubling. Gore's style of decision making was arrogant and overconfident and bordered on pathological resistance to advice. In making decisions for the campaign, Gore was often willing to overrule even a unanimous group of advisers. Gore aides told the *Washington Post*, "He always needs to prove that he knows more than anyone else in the room." As one aide said, "He has trouble trusting someone [else] who by the very fact that Al Gore is in the room is by definition not the smartest person in the room."[24] Gore's self-assertive decisions were not always good ones. Flying in the face of conventional wisdom, Gore disdained to make the economic and policy accomplishments of the Clinton administration a central theme of his campaign. Few observers defended this strategy.

If a presidential candidate surrounds himself with advisers whose collective advice he regularly dismisses, it should raise questions about his effectiveness as a manager and the soundness of his personality. The evidence is far from sufficient to conclude that Gore would have refused to listen to advice in, say, a national security crisis with potentially calamitous

consequences for the nation. Nevertheless, the inability to use advisers effectively is certainly one of the most dangerous failings of a president. Yet these
insider concerns about Gore's decision making played no significant role in
the campaign. Bush did not chastise Gore for hiring advisers he would not
listen to, and the media did not ask hard questions about his management
style.

Bush also encountered criticisms of his personal qualifications for the
office, but, as with Gore, the media and others largely overlooked some of
the most telling weaknesses. In some areas, perhaps surprisingly, the voters
showed a degree of sophistication. During the primaries, Bush confirmed
rumors that he had a history of alcohol abuse, illicit drug use, and other personal failings. He also gave assurances (which were never contradicted) that
he had overcome these frailties and put his life in order before beginning his
political career. He declined, however, to divulge details such as when, exactly, he had last used illicit drugs. In late October, days before the general election, a newspaper broke the story that Bush had been convicted of drunk driving in Maine in 1976. Bush again admitted to the past misbehavior and
denied its relevance to the election. Meanwhile, neither the Gore campaign
nor the media tried to link Bush's personal conduct to his likely performance
as president, and polls showed that few voters considered the matter relevant.[25] Had this issue received greater scrutiny, the candidates or the media
might have discussed whether there was a significant danger of Bush relaps-
ing into alcohol abuse while in office. But such a discussion probably would
have confirmed the voters' judgment that it would not.

The central issue concerning Bush's qualifications, however, was
whether he was sufficiently interested in and knowledgeable about government and public policy to perform credibly as president. Although this issue
received considerable attention in various forums, none of it was very revealing. In an incautious moment, Bush allowed a radio/television reporter to
quiz him on-air about the names of the leaders of Taiwan, Chechnya, Pakistan, and India. Bush's inability to name them was a major embarrassment
that came back to haunt him frequently during the campaign. Yet none of
those leaders had figured prominently in major issues of American foreign
policy, and it was unlikely that many governors, members of Congress, or
even reporters knew their names either.[26]

The Gore campaign tried another tack to exploit the competence issue,
arguing that Bush's comparatively short, six-year tenure as governor of Texas
was insufficient experience for the presidency.[27] Although this was indeed
modest experience compared with that possessed by most presidents, it was
not far out of line with the experience Ronald Reagan or Bill Clinton brought
to office; each had served as a governor only a few years more than Bush. The
Gore campaign's argument, then, was patently weak. Quite likely, it had
hoped that voters would interpret the charge in light of media commentary
that Bush was poorly informed—that is, that Gore would say "inexperienced" and voters would hear "ignorant."

The candidates' knowledge and understanding were most prominently on display in the televised presidential debates.[28] Undoubtedly aware of Gore's previously demonstrated capability in such contests, Bush initially resisted agreeing to the debates planned by the Commission on Presidential Debates. But in doing so, he was overlooking the leveling effect of extensive rehearsal, debate formats that allow the candidates to speak largely from prepared answers, and an audience whose demand for accurate and specific information is minimal. Presidential debates have rarely penalized lack of knowledge. In 1976 President Gerald Ford, debating Jimmy Carter, made a verbal slip, refused to acknowledge it, and ended up insisting ludicrously that Poland was at the time a free country. It cost him heavily. But in 1980 Ronald Reagan, the clear underdog to Jimmy Carter on perceived competence, did better than expected in the public's judgment and profited handsomely from debating. Twenty years later, under criticism, Bush reluctantly agreed to the debates and earned the same underdog's reward for performing competently. Although most commentators were impressed with Gore's mastery of the issues, they observed that Bush appeared to hold his own and to exceed expectations. The public agreed. The exit polls showed that a majority of Americans thought that Bush knew enough to be president.[29]

None of these manifestations of the competence issue revealed clearly what was true and significant about Bush: that as governor he was relatively unengaged in the substance of public policy and governmental processes, and that by comparison with most national political leaders, he was notably uninformed. As governor, Bush typically put in shorter hours than a civil service clerical worker. In making policy decisions, he relied on staff to provide short memos with recommendations. He also kept briefings short, often under fifteen minutes. Judging from insiders' reports, it was not Bush's practice to hear out advocates of alternative policies or to probe the grounds for staff recommendations.[30]

Whatever his involvement in Texas issues, Bush evidently paid less attention to national affairs and especially foreign policy. One revelation of his unawareness appeared trivial on the surface: Bush referred to the people of Greece as "Grecians" instead of "Greeks." But (unlike the quiz on obscure world leaders) this mistake probably was indicative of a habitual lack of attention to foreign affairs. Even an occasional viewer of national television news would have heard the correct term many times over a period of years and would have been unlikely to come up with the term *Grecian*—familiar to Americans mainly from advertisements for a men's hair-coloring product.[31]

Another episode was even more revealing of Bush's inattentiveness. At an early November campaign event, Bush castigated the Democratic ticket for wanting the federal government to control Social Security, "like it's some kind of federal program."[32] But Social Security is and has always been entirely a federal program. Not just a governor but anyone who had spent a significant amount of time discussing or reading about national domestic policy would have remembered this, one of the most basic features of the nation's largest domestic program. No one ever gave Bush a fair-minded quiz on his knowledge of policy and government, but it is evident that he would have scored very low for an aspiring national leader.

Leaving programs and policies aside, Bush's main strength as a candidate was that voters found him likable and trustworthy and saw him as a strong leader. Some of this advantage reflected his political success as governor of Texas during a period of sustained national prosperity that made state politics an easy arena in which to succeed. Even more important, it reflected voters' impressions of Bush as a person—their reactions to such signals as body language, facial expressions, and tone of voice. These impressions are far from reliable as grounds for predicting performance or behavior.[33] But in Bush's case they may have captured useful information. Close observers of Bush generally liked him and, apart from his disposition not to work very hard, had high regard for his personality and leadership style. An adviser described Bush to the *Washington Post* as "a man confident enough to show what he doesn't know, an executive who expects his advisers to know more than he does about their areas of expertise, and a leader willing to force those around him to rethink what they know."[34] In addition, there were no revelations about Bush that raised doubts about his emotional stability.

In the end, Bush's success as a vote-getter rested heavily on his besting Gore in the contest of personal qualities. Independent voters, who determined the election, more resembled Gore supporters than Bush supporters in their opinions about issues, which should have given Gore a large advantage. But the Pew Research Center polls showed a widening "likability" gap favoring Bush as the fall campaign progressed, culminating in a nine-percentage-point (48–39) Bush advantage by late October. Voters consistently viewed Bush as the stronger leader and as more capable of getting things done.[35] Thus the candidate with the generally lesser conventional qualifications for the presidency won critical popular support on the strength of the voters' judgment of his qualifications.

Commitments

The election campaign establishes the commitments that the president-elect will bring into office. The president's chances for success in governing will depend partly on whether those commitments, made in the heat of the campaign, still make sense substantively and politically after the election.

Varieties of Commitment

Political cynics like to suggest that campaign promises are made to be broken and have virtually no significance after the election. But, in fact, presidents work hard to fulfill most of the promises they made during the campaign.[36] Looking at the presidencies from John F. Kennedy through Reagan's first term, Jeff Fishel found that presidents, on average, submitted legislation or signed executive orders consistent with roughly two-thirds of their campaign promises. Even the lowest-scoring president, Reagan, acted on more than half of his 1980 promises, including some of the most dramatic and important ones.[37]

Presidential candidates make commitments partly by promising specific actions, such as Carter's 1976 pledge to create a Department of Education and Reagan's 1980 vow to cut income taxes by 30 percent. They also make promises implicitly by attacking the proposals, past actions, and alleged intentions of the opposing candidate, as in Lyndon Johnson's devastating attack in 1964 on Republican candidate Barry Goldwater's purported plan to abolish Social Security; the promise implicit in such attacks is to act differently. But whether a promise is explicit or implicit, it is politically costly for presidents to go back on their word, and they try hard to avoid doing so.

Presidential promise making and promise keeping are generally constructive for popular control of government—which is the whole point of democratic elections. They give voters some confidence that what they see in a candidate is what they will get if they elect that candidate as president. Moreover, the winner's promises sometimes have a larger effect. If a presidential candidate campaigns largely on issues and wins the election by a comfortable margin, the promises made during the campaign become the new president's "mandate." [38] Johnson's landslide victory in 1964, for example, was viewed as a mandate for his Great Society programs.

Very often, however, the effect of such promises is less benign, reflecting the voters' lack of sophistication and the superficiality of the campaign debate. In pursuit of votes, a candidate may make promises that serve the needs of the campaign but that are problematic, at best, from the standpoint of governing. Such promises may exploit the voters' limited information or appeal to their emotions, stereotypes, or wishful thinking. These campaign-driven, sound-bite promises may call for policies that in all likelihood are not feasible, would have unacceptable costs, or would accomplish little while distracting attention from genuinely constructive options. After the election, a president who has made such promises will face pressure to make good on them. He may fail to deliver, may use precious time and political support in pointless efforts to enact infeasible legislation, or, still worse, may deliver on the promises and harm the country.

Such problems do not arise from mere puffery—claims that are so vague or obviously hyperbolic that they have no specific implications. Nixon's famous promise to "bring us together" or Kennedy's vow to "get this country moving again" created no constraints on their actions as president. Nor can misleading promises be identified with anything approaching perfect objectivity. Yet based on discussions among the informed, especially nonpartisan commentators, campaign claims can, very roughly, be arrayed on a continuum from the unexceptionable to the almost completely unbelievable. Virtually everyone now understands that Reagan's 1980 campaign promise to balance the budget while cutting taxes 30 percent and raising defense spending was little more than a fantasy. So was Bush's 1988 promise to reduce the deficit with no new taxes. In much the same way, Democrats have engaged in demaguery on entitlement programs and environmental protection. In the 1990s, major policy proposals seemed increasingly to reflect a sound-bite mentality: a two-year limit on welfare, "three strikes and you're out" for criminal sentencing, and legislating the death penalty for a proliferating number of crimes.

To provide the basis for successful presidential governance, the candidates should impose some discipline on their claims and promises and keep them reasonably connected with reality. And the campaign debate and media coverage should provide enough scrutiny of the candidates' positions to induce such discretion or, failing that, to help the voters discount the exaggerations.[39] Simply put, there should not be a vast gulf between the rhetoric of the campaign and the realities of governing.

Commitments and the 2000 Campaign

The 2000 presidential campaign presented the two major-party candidates with the novel problem of defining a domestic agenda for a time of budget surpluses and economic prosperity, with no downturn then visible on the horizon. Nine years of strong economic growth had cut unemployment to record low levels, and the Federal Reserve had used interest rates to help keep inflation in check. Meanwhile, government revenues had repeatedly outpaced economic projections, and a federal budget deficit of more than $250 billion per year had been transformed, with help from some Clinton-initiated policy changes, into annual surpluses that were projected to add up to $4.6 trillion during the next decade.[40] The candidates, with sufficient caution, could have promised a combination of tax cuts and new spending without exceeding the financial resources that seemed likely to be available to pay for them. But in fact, the competition of the election led both candidates, especially Bush, to make the same kinds of problematic commitments that presidential candidates had often made in harder times.

The main difficulty was the political temptation to spend money that might never materialize. The Congressional Budget Office (CBO) based its projections for the federal surplus on economic assumptions that were prone to change. For example, it assumed a healthy 2.7 percent annual growth rate, with no recession, for the next decade. If that occurred, the country would have experienced nineteen years of uninterrupted economic growth. The projected surplus also was based the assumption that future Congresses and administrations would keep spending at current levels, adjusted for inflation. Instead, Clinton and the 106th Congress were busily spending down the surplus themselves, and the 2001 budget exceeded the 2000 budget by 8.5 percent.[41] The bipartisan Concord Coalition reported that discretionary outlays had increased 5.5 percent annually since 1998 and estimated that if the pace continued, the ten-year surplus would amount to only $712 billion, not the

$4.6 trillion projected by the CBO. In October, the Brookings Institution predicted a surplus of just $352 billion.[42] Observed Senator McCain, "We've got a surplus evaporating."[43]

Both candidates nevertheless proposed and continued to defend costly plans to reduce taxes substantially, expand Medicare to cover prescription drugs, and reform the Social Security system. Gore's proposals, somewhat more cautious than Bush's, set aside a $300 billion "surplus reserve" in case the projected surpluses were smaller than expected. But he still called for $818 billion in new spending, $200 billion for new retirement savings accounts, and $480 billion in tax cuts—more than enough to overspend the surplus if the economy slowed down.[44]

The centerpiece of Bush's program was a sizable across-the-board tax cut, along with elimination of the estate tax and the so-called marriage penalty, a doubling of the child tax credit to $1,000, and an expanded deduction for charitable giving. The cost of these cuts was estimated at $1.6 trillion ($1.3 trillion in lost revenue plus $300 billion in increased interest payments—the result of paying off less of the national debt).[45] Pointing to the CBO's optimistic forecast, the Bush camp argued that the plan would leave plenty of money to shore up Social Security, expand Medicare, increase discretionary spending (especially on defense), and reduce the debt. Yet, as others pointed out, if the cautionary forecasts of the Concord Coalition or the Brookings Institution proved more accurate, the Bush tax cut would drain resources from discretionary programs and push the federal government back into deficit spending. Bush's tax proposal was criticized as reckless or unrealistic by many economists.[46]

In a disappointment to the Bush campaign, the proposed tax cut was not very popular with the voters either. In September, a Pew Research Center poll showed that the public opposed Bush's tax program by a 58 percent to 40 percent majority.[47] Gore repeatedly attacked the plan as a "risky scheme" designed to benefit the rich. But as much as anything, the public had learned from nearly two decades of struggling with federal budget deficits to be wary of politicians pushing large tax cuts. Even so, tax cuts were important for Bush's conservative constituencies, and he stuck with the program throughout the campaign.

Bush's second major commitment was to partially privatize the Social Security system. He repeatedly promised neither to increase payroll taxes nor to reduce Social Security benefits for retirees or near-retirees.[48] Yet he also proposed to create new personal retirement accounts to be controlled by the individual account holder and funded by diverting a portion of his or her payroll taxes from the main trust fund. The idea was largely to enable Social Security participants to benefit from the high rates of return that were available in the stock market, although critics pointed out that such returns are associated with considerable risk. In any case, Bush omitted important details of his program—notably, how he would make up for the loss of revenue in the trust fund.

The other major commitments Bush made during the campaign either were not specific enough to limit his discretion as president (such as to "end the bickering" and "get things done") or enjoyed bipartisan support and probably were feasible, such as mandatory educational testing and some form of Medicare prescription drug coverage. Bush's commitments on Social Security privatization and especially tax cuts, however, were likely to prove problematic after the inauguration. Either one had the potential to draw Bush into a protracted, unsuccessful struggle to enact it or, if enacted, to have adverse economic effects that Bush and other policy makers would then have to deal with. That the elder president Bush had blatantly broken a campaign pledge to oppose taxes, at great cost to his 1992 reelection effort, made it even harder for George W. Bush to back off his own tax proposals. The first signs of difficulty emerged only two days after the disputed Florida outcome was finally resolved and Gore conceded the election. Two Republican leaders, House Speaker Dennis Hastert and Majority Whip Tom DeLay, publicly opposed across-the-board tax cuts.[49] Bush replied that he would not give up the program, setting the stage for a potentially bruising battle between the president and Congress.

Support

The results of presidential and especially congressional elections go far toward determining whether presidents will have adequate political support for their policies. Such support is crucial to their chances for policy success. In particular, a "presidency of achievement," such as those of Wilson, Franklin Roosevelt, Johnson, and Reagan, depends on a highly supportive political environment.[50]

Support in Washington for a president's policies is not critical for his popular success in the country, however. Clinton staged a political comeback in 1995 and 1996 largely by opposing the aggressive conservatives who controlled Congress. Nor is such support essential for success in governing. In fact, the government often works fairly well when the president and Congress are controlled by different political parties.[51] Provided that the two parties are reasonably disposed to cooperate, presidents may negotiate with an opposition-party Congress to deal effectively with national problems even if they cannot enact their own preferences.[52]

Elections and Sources of Support

Elections affect support for the president's policies in several ways. Most important, they determine the partisan and ideological balance in Congress. As considerable research demonstrates, presidential influence in Congress depends more on that balance than on presidential characteristics such as popularity or leadership skill.[53] The effects of the composition of Congress on the president's influence were highly evident during Clinton's first term. In 1993 and 1994, when he enjoyed Democratic majorities in both the House and the Senate, Clinton got his way more than 85 percent of the time in each house on roll-call votes on which he took a position. After losing both houses to the Republicans in the 1994 midterm elections, his success rate dropped precipitously. In 1995, Clinton won only 26 percent of the roll calls in the House, the lowest success rate of any president on record, and 49 percent in the Senate. As both Clinton and congressional Republicans moved toward the center in 1996, Clinton had more success, winning 53 percent of the important votes in the House and 58 percent in the Senate. These success rates were still low by historical standards, however, even for presidents who faced Congresses controlled by the opposition party.[51]

In addition, the congressional elections are an important barometer of national opinion on the president's policies and the role of government. The campaigns of the nearly one thousand House and Senate candidates constitute a massive and highly visible test of which issues and themes work best in the prevailing climate of opinion. If, for example, Democratic congressional candidates constantly stress their association with the Democratic nominee for president, campaign on his or her policies, and are elected along with the presidential nominee in large numbers, the results will be interpreted in Washington as powerful evidence of national support for the president's agenda. But if Democratic congressional candidates avoid speaking their standard bearer's name and campaign largely on Republican themes, their strategy indicates that Democrats have surrendered in the ideological battle.[55]

To a lesser degree, how the president got elected also affects congressional support for his agenda. For one thing, did the president campaign primarily on the issues? Another factor is the effect of the campaign on what Richard E. Neustadt calls the president's professional reputation and prestige.[56] For example, presidents who have suffered effective attacks on their character or competence, have endured embarrassing gaffes or scandals, and have been viewed by many voters as the lesser of two evils will have a diminished ability to rally support. During Clinton's first term the questions raised in the 1992 campaign about his avoidance of military service in Vietnam undermined his credibility as commander in chief. This lack of credibility helped to defeat his effort to end the ban on homosexuals in the armed forces.

The most important aspect of the president's manner of election is the margin of victory. Presidents who win landslides are given credit for their popularity and for their ability to rally public support. As a result, they receive longer or more generous honeymoons with Congress. In 1981, Reagan's economic program derived powerful momentum from his late surge in which he overtook Carter and won the election by a ten-percentage-point margin in the popular vote.

The elections also shape the disposition of the two parties to collaborate in effecting policy change. If the campaign was ideologically divisive and featured brutal negative attacks, the parties are likely to carry the spirit of partisan warfare into government. If centrist campaign strategies were more prominent and negative attacks more restrained, the potential for bipartisan cooperation is greater. The parties draw lessons about the rewards for confrontation or cooperation from how the voters respond to those strategies. In 1995, congressional Republicans adopted an exceptionally aggressive partisan posture partly because their obstruction of Clinton during his first two years had seemed to pay off in the 1994 elections.

The potential for bipartisanship also depends on what kinds of members are elected to Congress: moderates or ideologues. For some years, a gradual realignment of the party system has been weeding the moderates— liberal Republicans and conservative Democrats—out of Congress, especially in the House. This realignment has shrunk the base for bipartisan coalitions.[57]

In sum, elections can provide the necessary support for a successful presidency in more than one way. To set the stage for substantial policy achievements guided by the president's own agenda, the president needs to campaign on the issues, avoid significant damage to his image, and win the election by a large margin. In addition, congressional candidates of the president's party must link themselves with the president, campaign on the same issues, and win their elections in large numbers. Alternatively, to achieve governing success through negotiation and compromise, the parties must avoid polarizing, highly ideological campaigns and vicious negative attacks; the campaigns must expose and penalize confrontational tactics; and the voters must send a healthy number of moderates to Congress.

Support and the 2000 Election

The 2000 elections gave George W. Bush an extraordinarily complex, unpredictable situation with respect to popular and congressional support, along with one of the most ambiguous mandates in the history of the presidency. Even more than for most presidents, support for Bush and his opportunity for achievement will depend on how he deals with this situation: how he presents himself, whom he looks to for support, and what kind of agenda he emphasizes. In the end, a presidency of substantial accomplishment is possible.

Bush assumed the presidency under a cloud of doubt that he was legitimately elected. He lost the national popular vote to Gore by about 0.5 percent and won the electoral vote 271–266, the narrowest margin since 1876. Most important, Bush was elected only after a prolonged controversy over recounting ballots in Florida that finally was resolved in his favor by a Supreme Court decision widely criticized as partisan. African American leaders complained that irregularities in Florida had prevented thousands of African Americans from voting—presumably, mostly for Gore—and members of the Congressional Black Caucus walked out of the congressional ceremony that certified Bush as the winner in the electoral college.

Nevertheless, most Americans accepted the result. A mid-December Gallup poll found that 83 percent accepted Bush's legitimacy, including 68 percent of Gore's voters. The conflict-ridden process of Bush's election will probably reduce his influence, but only in a small way. When Bush asks Congress or the public to support his agenda, opponents may say that because he did not "really" win the election, he does not "speak for the American people." This argument is likely to sway only a few members of Congress, or a small fraction of the public, and only once in a while. After all, neither legislators nor voters tend to give presidents much deference just because they were elected president.[58]

In defining Bush's influence, what matters far more is the excruciatingly close outcome of the congressional elections. Bush is the first Republican president since Dwight D. Eisenhower to have the benefit of a Republican-controlled Congress.[59] But the Republican control is not only extremely narrow but also tenuous. Republicans control the House by just ten seats (221–211), and their control of the Senate, which is divided 50–50, rests on the vice president's tie-breaking vote. It also rests on the health of two aging Republican senators from states with Democratic governors who presumably would appoint Democratic replacements if the senators died or resigned.[60] In view of the fact that presidents since the late 1960s more often than not have faced Congresses controlled by the opposition party, Bush's prospects for support in Congress are, in terms of party strength, above average. But he cannot expect support for sweeping conservative measures or for sweeping measures of any kind.

Equally important, during the campaign Bush was unable to develop strong public support for his policy agenda. His most popular major proposal was for the partial privatization of Social Security. Yet in the exit polls, just 57 percent of voters supported creating separate retirement accounts with investments controlled by individual owners. As Clinton learned so painfully in his health care plan debacle of 1993, such a soft majority can easily vanish when legislative debate draws the public's attention to counterarguments. In fact, with stock prices sinking before the inauguration, the risks of the market were certain to receive more attention. As for tax cuts, only 51 percent of respondents in the exit polls supported Bush's proposal for an across-the-board tax cut, and when asked what the top priority for using the budget surplus should be, only 28 percent chose cutting taxes. Six in ten voters opposed Bush's position on gun control, and nearly eight in ten opposed school vouchers, which he favors. Bush worked hard to sell his policies during the campaign, but apart from his strongest supporters, the voters did not buy them. The exit poll results underline how much Bush's success in the election turned on voters' preference for him as a candidate and leader, an important asset for his presidency. The downside, from Bush's perspective, was that he could not count on initial public support for the main items on his policy agenda.[61]

From another perspective, however, there was exceptionally strong support in Congress and in the country for the central message of Bush's presidential campaign—his promise to be a moderate conservative who would work with both parties to get things done. Bipartisan cooperation has been quite limited in recent years because of the growing ideological polarization in Congress and the intense partisan conflict of Washington politics. But the public has wearied of such politics, and politicians took the cue in the 2000 congressional campaign. Many Democratic congressional candidates ran as centrist "New Democrats." The party even nominated some conservative House candidates who favored gun owners' rights or opposed abortion. On the Republican side, some hard-line conservative House members—such as Clinton scourge Bob Barr of Georgia—trimmed their ideological sails and ran for reelection as moderates.[62] In the Senate races, five conservative Republican incumbents were defeated, while the three New England moderate Republicans who were up for reelection skated to victory.[63] Moderates gained strength in Congress for the first time in decades. The success of moderate candidates mirrors and reinforces the closely balanced party divisions in both houses of Congress and ensures that the balance of power has shifted toward the center in Congress. "The president, whoever he is, will have to look to moderate centrists to get his agenda passed," said conservative Democratic senator John Breaux of Louisiana shortly after Election Day.[64]

As always, centrist presidential leadership will face serious obstacles, especially from the ideological extremes. With what they consider a "stolen" election etched in their memory, liberal Democrats have more taste for defeating Bush's agenda than for working with him. Indeed, the razor-thin margin of Republican control in Congress gives congressional Democrats a strong incentive to make things hard for Bush and focus on regaining majority status in the 2002 midterm elections. At the same time, many conservative Republicans will see their party's control of the presidency and Congress as an opportunity to effect the conservative policy revolution that they believed would follow their takeover of Congress in the 1994 midterm elections. "The things we have been dreaming about we can now do," predicted the House's conservative majority whip, Tom DeLay.[65]

In all, Bush faces a delicate situation. In appealing for support, he cannot trade heavily on his legitimacy as president. He will need help from politicians and citizens who only reluctantly concede that the processes that deposited him in the Oval Office were constitutionally valid. And he will need to emphasize the moderate elements of his policy agenda. Especially in the Senate, where forty-one senators can sustain a filibuster, the Democrats will be able to block hard-line conservative bills almost effortlessly. Bush's need to pursue a moderate course is also his opportunity. The political rationale for a problem-solving, centrist agenda has rarely, if ever, been more compelling. The House, the Senate, and the public are each positioned at the dead center of the political spectrum. Odd though it sounds, Bush has the chance to lead a bold experiment in moderate government.

The Prospects for the George W. Bush Presidency

The 2000 elections produced a president whose prospects for political, policy, and governing success are unusually precarious. Although Bush was appealing and persuasive to most voters and his personality has important strengths, his work effort, level of attention, and knowledge of government and policy are all modest for a contemporary political leader. His presidency will test whether a president can make up for such limitations through a concerted strategy of delegation. In the optimistic assessment of Texas state senator David Sibley, "Bush is a delegator. In war terms he's going to be the general who decides which mountains you take, but he's not going to be telling the lieutenant which machine-gun nest you charge first." [66] Unfortunately, at least in the presidency, delegation is not as simple as this statement implies. [67] Even fully engaged, deeply informed presidents often have great difficulty getting subordinates to serve their interests effectively.

During the transition period, which was shortened by the long delay in resolving the election, Bush dealt with the complexities of delegation by turning over a large share of his major decisions and management responsibilities to Vice President–elect Richard B. Cheney. An experienced Washington hand, Cheney was certainly capable of taking charge. On the whole, the Bush transition and the first days of his presidency went notably smoothly, winning general acclaim for a well-managed, politically astute operation. [68] But it was not clear whether this pattern would ultimately serve Bush's objectives. It led to media criticism of Bush for his lack of engagement—including a joke, referring to Cheney's heart troubles, that Bush was "a heart beat away from the presidency."

Bush's chances for success also will turn on his ability to resist pressure from conservative Republican constituencies and occupy the moderate position that offers his only hope of working effectively with the 107th Congress. That Bush will choose to do so cannot be taken for granted. Bush's immediate predecessor was a case in point. Elected as a centrist "New Democrat," Clinton was virtually captured by the liberal wing of the Democratic Party for the first two years of his presidency. That mistake contributed heavily to the huge Democratic losses in the 1994 elections. Bush's choices between moderate and hard-line conservative positions may determine whether he escapes a similar fate.

Notes

1. The authors assume that the general category of president includes women. For simplicity of expression, however, we sometimes rely on the convention of the generic *he* to refer to persons of either sex.
2. See Richard E. Neustadt, *Presidential Power: The Politics of Leadership* (New York: Wiley, 1960); James David Barber, *The Presidential Character* (Englewood Cliffs, N.J.: Prentice-Hall, 1972); Fred I. Greenstein, *The Presidential Difference: Leadership Style from FDR to Clinton* (New York: Free Press, 2000); and Marc

Landy and Sidney M. Milkis, *Presidential Greatness* (Lawrence: University Press of Kansas, 2000).

3. Donald R. Kinder, Mark D. Peters, Robert P. Abelson, and Susan T. Fiske, "Presidential Prototypes," *Political Behavior* 2 (1980): 315–337. Also see Stephen J. Wayne, "Great Expectations: What People Want from Presidents," in *Rethinking the Presidency,* ed. Thomas E. Cronin (Boston: Little, Brown, 1982); Stanley A. Renshon, *The Psychological Assessment of Presidential Candidates* (New York: New York University Press, 1996); and George C. Edwards and Stephen J. Wayne, *Presidential Leadership: Politics and Policy Making* (New York: St. Martin's Press, 1999), 105–107.

4. Fred Greenstein's analysis of the last eleven presidents based on six qualities that influence presidential performance exemplifies this approach and largely mirrors our own list of relevant qualities. Greenstein, *Presidential Difference.* See also Erwin C. Hargrove and Michael Nelson, *Presidents, Politics, and Policy* (Baltimore: Johns Hopkins University Press, 1984); and Paul J. Quirk, "Presidential Competence," in *The Presidency and the Political System,* 6th ed., ed. Michael Nelson (Washington, D.C.: CQ Press, 2000).

5. Our discussion here follows closely our account in Paul J. Quirk and Sean C. Matheson, "The Presidency: Elections and Presidential Governance," in *The Elections of 1996,* ed. Michael Nelson (Washington, D.C.: CQ Press, 1997). It has been amended in modest ways to address issues that arose in the 2000 election.

6. Barbara Kellerman, *The Political Presidency* (New York: Oxford University Press, 1984).

7. Samuel Kernell, *Going Public: New Strategies of Presidential Leadership,* 3d ed. (Washington, D.C.: CQ Press, 1997).

8. Richard Rose, "Learning to Govern or Learning to Campaign?" in *Presidential Selection,* ed. Alexander Heard and Michael Nelson (Durham: Duke University Press, 1987).

9. Michael Nelson, "Who Vies for President?" in *Presidential Selection.*

10. See David Broder, "Al Gore: A Close Second," *Washington Post* National Weekly Edition, September 2–8, 1996, 6–7.

11. James David Barber, *The Presidential Character* (Englewood Cliffs, N.J.: Prentice-Hall, 1972).

12. Jeffrey Tulis, "On Presidential Character," in *The Presidency in the Constitutional Order,* ed. Jeffrey Tulis and Joseph M. Bessette (Baton Rouge: Louisiana State University Press, 1977), 287.

13. See, for example, Christopher Peterson and Fiona Lee, "Reading between the Lines: Speech Analysis," *Psychology Today,* September/October 2000, 50–51.

14. Stanley A. Renshon, *The Psychological Assessment of Presidential Candidates* (New York: New York University Press, 1996).

15. Dean K. Simonton, *Why Presidents Succeed: A Political Psychology of Leadership* (New Haven: Yale University Press, 1987), 230–232. Although there is some evidence that a president's motivation (generally conceived as the desire for power, achievement, or affiliation) influences his behavior, no clearly preferable motivation has been established. David G. Winter and Abigail J. Stewart, for example, found that desire for power, a trait most Americans express concern about, is strongly correlated with greater presidential success. The only two traits that clearly seem to be desirable in a president are open-mindedness and intellectual sophistication. See David G. Winter and Abigail J. Stewart, "Content Analysis as a Technique for Assessing Political Leaders," in *A Psychological Examination of Political Leaders,* ed. Margaret G. Hermann (New York: Free Press, 1977), 28–62.

16. Also see Alexander L. George and Juliette L. George, *Woodrow Wilson and Colonel House* (New York: Day, 1956).

17. Reagan's presidency is also a reminder that age and health are relevant to presidential performance. Other things being equal, the nation certainly should prefer to avoid choosing a president who is likely to die or suffer a disabling illness during his term of office. Reagan exhibited striking deficiencies of memory and factual knowledge as early as the 1980 campaign and throughout his presidency. By the end of his second term, his increasingly severe lapses provoked press speculation that he was becoming senile. By the mid-1990s, Reagan, whose Alzheimer's disease had advanced, was unable to make public appearances. Because Alzheimer's disease can run its course for twenty years or more, it is possible that Reagan's forgetfulness and simplistic thinking were caused by the disease throughout his presidency, although the evidence is certainly not conclusive. See Edmund Morris, *Dutch: A Memoir of Ronald Reagan* (New York: Random House, 1999), 662, 837.

18. Elizabeth Drew, *On the Edge: The Clinton Presidency* (New York: Simon and Schuster, 1994).

19. Indeed, Michael Barone and Grant Ujifusa predicted well before the general election campaign that character would be "perhaps the most important consideration in a post-Clinton election." Michael Barone and Grant Ujifusa, *The Almanac of American Politics 2000* (Washington, D.C.: National Journal, 2000), 1510.

20. David Moore, "Gore and Bush in 2000?" Gallup poll, September 12, 1997, online at http://www.gallup.com/poll/releases/pr970912.asp.

21. Federal Election Commission reports, January 31, 2000, and February 20, 2000, online at http://www.fec.gov.

22. Federal Election Commission figures are available at http://www.fec.gov/finance/precm8.htm.

23. Pew Research Center for the People and the Press, November 1, 2000, online at: http://www.people-press.org/loct00rpt.htm.

24. John F. Harris, "Gore as President: Politics vs. Policy," *Washington Post,* October 29, 2000, A1.

25. In a November 5 Gallup poll conducted just after news of his 1976 drunk driving arrest broke, 87 percent of Americans said the revelation would not influence their voting decision, and 77 percent found it irrelevant to Bush's ability to serve as president. Poll results are available at: http://www.gallup.com/poll/releases/pr001105.asp.

26. The right answers were: Lee Teng-hui (Taiwan), Aslan Maskhadov (Chechnya), Pervez Musharraf (Pakistan), and Atal Behari Vajpayee (India).

27. Katharine Q. Seelye and Richard Perez-Pena, "Gore Team Renews Criticism of Bush as Inexperienced," *New York Times,* October 30, 2000.

28. Debates also test special talents, such as verbal facility and quick thinking under pressure, which are not core presidential skills.

29. Voter News Service "Exit Polls," November 7, 2000, online at http://www.cnn.com/ELECTION/2000/epolls/US/P000.html.

30. James A. Barnes, "How Bush Would Govern," *National Journal,* October 28, 2000; and Michael Tutty, "Bush as Texas Sees Him: Lean, Not Lightweight," *Wall Street Journal,* December 14, 2000, A16.

31. The first definition of *Grecian* is, in fact, "Greek," but it is not used to refer to the people, leaders, policies, events, or language of contemporary Greece. The hair-coloring product is Grecian Formula, said to color "only the gray."

32. "Complete Bushisms," *Slate,* November 2, 2000, online at http://www.slate.com.

33. See Robert Frank, *The Passions within Reason: The Strategic Role of Emotions* (New York: Norton, 1988), for a discussion of how and why such signals play a larger role in interpersonal relations.

34. Dan Balz and Terry M. Neal, "Bush as President: Questions, Clues, and Contradiction," *Washington Post,* October 22, 2000, A1.
35. Pew Research Center poll, November 1, 2000, online at http://www.people-press.org/loct00que.htm.
36. Jeff Fishel, *Presidents and Promises* (Washington, D.C.: CQ Press, 1985).
37. Ibid., 38–39.
38. Much of the Washington community will assume that the voters endorsed those promises. See John H. Aldrich, "Presidential Selection," in *Researching the Presidency: Vital Questions, New Approaches* (Pittsburgh: University of Pittsburgh Press, 1993), 23–68.
39. On the limitations of media coverage, see Thomas E. Patterson, *Out of Order* (New York: Random House, 1994).
40. Allen Schick, *The Federal Budget: Politics, Policy, and Process* (Washington, D.C.: Brookings, 2000); and Eric Pianin, "Differences Aside, Candidates Rely on Same Forecast," *Washington Post,* October 23, 2000, A12.
41. Andrew Taylor and Daniel J. Parks, "An Immovable President Meets Irresistible Pork," *CQ Weekly,* October 7, 2000, 2318–2319.
42. Daniel J. Parks, "The Surplus and the Baby Boomers," *CQ Weekly,* October 14, 2000, 2388–2389.
43. Taylor and Parks, "An Immovable President," 2319.
44. Pianin, "Differences Aside."
45. Richard Stevenson, "Bush Tax Plan: The Debate Takes Shape," *New York Times,* August 26, 2000, A1.
46. "Poor Grades for Al and George," *The Economist,* September 30, 2000.
47. Pew Research Center poll, September 14, 2000, online at http://www.people-press.org/typo00que.htm.
48. For the full outline of the Bush Social Security plan, see George W. Bush, "Saving Social Security and Medicare" (campaign speech and publication), May 15, 2000.
49. Lizette Alvarez, "House Leader Differs with Bush on Across-the-Board Tax Cuts," *New York Times,* December 15, 2000, A1.
50. The term is from Hargrove and Nelson, *Presidents, Politics, and Policy.*
51. David R. Mayhew, *Divided We Govern: Policy Control, Lawmaking, and Investigations, 1946–1990* (New Haven: Yale University Press, 1992); and Paul J. Quirk and Bruce Nesmith, "Divided Government and Policymaking: Negotiating the Laws," in *The Presidency and the Political System,* 6th ed., ed. Michael Nelson (Washington, D.C.: CQ Press, 2000), 570–594.
52. Charles O. Jones, *The Presidency in a Separated System* (Washington, D.C.: Brookings, 1994).
53. Jon R. Bond and Richard Fleisher, *The President in the Legislative Arena* (Chicago: University of Chicago Press, 1990); George Edwards, *At the Margins: Presidential Leadership of Congress* (New Haven: Yale University Press, 1989); and Mark Peterson, *Legislating Together* (Cambridge: Harvard University Press, 1996).
54. Jon Healey, "Clinton Success Rate Declined to a Record Low in 1995," *Congressional Quarterly Weekly Report,* January 27, 1996, 193–198; and Carroll J. Doherty, "Clinton's Big Comeback Shown in Vote Score," *Congressional Quarterly Weekly Report,* December 21, 1996, 3427–3430.
55. For a fuller discussion of systemic influences on presidential performance, see Stephen Skowronek, *The Politics Presidents Make: Leadership from John Adams to George Bush* (Cambridge: Belknap Press, Harvard University Press, 1993), and Hargrove and Nelson, *Presidents, Politics, and Policy.*
56. See Neustadt, *Presidential Power*; and Richard E. Neustadt, *Presidential Power and the Modern Presidents: The Politics of Leadership from Roosevelt to Rea-*

gan (New York: Free Press, 1990). Neustadt's emphasis on the president's personal attributes has been seriously challenged, at least with respect to leadership of Congress. Also see Bond and Fleisher, *President in the Legislative Arena*; Edwards, *At the Margins*; and Peterson, *Legislating Together*.

57. Joseph Cooper and Garry Young, "Partisanship, Bipartisanship, and Crosspartisanship in Congress since the New Deal," in *Congress Reconsidered*, 6th ed., ed. Lawrence C. Dodd and Bruce I. Oppenheimer (Washington, D.C.: CQ Press, 1997), 246–273.

58. Benjamin I. Page, Robert Y. Shapiro, and Glenn R. Dempsey, "What Moves Public Opinion?" *American Political Science Review* 81 (March 1987): 23–44; and Edwards, *At the Margins*.

59. Eisenhower entered office with a similarly narrow congressional majority: 48–47 in the Senate and 221–211 in the House.

60. At the time of the election, Sen. Jesse Helms, R-N.C., was seventy-nine, and Sen. Strom Thurmond, R-S.C., was ninety-eight, and both had recurring health problems. Indeed, of the nine senators over age seventy, seven come from states with Democratic governors.

61. Voter News Service "Exit Polls."

62. "Running toward the Middle," *National Journal*, October 21, 2000.

63. Andrew Taylor, "Searching for the Vital Center," *CQ Weekly*, November 11, 2000, 2641–2645.

64. Alan K. Ota, "New Democrats Looking for Larger Role in the 107th Congress," *CQ Weekly*, November 11, 2000, 2644.

65. Quoted by E. J. Dionne, "Bush's Choice," *Washington Post*, December 19, 2000, A39. Edward Walsh, "Despite Successes, Republicans Face Hurdles," *Washington Post*, December 15, 2000, A26.

66. Barnes, "How Bush Would Govern."

67. Quirk, "Presidential Competence."

68. Richard L. Berke, "Bush's First Week in Office Garners Respectful Reviews," *New York Times*, January 28, 2001, A1, A15.

8

Congress: Elections and Stalemate

Gary C. Jacobson

The contests for control of the House of Representatives and Senate
in 2000 were as tight as the contest for the White House. As voters went
to the polls on the morning of November 7, the outcomes of these elections
were as uncertain as they had been at the beginning of the election year. Any
combination of unified or divided partisan control of Congress (and the
White House) was still conceivable. As with the race for the presidency, the
contest for the House, where the Democrats needed to gain only seven seats
in order to take control, remained too close to call. Democrats were also
given an outside chance to take the Senate. The final result—unified but
tenuous Republican control of both houses (and both branches)—was not
surprising, but neither would any of the other possible outcomes have been
surprising.

The election left the Senate divided exactly in half, with Republicans
and Democrats each holding fifty seats. The Republicans maintained control
because Republican Dick Cheney was elected vice president. As such,
Cheney presides over the Senate and can vote to break ties. Democrats
picked up two House seats, narrowing the Republican majority to 221 to
212 (the two independent House members split on which party they routinely support) but falling short of the seven-seat gain they needed to win
control (Table 8-1).

For the first time since before the New Deal, Republicans have won control of both houses in four straight elections, but by margins so narrow as to
belie any notion that they now enjoy a "natural" majority in Congress or the
nation. Figure 8-1 shows how small the Republican House margins have
been since 1994 compared with the margins usually enjoyed by Democrats
during the era of Democratic dominance initiated by the 1932 election.
Indeed, these House majorities are the narrowest produced by any four consecutive elections in American history. Figure 8-2 shows that small Senate
majorities have been rather more common over the years, as have shifts in
partisan control, although only once before, in 1880, did a Senate election
result in a tie between the parties. Among elections since 1932, only 1952
compares to 2000 in leaving both houses so closely balanced between the
parties; it was also the last election that produced a unified Republican government.

Table 8-1 Membership Changes in the House and Senate in the 2000 Elections

	Republicans	Democrats	Independents	Vacant
House of Representatives				
Elected in 1998	223	211	1	
At the time of the 2000 election	222	209	2	2
Elected in 2000	221	212	2	
Incumbents reelected	193	199	2	
Incumbents defeated	4	2		
Open seats retained	20	4		
Open seats lost	5	6		
Senate				
After the 1998 election	55	45		
At the time of the 2000 election	54	46		
After the 2000 election	50	50		
Incumbents reelected	13	10		
Incumbents defeated	5	1		
Open seats retained	0	3		
Open seats lost	1	1		

Source: Compiled by the author.

Rather than break the partisan stalemate that prevailed in Washington during the second Clinton administration, voters reinforced it. Instead of delivering a clear-cut verdict on the performance of either the Democratic administration or the Republican Congress, the electorate divided down the middle. The resulting configuration would suggest a continuation of legislative gridlock, even if the fight over Florida's electoral votes had not inflamed partisan passions and further polarized the congressional parties. By resurrecting battle lines formed during the 1998–1999 Clinton impeachment struggle, the Florida conflict further reduced prospects for bipartisan cooperation under the new government.

Why were the elections so inconclusive? Why, contrary to most predictions, did Democrats come closer to winning the Senate than the House? What do the election results tell us about the current state of American politics? What do they portend for the 107th Congress and for the 2002 elections?

My purpose in this chapter is to begin to answer these questions. To do so, I first consider the context of the election, the long- and short-term electoral forces prevailing in 2000. I then examine the conditions that shaped the House elections, including impeachment politics and term limits. Next, I consider whether the presidential campaigns may have influenced Senate elections, even though nationally the race for president was a dead heat. Finally, I speculate about the prospects for governing under the incoming administration and whether the 2002 elections will break the stalemate.

Figure 8-1 House Margins, 1932–2000

Democratic seats minus Republican seats

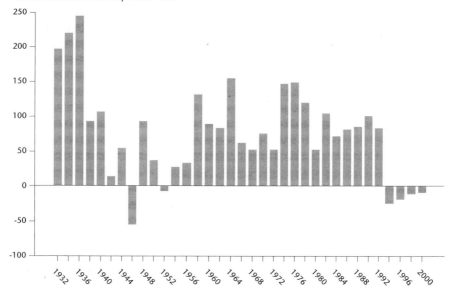

Source: Norman J. Ornstein, Thomas E. Mann, and Michael J. Malbin, *Vital Statistics on Congress, 1999–2000* (Washington, D.C.: CQ Press, 2000), Table 1-19; 2000 data compiled by the author.

Figure 8-2 Senate Margins, 1932–2000

Democratic seats minus Republican seats

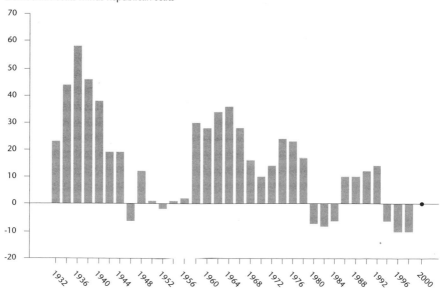

Source: Norman J. Ornstein, Thomas E. Mann, and Michael J. Malbin, *Vital Statistics on Congress, 1999–2000* (Washington, D.C.: CQ Press, 2000), Table 1-19; 2000 data compiled by the author.

Prelude to Stalemate

Congressional elections are shaped by a combination of long- and short-term electoral forces. The most powerful long-term electoral force is partisanship. Although independent "swing" voters get most of the attention during election campaigns, the vast majority of votes are cast by people who identify themselves as Republicans or Democrats and vote accordingly. Moreover, party-line voting has been on the rise during the past two decades, and exit polls indicate that the 2000 election extended that trend.[1]

Partisanship is a long-term electoral force because, except under the most unusual circumstances, the distribution of Republicans and Democrats in the electorate changes only slowly, if at all, from one election to the next. Short-term forces, arising from more transient conditions, thus produce most shifts in congressional party fortunes. For example, a deep recession cost the Republicans twenty-six House seats in 1982, and in 1994 Clinton's unpopularity contributed to the Republicans' fifty-two-seat gain, which gave them control of the House.

Short-term electoral forces favored neither party in 2000, so the outcomes reflected the underlying partisan balance in the electorate with unusual clarity. The results show that the two major parties are more evenly matched than at any time since the nineteenth century. The substantial popular majority that Democrats had enjoyed since the New Deal was gone by the mid-1980s. Since then, they have retained a small edge in party identification in most polls, but, because self-identified Republicans are more likely to vote and are more loyal to their party, the electoral balance is nearly even.[2]

The 2000 elections, then, accurately reflected the close partisan division that now prevails in the United States. They did not, however, reflect the intense polarization between the parties that has also characterized national politics during the past decade.[3] Quite the contrary; the battles for control of the White House and Congress were fought in swing states and districts and for the support of independent-minded swing voters, circumstances in which partisan appeals were muted. Ironically, the furious partisan contest for control of the federal government was conducted with almost no mention of party at all in the campaigns that decided the outcome.

Neutral National Forces

If nothing else, the razor-thin electoral margin separating George W. Bush and Al Gore in the presidential race confirms that no partisan tide was running in 2000. Neither party benefited nationally from presidential coattails. Nor had there been any sign during the months leading up to the election that conditions in the fall would favor either party. Unlike 1994, but like 1996 and 1998, the electoral environment in 2000 broadly favored the congressional status quo.

The robust economy, which grew even faster during the second Clinton administration than it had during the first, produced widespread public satisfaction with the performance of government and the direction of the country. Growing real incomes, low unemployment, and low inflation left a large majority of families better off financially, and even the sharp rise in energy prices during the summer did little to dampen economic optimism. The huge federal budget deficits of the early 1990s had, by the end of the decade, become huge budget surpluses. The robust economy combined with the welfare reforms enacted in 1996 to cut the proportion of Americans on welfare by more than half. Low unemployment contributed to the sharp drop in violent crime reported in the 1990s.

The American public was well aware of these trends and gave both the economy and the president high marks. In an October 2000 Gallup Poll, more than 70 percent of the public rated the economy as excellent or good, and more than 70 percent approved of Clinton's economic performance. Twice as many Americans said they were satisfied as dissatisfied with the direction of the country. This was good news for the Democrats, but Clinton had to share credit with the Republican-controlled Congress, in which the incumbents of both parties stood to benefit from the generally high levels of public satisfaction. As Figure 8-3 shows, Clinton was by no means the only politician to benefit from the economic improvements that occurred during his administration.

Although Clinton and the Republican Congress were often at odds with each other—most dramatically during the 1995 showdown over the budget

Figure 8-3 Approval of Congress and Clinton (Quarterly Averages)

Percentage approving

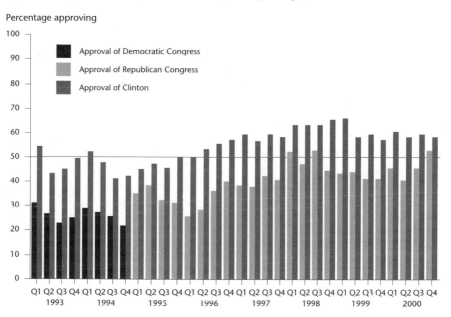

Quarter and Year

and the 1998–1999 effort to impeach Clinton and remove him from office—public approval of the president and Congress showed a strong tendency to move up and down together during the Clinton years. This was true regardless of which party controlled Congress. During the eight quarters of unified government in 1993 and 1994 (shown in the striped columns of Figure 8-3), the quarterly averages of congressional and presidential approval ratings were correlated at .73; during the twenty-four quarters of divided government, they were correlated at .77. The average difference between presidential and congressional approval ratings was actually wider during Clinton's first two years as president (twenty-one percentage points) than during his final six (seventeen percentage points). At the time of the 2000 election, both Clinton and Congress were enjoying unusually high levels of approval by historical standards. The most plausible reason why public approval of the president and a Congress dominated by his enemies moved in rough parallel is that many Americans evaluate both branches by the same criteria, namely, the economy and the general state of the nation.

The House Elections

The high level of public satisfaction with Congress and the absence of a discernable partisan tide were good omens for congressional incumbents in 2000. Incumbents almost never lose unless they face high-quality challengers blessed with abundant campaign resources and potent issues that can undermine an incumbent's standing with his or her constituents.[4] With a satisfied electorate and with neither party surging, issues that could be used effectively against incumbents were scarce. Without exploitable issues, the best potential challengers (typically, those pursuing long-term political careers) were, as always in such an environment, reluctant to run. Their reluctance was reinforced by knowledge that campaign contributors would be skeptical of their chances of winning and therefore unlikely to invest in their challenges.[5] Under these conditions, only the most vulnerable House incumbents—a small number—attracted formidable challenges.

As a consequence, the battle for the House focused on a few hotly contested races, most of them for open seats, which tend to be more competitive because neither candidate enjoys the advantages of incumbency.[6] Only nine of the four hundred seats defended by incumbents were listed as either "toss-up" or leaning toward the challenger's party in Congressional Quarterly's November handicapping.[7] Even if districts rated as only "leaning" toward the incumbent's party are added, the number of incumbents estimated to be in danger was just thirty-four. In contrast, eleven of the thirty-five open seats were rated toss-ups, and eight others were classified as leaning toward one of the parties. Therefore, fewer than 9 percent of the incumbent-held seats were in play in 2000, compared with more than half of the open seats.

The narrow focus of competition was reflected in the distribution of politically experienced candidates. Only 17 percent of Republican incumbents and 20 percent of Democratic incumbents faced challengers who had ever held elective public office, a blunt but serviceable measure of candidate quality.[8] The experienced challengers were, as always, concentrated in competitive races—indeed, they were one reason why these contests were classified as competitive; challengers to 59 percent of the incumbents in races rated toss-up or leaning had held elective office, compared with 15 percent of challengers to incumbents in the noncompetitive races. As usual, high-quality candidates flocked to open seats, in which 57 percent of the Democrats and 68 percent of the Republicans had held prior elective office.

Many of the open seats were not particularly competitive, however. Almost half were quite safe for the party of the departing incumbent because of the district's underlying partisan makeup. Most of these safe seats were held by Republicans, which meant that, although Republicans had to defend twenty-five open seats compared with the Democrats' ten, the Republicans actually ended up on election day with a net gain of one open seat. Seventeen of the open Republican districts had given Republican presidential candidate Bob Dole a majority of their votes in 1996, and three more had gone to Clinton with less than his national average of 54 percent of the major party vote. Democrats won only one of these twenty seats (Utah's Second District), while taking four of the five Republican districts where Clinton had won more than 54 percent of the major party vote in 1996. Republicans won all six of the open Democratic seats where Clinton had received less than 58.5 percent, while Democrats retained all four seats where Clinton's vote had exceeded that margin.

In addition to widespread public contentment and the absence of a national partisan tide, several other circumstances helped to narrow the range of competition for House seats in 2000. The first was a legacy of the 1994 election. Republicans picked up fifty-two House seats in 1994 and kept a large majority of them in the next two elections because most of the seats they had taken were seats that, according to presidential voting patterns, should have been theirs in the first place.[9] After 1994 the number of seats in the "wrong" party's hands dropped sharply, making it much more difficult for either party to take seats from the other in the absence of strong sentiment in its favor. Second, Democrats who had survived the Republican wave in 1994, and Republicans who had held on after it receded in 1996 and 1998, were unlikely to be vulnerable in the neutral conditions that prevailed in 2000.

Finally, 2000 was the fifth and final election under the current national apportionment of House districts, which was governed by the 1990 census. Figure 8-4 indicates that, if we use Congressional Quarterly's preelection ratings as an indicator and the 1980s and 1990s as representative decades, competition appears to decline over the course of each reapportionment cycle. Although election-specific considerations certainly affect the level of competition in every election (1994 and 1996 stand out), competition was at or near its high right after new district lines were drawn in these two reapportionment cycles, tended to decline thereafter, and reached its lowest point in the cycle's

Figure 8-4   Competitive House Elections, 1982–2000

Number of competitive contests

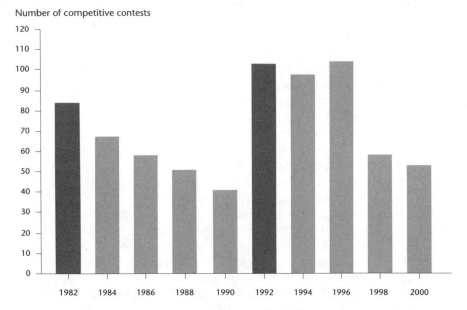

Note: Competitive races are those classified by Congressional Quarterly as "toss-ups" or "leans Democratic (Republican)"; uncompetitive races are those classified as "safe" or "Democrat (Republican) favored." Darker bars represent first election after redistricting.

final election. The pattern suggests that political learning occurs; vulnerable incumbents who survive one or two strong challenges cease to be inviting targets. The pattern also reflects retirements; years ending in "2" always produce a bumper crop of retirements as incumbents leave the House rather than contend with redrawn districts, while some members apparently put off retirement for a term or two pending reapportionment. The number of voluntary departures from the House in 2000, thirty-two, was the lowest of the decade.

The narrow range of competition in the 2000 House elections was also evident in the distribution of campaign money. By October 17, the Federal Election Commission's deadline for reporting interim campaign contributions and expenditures, candidates in the forty-eight seats classified as toss-ups or leaning had already spent an average of more than $1 million apiece. As usual, safe incumbents also reported that they had abundant funds, while nonincumbents in contests not considered competitive were starved for resources, reporting average expenditures through October 17 of approximately $100,000 or about one-fifth of what it now typically costs to mount a competitive House race.[10]

The focus of campaign donors who supported challengers in the small number of competitive races involving incumbents is apparent from Figure 8-5, which displays the Gini coefficient of inequality for the distribution of campaign expenditures by House challengers from 1972 to 2000. The Gini

Figure 8-5 The Concentration of Challengers' Spending in House Races, 1972–2000

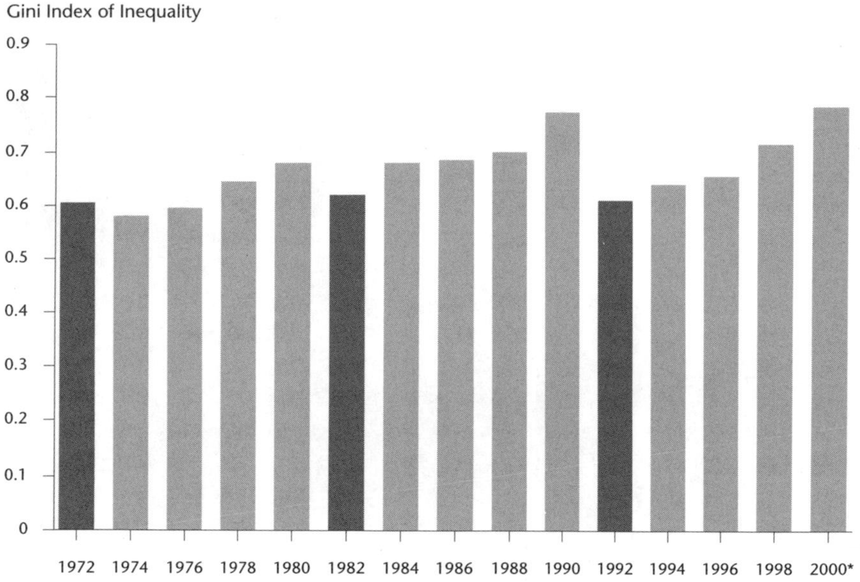

Gini Index of Inequality

Note: The Gini coefficient for the first election in each cycle is shown by darker bars

*Based on data through October 17.

coefficient takes values from 0.0 (complete equality; each candidate gets the same amount of money) to 1.0 (complete inequality; one gets everything, the rest, nothing).[11] Spending data reported through October 17 show the most skewed distribution of challenger resources ever. Notice also that the concentration of financial resources increases over the course of each reapportionment cycle, mirroring the decline in competitive races observed in Figure 8-4; the only year with the Gini coefficient coming close to that for 2000 is 1990, another year at the end of a reapportionment cycle.

Overall, the amount of funding available to House candidates in 2000 was the highest in history and, in contrast to past elections, neither party enjoyed an appreciable financial advantage. As Figure 8-6 shows, the candidates of the majority party (Democrats 1990–1994, Republicans 1996–1998) normally raise, on average, more money than their opponents. In 2000, however, the Republican advantage was minimal, reflecting contributors' view that the Democrats had a good chance of becoming the majority party. Significantly, donations by corporate and business associations to each party's congressional party campaign committee, which had favored the Republicans by almost two to one in the 1997–1998 election cycle, were evenly divided during the first half of 2000.[12]

The competitive, high-spending House districts were also the main targets of independent and "voter education" campaigns operating outside the

Figure 8-6   Contributions to House Candidates

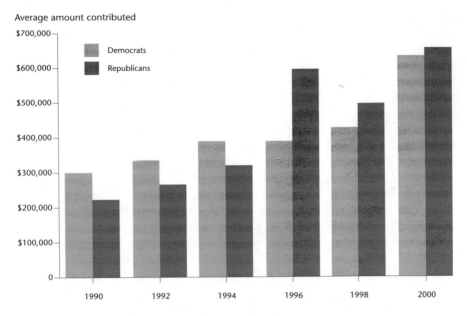

Average amount contributed

Source: Federal Election Commission.

Note: All figures are for twenty days prior to the election.

candidates' purview. Party units, labor unions, and the U.S. Chamber of Commerce, as well as narrower special interest groups such as the Sierra Club, the National Rifle Association, and Handgun Control, Inc.—indeed, even private individuals—got into the act. Some bought broadcast ads, others organized phone banks, and still others sent targeted mailings to selected audiences or mobilized their members to vote on election day.[13] The net effect of all this spending was an expensive standoff.

The Legacy of Impeachment

One potential source of a swing to the Democrats in 2000, and therefore one reason they were given a good chance to retake the House, was the Republicans' failed attempt to impeach and remove Bill Clinton from the White House. The House vote in December 1998 to impeach Clinton divided the parties almost perfectly, with 98 percent of the House Republicans voting for at least one of the four proposed articles of impeachment, and 98 percent of House Democrats voting against all four. The impeachment vote put congressional Republicans in some political danger. Clinton's approval ratings peaked just as they were trying to drive him from office, and every one of the dozens of polls taken on the issue found that the American people opposed impeachment and removal, typically by a margin of nearly two

Figure 8-7 District Presidential Vote and Republican Support for the Impeachment of Bill Clinton

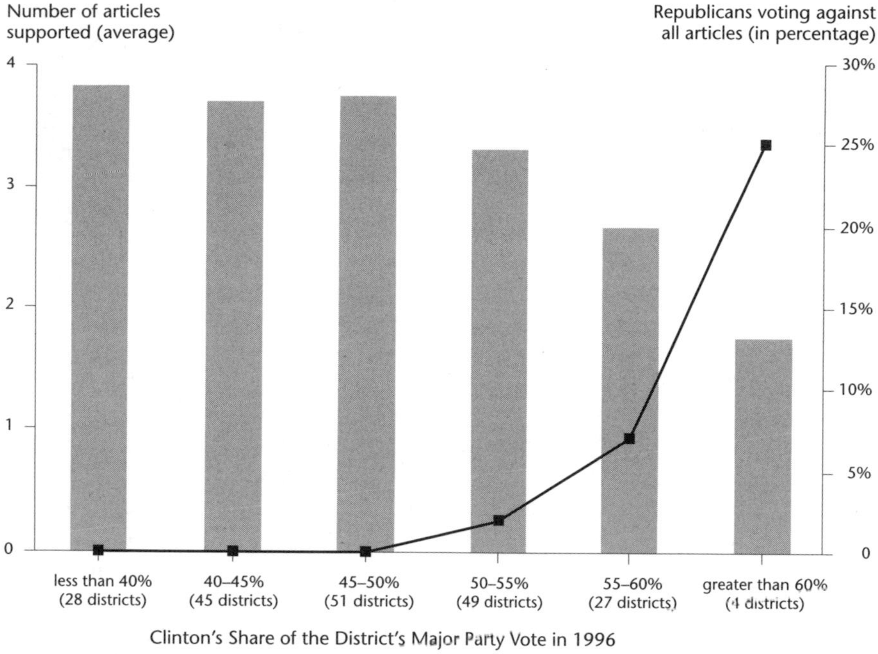

Number of articles
supported (average)

Republicans voting against
all articles (in percentage)

less than 40%
(28 districts)

40–45%
(45 districts)

45–50%
(51 districts)

50–55%
(49 districts)

55–60%
(27 districts)

greater than 60%
(4 districts)

Clinton's Share of the District's Major Party Vote in 1996

Note: The vertical bars indicate the average number of articles of impeachment supported; the line indicates the percentage of Republicans voting against all four articles of impeachment. The number of districts in each category is indicated below each vertical bar.

to one.[14] In effect, Republicans gambled that a partisan move to impeach and remove a popular president in the teeth of public opinion would be forgiven, forgotten, or even applauded by the time the 2000 elections rolled around.

The Republicans' success in maintaining control of the House and (barely) the Senate suggests that they won this gamble. Although Americans continued to give Clinton high approval ratings through the end of his term, no general backlash against the Republican effort to oust him occurred in the 2000 elections. Indeed, what is striking is how little attention the issue received in most campaigns. It may be tempting to interpret this as an example of Americans' short political attention span, but a number of other factors are probably more important. As Figure 8-7 indicates, House Republicans did not totally ignore their constituents when voting on impeachment. Although only four of them voted aga--inst every article, more than a third voted against at least one of the four articles. The higher Clinton's 1996 vote was in a district, the fewer articles its Republican representative was likely to support. Such gradations allowed members to display a more "moderate" stance on impeachment if they chose to do so. Moreover, although polls showed that most constituents of House Republicans opposed impeachment, those constituents who had actually voted for the House Republicans supported impeachment by a two-to-one margin.[15]

Finally, Republicans may have escaped punishment at the polls for their widely unpopular move simply because it failed. Indeed, the expectation that it would fail was the basis of an argument used by Republican leaders to persuade moderate Republicans from Democratic-leaning districts to vote for impeachment. As one of House Majority Whip Tom Delay's associates put it, "If, as we all assume, Clinton will survive in the Senate, moderates who vote to impeach won't have to worry about a backlash."[16] Because most voters got what they wanted—namely, the continuation of the Clinton presidency—they were not inclined, almost two years after the fact, to punish Republicans wholesale for their attempt to remove him. Just as good times helped Clinton to survive the impeachment process, the strong economy and positive social climate in 2000 probably helped to protect the Republicans in Congress by maintaining public contentment with the status quo.

This is not to say that impeachment politics had no lingering effects on the election. A vote for impeachment galvanized early and formidable Democratic opposition to a few Republican incumbents, although mainly in the kind of swing districts where strong challenges were likely to arise anyway. Three of the four Republican incumbents who lost fell into this category: Californians Brian Bilbray and James Rogan, both of whom represented districts where Clinton had won 55 percent of the major party vote in 1996, and Jay Dickey of Arkansas, who represented a district that had given Clinton 66 percent of its major party vote in 1996 and that includes Hope, the town where Clinton was born. Each of the three was defeated by a popular state legislator with a lavishly funded campaign. Rogan, who was prominent among the thirteen managers who presented the House impeachment case at the Senate trial, and Adam Schiff, his victorious opponent, became poster children for rival pro- and anti-impeachment activists nationwide. They ended up conducting the most expensive House race in history; through October 17, Rogan had spent more than $5.7 million and Schiff, more than $3.3 million.

None of the other House managers lost their reelection bids, although on average their vote was about six percentage points lower than what other similarly situated Republican incumbents received, a consequence of attracting significantly better funded challengers than their district's political circumstances would otherwise have warranted.[17] Their lower vote shares were not decisive, however, because aside from Rogan, only one impeachment manager, Steve Chabot of Ohio, did not represent a safe Republican district. (Chabot won with 55 percent of the vote against a weak opponent.) One other House manager suffered a defeat on November 7: Bill McCollum of Florida, who had left the House to run for the Senate.

Besides impeachment, another unusual feature of the 2000 House elections was that the time to retire had come for the ten Republicans and one Democrat who had promised voters in 1994 to limit themselves to three

House terms. Three of the Republicans and the lone Democrat reneged and were reelected handily anyway. Although still approving overwhelmingly of legislative term limits, generally satisfied voters were of no mind to impose them on their own incumbents, even the pledge-breakers. Democrats picked up two seats from the seven Republicans who kept the pledge; in both cases, the districts already leaned Democratic. New Republicans easily won the other five districts, which had moderately to strongly Republican inclinations. Had it not been for Republicans who kept their term limit pledges, the Democrats would have made no net gain at all in the House elections.

House Republicans executed a successful defensive campaign strategy in 2000 that left them with a reduced but still secure majority. Ironically, their approach was almost the exact opposite of their winning plan in 1994. Rather than campaign as a team pledged to a common program, as they had with the Contract with America, Republican campaigns in 2000 centered on individual candidates and locally important issues.[18] Instead of boldly challenging Clinton, congressional Republicans sought, after impeachment, to avoid confrontations with the president at all costs. If the voters' decision was framed as the Republican Congress versus the Clinton administration, they feared, with good reason, that they would lose. As one Republican strategist put it, "I don't think it's in the interest of the Bush campaign or congressional Republicans [for Congress] to be an issue in November. What both of them should want is for Congress not to be an issue and to be invisible."[19] Democrats did try to make the Republican Congress an issue, but the Republicans carefully avoided battles that would remind voters either of the 1995 government shutdown or impeachment, softening their rhetoric and rolling out the pork barrel, as both parties "joined hands in an election year spending spree on roads, courthouses, schools, rivers, runways, and research."[20]

The House Republicans' low profile and local focus contributed to a tideless election that, like the presidential race, provided a clear expression of the underlying partisan division in the American electorate. Relatively few seats changed party control (seventeen, tied for third lowest among the twenty-seven post–World War II congressional elections), but on balance the changes that occurred increased the partisan match between districts and members. After the election, three fewer House seats were held by a party whose 1996 major party presidential vote in the district fell more than two percentage points below the national average, continuing the decade-long decline in the number of seats held by the "wrong" party. By this measure, only forty-nine such seats remained after the 2000 election, compared with eighty-one after the 1992 election and sixty-two after the 1996 election.[21]

The Senate Elections

Unlike the House elections, the Senate elections shook up the status quo in 2000. Republicans lost five seats, leaving the Senate evenly divided between the parties for only the second time in U.S. history. The Democrats had picked up one seat in July, when Republican Paul Coverdell of Georgia died and Georgia's Democratic governor appointed Democrat Zell Miller to take his place; Miller easily won a special election on November 7 to fill out the remaining four years of Coverdell's term. The Democrats gained four additional seats on election day, defeating five incumbent senators to the Republicans' one, with each party losing a single open seat.

The differences between the House and Senate results, although noteworthy, are not exceptional. Of the 403 House incumbents who sought reelection in 2000, all but nine succeeded (three lost in primaries, six in the general election), a 98 percent success rate. By comparison, the success rate for the twenty-nine Senate incumbents who ran in 2000 was only 79 percent. On average, Senate incumbents are about three times as likely to lose as House incumbents, but only on average. Reelection rates of senators vary widely from year to year, ranging in post–World War II elections from a high of 97 percent in 1990 to a low of 55 percent in 1980.

The main reason senators are more likely than representatives to face stiff competition and to suffer defeat at the polls is that a larger proportion of states than districts have a roughly even partisan balance, making them winnable by either party. Indeed, since 1980 no fewer than forty of the fifty states have been served by senators from both parties, and of the remaining ten states only one (Hawaii) did not elect at least one governor of the party opposite their senators'. In addition, brighter electoral prospects attract a larger number of the talented, well-funded challengers who are essential for competitive contests. As a result, in the average election year, about half the Senate races are hotly contested compared with fewer than 15 percent of the House races.[22] The 2000 election was fairly typical in this regard, with ten seats won with less than 55 percent of the major party vote, and sixteen seats won with less than 60 percent. Table 8-2 lists the results of the individual races.

Senators run on a six-year rather than a two-year cycle, and that can also lead to different patterns of competition in House and Senate races. When a strong partisan tide in an election produces large House and Senate gains for a party, the representatives who ride in on the surge are at risk two years later. The senators can wait six years before they face reelection under circumstances likely to be less helpful than those prevailing when they were first elected. For example, Republicans had an excellent year in 1980, picking up thirty-four House seats and twelve Senate seats, and winning a majority in the upper chamber for the first time since 1952. They quickly gave up most of their House gains, losing twenty-six seats after only two years, but they did not suffer significant losses in the Senate until 1986, when the class of 1980 faced its first test and the Democrats picked up eight seats to regain majority control.

The 2000 Senate elections were the first test for several staunchly conservative Republicans who were first elected in 1994. Three of the five Republican losers in 2000—John Ashcroft of Missouri, Rod Grams of

Table 8-2   Senate Election Results

State	Vote Total	Percentage of Total Vote
Arizona		
Jon Kyl (R)	1,108,196	79
California		
Dianne Feinstein (D)	5,932,522	56
Tom Campbell (R)	3,886,853	37
Connecticut		
Joseph I. Lieberman (D)	828,902	63
Philip Giordano (R)	448,077	34
Delaware		
Thomas Carper (D)	181,566	56
William V. Roth Jr. (R)	142,891	44
Florida		
Bill Nelson (D)	2,989,487	51
Bill McCollum (R)	2,705,348	46
Georgia		
Zell Miller (D)	1,413,224	58
Mack Mattingly (R)	920,478	38
Hawaii		
Daniel K. Akaka (D)	251,215	68
John S. Carroll (R)	84,701	23
Indiana		
David L. Johnson (D)	683,273	32
Richard G. Lugar (R)	1,427,944	67
Maine		
Mark Lawrence (D)	197,183	31
Olympia J. Snowe (R)	437,689	69
Maryland		
Paul Sarbanes (D)	1,230,013	63
Paul Rappaport (R)	715,178	37
Massachusetts		
Edward M. Kennedy (D)	1,889,494	73
Jack E. Robinson (R)	334,341	13
Michigan		
Debbie Stabenow (D)	2,061,952	49
Spencer Abraham (R)	1,994,693	48
Minnesota		
Mark Dayton (D)	1,181,553	49
Rod Grams (R)	1,047,474	43
Mississippi		
Troy Brown (D)	314,090	32
Trent Lott (R)	654,941	66
Missouri		
Mel Carnahan [a] (D)	1,191,812	50
John Ashcroft (R)	1,142,852	48
Montana		
Brian Schweitzer (D)	194,430	47
Conrad Burns (R)	208,082	51
Nebraska		
Ben Nelson (D)	353,093	51
Don Stenberg (R)	337,977	49
Nevada		
Ed Bernstein (D)	238,260	40
John Ensign (R)	330,687	55

(Continued)

Table 8-2 *Continued*

State	Vote Total	Percentage of Total Vote
New Jersey		
Jon Corzine (D)	1,511,237	50
Bob Franks (R)	1,420,267	47
New Mexico		
Jeff Bingaman (D)	363,744	62
Bill Redmond (R)	225,517	38
New York		
Hillary Rodham Clinton (D)	3,422,027	55
Rick A. Lazio (R)	2,681,221	43
North Dakota		
Kent Conrad (D)	176,470	62
Duane Sand (R)	110,420	38
Ohio		
Ted Celeste (D)	1,595,066	36
Mike DeWine (R)	2,665,512	60
Pennsylvania		
Ron Klink (D)	2,154,908	46
Rick Santorum (R)	2,481,962	52
Rhode Island		
Bob Weygand (D)	161,023	41
Lincoln Chaffee (R)	222,588	57
Tennessee		
Jeff Clark (D)	621,152	32
Bill Frist (R)	1,255,444	65
Texas		
Gene Kelly (D)	2,030,315	32
Kay Bailey Hutchison (R)	4,082,091	65
Utah		
Scott N. Howell (D)	242,569	32
Orrin G. Hatch (R)	504,803	66
Vermont		
Ed Flanagan (D)	73,352	25
James M. Jeffords (R)	189,133	66
Virginia		
Charles S. Robb (D)	1,296,093	48
George F. Allen (R)	1,420,460	52
Washington		
Maria Cantwell (D)	1,199,437	49
Slade Gorton (R)	1,197,208	49
West Virginia		
Robert C. Byrd (D)	469,215	78
David T. Gallaher (R)	121,635	20
Wisconsin		
Herb Kohl (D)	1,563,238	62
John Gillespie (R)	940,744	37
Wyoming		
Mel Logan (D)	47,087	22
Craig Thomas (R)	157,622	74

Source: OnPolitics Elections 2000, online at http://www.washingtonpost.com/wp-dyn/politics/elections/, January 2001.

Note: **Bold face** denotes incumbent. The Hawaii and Washington election results were not yet certified as we went to press.

[a]Carnahan died October 16; his wife, Jean Carnahan, was appointed to replace him until the next general election in 2002.

Minnesota, and Spencer Abraham of Michigan—were members of this class. All three were burdened with images that put them well to the right of their constituents. Part of the reason Democrats pulled even in the Senate is that the strong Republican current that had prevailed in 1994 was no longer running.

The other Republican incumbents who lost in 2000 were William Roth of Delaware and Slade Gorton of Washington. Roth's bid for a sixth term at age seventy-nine faltered when he fainted during two public appearances late in the campaign, a sign that he might not be up to the job physically. He lost to Thomas Carper, a popular governor and former U.S. representative. Gorton had the rare experience of losing as a Senate incumbent for the second time. Elected in 1980, defeated in 1986, then elected to Washington's other Senate seat in 1988 and 1994, Gorton lost to Maria Cantwell, a former member of Congress turned Internet executive, in a contest so close that it took almost as long to resolve as the presidential race in Florida.

The Democrats lost one Senate incumbent, Charles Robb of Virginia. Robb had survived the Republican tide in 1994, defeating Oliver North, the most visible figure in the Iran-contra affair and later a flamboyantly conservative talk-show host, but he was unable to prevail against Republican George Allen, a popular former governor. Robb's defeat, combined with the standoff in open seat contests—each party picked up one from the other, with Republican John Ensign winning a Nevada seat and Democrat Bill Nelson, a Florida seat—killed the Democrats' hopes of a Senate majority in 2000. When the Senate is divided 50–50, the vice president casts the tie-breaking vote on organizational matters, such as which party's members will chair Senate committees. Bush's victory meant that vote would be cast by Republican Dick Cheney. Had Gore won, his running mate, Joe Lieberman, would have had to resign his Connecticut Senate seat to become vice president. John Rowland, the Republican governor of Connecticut, would have appointed his successor, no doubt choosing someone from his own party and giving the Republicans a 51–49 majority.

The 2000 Senate elections produced several historic firsts. By winning the New York Senate seat left open by the retirement of Democrat Daniel Patrick Moynihan, Hillary Rodham Clinton became the first presidential spouse to be elected to any public office, let alone the Senate. In Missouri, Ashcroft lost to a dead man. Ashcroft's opponent, Democratic governor Mel Carnahan, had been killed in a plane crash on October 16. The Democratic lieutenant governor thereby became governor and quickly promised voters he would appoint Carnahan's widow, Jean Carnahan, to the seat if the late governor, whose name remained on the ballot, won, which he did. Finally, victories by Clinton, Cantwell, Carnahan, and Debbie Stabenow (who defeated Abraham in Michigan) raised the number of women in the Senate from nine to thirteen, an all-time high. Considering that until 1992 no more than two women had ever sat in the Senate at the same time, these gains extended a notable trend.

Figure 8-8   Contributions to Senate Candidates

Average amount contributed

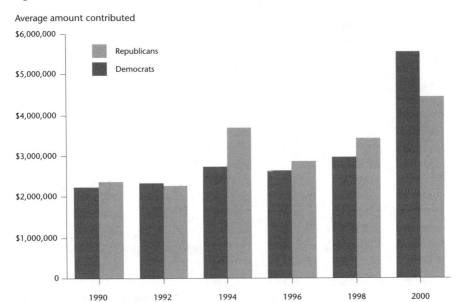

Source: Federal Election Commission.

Note: All figures are for twenty days prior to the election.

Like the battle for the House, the battle for the Senate stimulated record political fund-raising. Contributions through the October 17 reporting deadline ran well ahead of previous elections for the equivalent period (Figure 8-8). On average, Democrats raised more than Republicans, but only because of the $54 million reported on that date by Jon S. Corzine, a former Wall Street executive who eventually spent more than $60 million from his personal fortune on his successful bid for an open New Jersey Senate seat. Corzine easily broke the record for spending by a single campaign for any congressional office, but for total spending in a Senate race, the New York campaigns ended up on top. With the polarizing figure of Hillary Clinton on the ballot, the New York Senate election attracted national attention from contributors. Through October 17, Clinton had raised more than $26 million, and her Republican opponent, Rep. Rick Lazio, more than $33 million. New Yorkers evidently do not object to electing newcomers to the state to represent them in the Senate, at least if they are famous enough; after John F. Kennedy's assassination, his brother and attorney general, Robert Kennedy, moved to New York and was elected to the Senate in 1964.

With the presidential election essentially tied, it would seem that neither party's Senate candidates could derive much of a boost from the top of the ticket. But although no national trend favored either party, some distinctive state currents generated by the presidential campaign probably affected several Senate races. In at least one instance, a presidential campaign gave decisive help to a Senate candidate: the huge effort to get out the union and minority vote that swung Michigan into the Gore column was essential to Stabenow's victory over Abraham.[23] More generally, there was a modest but observable relationship between statewide presidential and Senate results. The incumbent party lost six of fourteen Senate seats in states won by the other party's presidential candidate, but only two of nineteen seats in states won by its own party's presidential candidate. One of the two was in Florida, where Gore may actually have received the most votes (we will never know). The other was Missouri, which Bush won by a narrow margin. With the exception of Missouri's Ashcroft, every losing incumbent was from a state won by the other party's presidential candidate. Overall, twenty-four of thirty-four states cast a plurality of their votes for Senate and presidential candidates of the same party, precisely the same as in 1992 and 1996.

It is also possible to detect traces of the impeachment struggle in the Senate results. Twelve Republican incumbents represented states won by Clinton in 1996. The two who voted against conviction were reelected easily. Five of the ten voting for conviction lost, as did McCollum, the House impeachment manager who tried to move up to the Senate in Florida. Five Republican incumbents represented states that Dole had won in 1996; all of them voted for conviction, and all were reelected. This is not to say that impeachment was a decisive issue in any of these races, but votes for conviction may have contributed to the impression that Republican conservatives such as Grams, Abraham, Ashcroft, and McCollum were ideologically out of step with their pro-Clinton constituencies.

Regional Alignments

Like the national vote for president, the close national partisan balance in the House and Senate masks distinct regional differences in party strength. Not surprisingly, the regional divisions in the presidential vote also are apparent in House and Senate election results. After the 2000 elections, Republicans held 63 percent of the House seats and 67 percent of the Senate seats in the twenty-six states of the South, Plains, and Mountain West, of which Bush won all but New Mexico. The Democrats controlled 57 percent of the House seats and 69 percent of the Senate seats in the Northeast, Midwest, and West Coast, regions where Gore won nineteen of twenty-four states.

With the same partisan divisions marking the House, Senate, and presidency, the challenge of building the cross-party coalitions that the new administration will need to achieve anything would have been formidable under the best of circumstances. After the bruising partisan struggle over the Florida vote count, the challenge is even greater.

Prospects for the New Congress

With his tenuous and clouded victory, George W. Bush assumed the presidency not only bereft of a popular mandate but also without the normal, if temporary, deference the opposing party grants to the people's choice. His party does control both houses of Congress, but by margins so narrow that he cannot prevail with Republican votes alone. During the campaign, Bush promised bipartisan leadership of the kind he had provided as governor of Texas. But Congress is far more conflict-ridden and polarized along ideological and party lines than is Texas's part-time, amateur legislature. Figures 8-9 and 8-10, which display the distribution of ratings of Republican and Democratic members by the Americans for Democratic Action (ADA), a liberal interest group, document just how ideologically divided the congressional parties have become. The ADA scores register how often the member voted on the ADA's side on twenty key votes in 1999.

In the House, the median Democrat had an ADA score of 100, and the median Republican had a score of 5 or 10; 96 percent of Republicans had ADA scores below 50, and 97 percent of the Democrats had scores above 50. The Senate was even more sharply polarized. The Democrats' median score was 100, the Republicans' was zero, and every Republican was considerably less supportive of the ADA's positions than every Democrat. More compre-

Figure 8-9   House ADA Scores (1999)

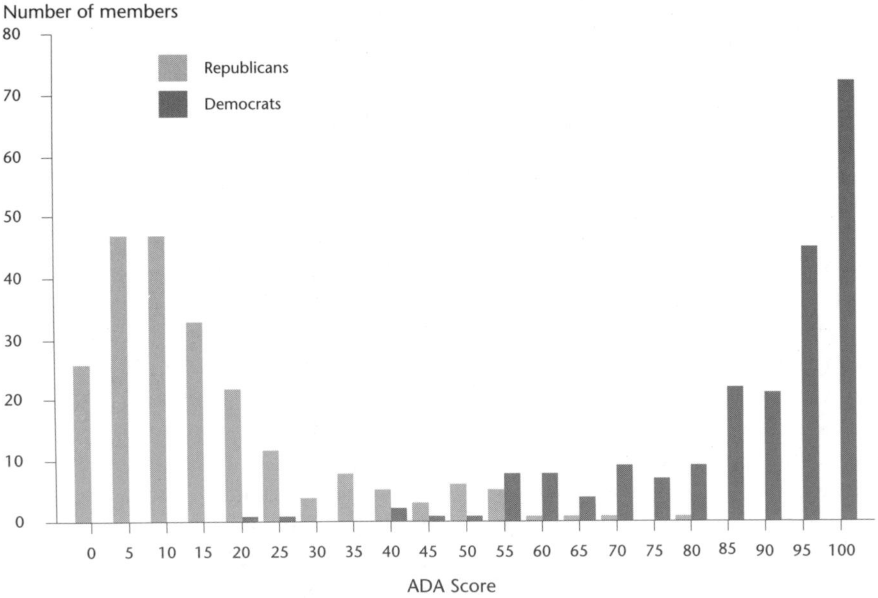

Source: http://adaction.org/1999vrhlq.html.

hensive analyses of voting patterns confirm that partisan polarization reached a forty-year high in the 1990s.[24]

The battle over Florida guaranteed that partisan tensions would be high in the 107th Congress. Unified Republican control of the government may intensify these tensions. Conservative Republicans in Congress, who kept a low profile during the election year to help Bush to victory, will be eager to move on issues where they had been stymied by Clinton's veto. Congressional Democrats will have no more reason to help Bush look good than did congressional Republicans who, after the 1992 election, tried everything possible to block Clinton's initiatives and embarrass his administration.

Plainly, the 2000 elections did nothing to help bring an end to legislative gridlock. Hope for cooperation lies only in the continuation of the economic boom that has produced ever larger projected budget surpluses. During the presidential campaigns, Bush and Gore differed more on means than on ends in addressing some major issues involving taxes and spending. Disputes over money often lend themselves to compromises that split the difference. A tax cut that lies somewhere between Bush's across-the-board income tax cut proposal and Gore's more narrowly targeted tax cuts is not hard to imagine. In addition, the accumulating surpluses allow for a variety of expensive demands—for tax cuts, prescription drug benefits, Social Security, and education funding—to be met simultaneously, inviting comprehensive

Figure 8-10 Senate ADA Scores (1999)

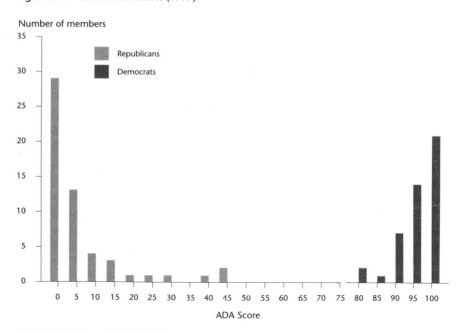

Source: http://adaction.org/1999vrhlq.html.

log-rolling between the parties. Although by no means easy to achieve, bipartisan deals on allocating surpluses should be more within reach than were the bipartisan deals on reducing the deficits that Congress and the president negotiated during the Reagan and Bush administrations.

Issues involving money are considerably more amenable to compromise than are social issues such as abortion, gay rights, gun control, and school vouchers. Moreover, differences between the parties' respective electoral constituencies on social issues leave little room for bipartisan agreement. If Bush and congressional Republicans push for changes demanded by their party's social conservatives, the prospects for bitter partisan conflict and legislative stalemate will grow.

Looking Forward to 2002

Stalemate and gridlock in Washington inevitably direct politicians' energies toward the next election, as they formulate strategies to persuade the voters to settle matters in their favor. The close partisan balance in the 107th Congress leaves both houses up for grabs in 2002. The Democrats' hopes of winning back the Senate may be encouraged by the partisan distribution of seats that will be contested in 2002. Democrats will have to defend only fourteen seats, while the Republicans must defend twenty-one. But only five of those Republican seats are in states won by Gore, only two more than the three seats that Democrats must defend in states won by Bush. Democrats may actually have a better chance to take over the Senate before the 2002 elections. Republican control rests on the doubtful health of two elderly senators, Strom Thurmond of South Carolina (born 1902) and Jesse Helms of North Carolina (born 1921). Each represents a state in which a Democratic governor would appoint his successors if he cannot serve out his term.

Even if no change in voters' sentiments occurs, the partisan balance in the House may be altered by the reapportionment and redistricting that must take place before the 2002 midterm in accordance with the 2000 census. Redistricting after the 1990 census clearly benefited the Republicans, because

Table 8-3   Redistricting Effects in 2002

Seat Change	Number of States	Won by Bush	Won by Gore	Average Vote for Bush
−2	2 (Pa., N.Y.)	0	2	42.5%
−1	8 (Conn., Ill., **Ind.**, **Mich.**, **Miss.**, **Ohio**, **Okla.**, Wisc.)	4	4	51.5%
0	32	20	12	53.6%
1	4 (Calif., **Colo.**, Nev., **N.C.**)	3	1	51.6%
2	4 (**Ariz.**, **Fla.**, **Ga.**, **Tex.**)	4	0	54.9%

Note: States won by Bush are in **bold** face.

the states that gained seats in the House were significantly more Republican than the states that lost them. In addition, the federal Voting Rights Act's charge to the states to design districts that are winnable by minority candidates worked as a pro-Republican gerrymander.[25] Indeed, the post-1990 reapportionment and redistricting was a major reason why Republicans finally gained control of the House in 1994.

Republicans should also benefit from the post-2000 reapportionment and redistricting. As in the 1990s, the states that gain seats are more Republican (as measured by the presidential vote) than the states that will lose seats. Gore won six of the ten states projected to lose seats, while Bush won seven of the eight states expected to gain seats (Table 8-3). Moreover, Republican governors and legislatures will control the redistricting process in a slightly larger number of the states where extensive changes in district lines are likely to be required. Republicans also will benefit from Democratic retirements if those members who were persuaded by Minority Leader Richard Gephardt to run one more time in order to help their party retake the House in 2000 now decide to step down.[26]

House Democrats' main hopes for 2002 lie in Bush's victory in 2000. With the exceptions of 1934 and 1998, the president's party has lost House seats in every midterm election since the Civil War. During the past half century, the Republicans have lost an average of twenty-four House seats in each of the seven midterm elections held during Republican administrations. The main reason that the Republicans did poorly in these elections was the economy. As Table 8-4 indicates, four of them were held in recession years (the years when the gross domestic product declined), two others in years of feeble economic growth, and only one in a year when the growth rate was even average (1986). Republicans lost an average of thirty-five seats in the recession years, only eight in the others.

The battle for control of the House in 2002, then, is likely to be determined mainly by the Bush administration's performance in managing the economy. If the economy continues to grow and Bush maintains decent pub-

Table 8-4   The Economy and Midterm Elections under Republican Presidents

Year	President	Election Year Change in GDP	House Seat Change	Senate Seat Change
1986	R. Reagan	3.1%	5 D	8 D
1990	G. Bush	1.2%	9 D	1 D
1970	R. Nixon	0.1%	12 D	2 D
1974	G. Ford	−0.6%	49 D	4 D
1954	D. Eisenhower	0.7%	19 D	2 D
1958	D. Eisenhower	−1.0%	49 D	15 D
1982	R. Reagan	−2.3%	26 D	1 R

Notes: GDP is the gross domestic product of the United States; D denotes Democratic gain, R denotes Republican gain.

lic approval ratings, redistricting may offset the usual midterm decline sustained by the president's party and the Republicans may hold on. But if history is any guide, the 2002 elections offer Democrats their best chance of retaking the Congress since they lost it in 1994.

Notes

1. Gary C. Jacobson, "The Elections of 2000 and Beyond," a supplement to *The Logic of American Politics,* by Samuel Kernell and Gary C. Jacobson (Washington, D.C.: CQ Press, 2001), 6–7.
2. Gary C. Jacobson, *The Politics of Congressional Elections,* 5th ed. (New York: Longman, 2000), 106–107.
3. Keith T. Poole and Howard Rosenthal, *Congress: A Political-Economic History of Roll Call Voting* (New York: Oxford University Press, 1997), chaps. 3 and 11.
4. Jacobson, *Politics of Congressional Elections,* 160.
5. Gary C. Jacobson and Samuel Kernell, *Strategy and Choice in Congressional Elections,* 2d ed. (New Haven: Yale University Press, 1983), chaps. 3 and 4.
6. During the past fifty years, the chances of defeating an incumbent have been about one in twenty. The chances of taking an open seat from the other party have been about one in four. See Jacobson, *Politics of Congressional Elections,* 37.
7. "CQ's House Race Ranking Update," *CQ Weekly,* November 4, 2000, 2584.
8. In postwar elections, the average proportion of experienced Democratic challengers is 25 percent, of Republican challengers, 17 percent.
9. Gary C. Jacobson, "Reversal of Fortune: The Transformation of U.S. House Elections in the 1990s," in *Continuity and Change in Congressional Elections,* ed. David Brady, John Cogan, and Morris P. Fiorina (Stanford: Stanford University Press, 2000), 15.
10. Jacobson, *Politics of Congressional Elections,* 42.
11. Hayward R. Alker Jr., *Mathematics and Politics* (New York: Macmillan, 1965), 36–42.
12. Karen Foerstel and Derek Willis, "DCCC Rakes in New Money as Business Hedges Its Bets," *CQ Weekly,* July 15, 2000, 1708–1712.
13. John Mintz, "Everybody Can Get Into the Act With Issue Ads," *Washington Post,* September 19, 2000, A-1.
14. Gary C. Jacobson, "Public Opinion and the Impeachment of Bill Clinton," *British Elections and Parties Review* vol. 10, ed. Philip Cowley et al. (London: Frank Cass, 2000), 1–31.
15. Ibid.
16. *Hotline,* December 8, 1998.
17. I determined this by regressing the Republican incumbent's vote in 2000 on the district's vote for Clinton in 1996, the Republican's vote in 1998, and whether or not the Republican was one of the impeachment managers. The estimated coefficient on "manager" is -6.1 (t=-3.35), but it shrinks to -2.3 and becomes insignificant if the challenger's level of spending is taken into account.
18. Bob Benenson, "Proudly Worn Party Label Missing in Key Contests," *CQ Weekly,* September 23, 2000, 2182–5.
19. Andrew Taylor and Karen Foerstel, "GOP's Hope for Graceful Exit Rides on Debt Reduction Plan," *CQ Weekly,* September 16, 2000, 2117.
20. Andrew Taylor, "Sound Like a Moderate, Vote Like a Conservative," *CQ Weekly,* August 5, 2000, 1930–4; Mike Christensen, "Congress' Cornucopia: A Sampler of Spending Add-Ons," *CQ Weekly,* October 7, 2000, 2322–2323.

21. Gary C. Jacobson, "A House and Senate Divided: The Clinton Legacy and the Congressional Elections of 2000," *Political Science Quarterly* 116 (Spring 2001), forthcoming.
22. Mark C. Westlye, *Senate Elections and Campaign Intensity* (Baltimore: Johns Hopkins University Press, 1991), 25.
23. "Michigan," *New York Times,* November 9, 2000, B16.
24. Poole and Rosenthal, *Roll Call Voting,* chap. 11.
25. Minority voters are primarily Democrats; packing them into minority-majority districts makes neighboring districts more Republican; see Jacobson, *Politics of Congressional Elections,* 10.
26. Karen Foerstel, "Gephardt's Charge," *CQ Weekly,* November 4, 2000, 2578.

9

The Postelection Election: Politics by Other Means

Michael Nelson

In 1990 Benjamin Ginsberg and Martin Shefter argued that the United States had entered an era of, as the title of their book put it, "politics by other means" in which elections had been supplanted by other forms of political conflict between contending interests.[1] As if to demonstrate that political scientists occasionally get things right, the 2000 presidential election fit Ginsberg and Shefter's argument almost to a tee. This was especially evident during the "postelection election"—the five weeks between November 7, when the voters went to the polls, and December 12, when the election was effectively decided by the U.S. Supreme Court. In the end, in fact, the Bush versus Gore election contest was less decisive in selecting the forty-third president of the United States than the *Bush v. Gore* Supreme Court case.

This chapter begins by summarizing Ginsberg and Shefter's analysis of politics by other means. It then reviews the events of the postelection election of 2000 and assesses the usefulness of their framework in explaining those events. The chapter concludes with a brief discussion of the first days of the Bush administration.

Politics by Other Means

"American politics has recently undergone a fundamental transformation," argue Ginsberg and Shefter in *Politics by Other Means*. As the subtitle of their book—*The Declining Importance of Elections in America*—suggests, competing political interests in American society no longer "seek to defeat their opponents chiefly by outmobilizing them in the electoral arena." Instead, "contending forces are increasingly relying on such institutional weapons of political struggle as legislative investigations, media revelations, and judicial proceedings to weaken their political rivals and gain power for themselves."[2]

Ironically, the main reason that institutional struggles have replaced elections as the primary form of political combat, according to Ginsberg and Shefter, derives from electoral politics itself. From the 1930s to the 1960s, political power still depended on winning elections. Like the Democratic majority forged by Andrew Jackson in the 1830s and the post–Civil War Republican majority that endured through the 1920s, the New Deal

Democratic coalition inaugurated by Franklin D. Roosevelt in the 1930s owed its power to an alliance of voters. The coalition, which was united mainly by economic self-interest, included southern whites, northern blacks, unionized workers, eastern and southern European ethnics, government employees, and middle-class liberals. When issues of race and civil rights rose to the fore of the national political agenda in the 1960s, however, the coalition broke apart.

Two equally matched party coalitions emerged from the breakup of the New Deal coalition. The Democrats remained the party of organized labor, African Americans and other racial minorities, government employees, and middle-class liberals, who now embraced several new causes such as feminism, environmentalism, and gay rights. The Republicans, long the party of business and wealth, added southern whites and many northern ethnic whites to their coalition by promoting a host of social issues (right to life, family values), racial issues (opposition to school busing and affirmative action), and patriotic issues (opposition to flag burning, support for high defense spending). Within the federal government, the Democrats became entrenched in nearly all of the domestic policy departments, and the Republicans developed a bastion of support in the military.

Neither the new Democratic nor the new Republican coalition, however, has been able to develop a stable majority in the electorate. From the late 1960s until the early 1990s, the Republicans usually controlled the presidency and the Democrats had an apparent stranglehold on Congress. Then, in 1992, the Democrats captured the White House and two years later the Republicans won control of Congress. Thus throughout the final third of the twentieth century, divided government in one form or another was the rule. Neither party was able to achieve primacy over the other by consistently winning elections.

According to Ginsberg and Shefter, once faced with electoral stalemate, the parties shifted their main arena of political conflict into the government itself. Evidence of the parties' de-emphasis on winning elections could be found, they contend, in declining voter turnout and the weakening of grassroots party organizations, which traditionally have mobilized voters to go to the polls. In their book and in subsequent writings, they demonstrate the shift of partisan conflict into government by examining two recent phenomena: bitter battles over presidential appointments and the "judicialization" of politics.[3]

With presidents of one party and Senates controlled by the other, presidential appointments that once would have been confirmed easily now generate bitter partisan battles. Republican Supreme Court nominees Robert Bork (nominated by Ronald Reagan in 1987) and Clarence Thomas (nominated by George Bush in 1991) were raked over the coals by the Democratic Senate. When Bill Clinton became president and the Republicans took charge of the Senate, many of his nominations for federal district and circuit court judgeships went unconfirmed. More surprisingly, presidential nominations for positions in the executive branch have been thwarted as well. For example, Bush became the first new president in history to have a cabinet nominee rejected by the Senate, and Clinton saw his initial choices for attorney general and assistant attorney general shot down even before the Senate Judiciary Committee finished its confirmation hearings. As Ginsberg and Shefter point out, the motives for these battles were partisan, but the arguments often were personal, involving charges of alcohol abuse, sexual misconduct, employment of illegal workers, or unorthodox political views. "Character assassination," they note, "has become a routine aspect of American politics."[4] Joined with onerous ethics laws enacted in the late 1970s, which force nominees both to disclose publicly much of their personal and financial history and to accept substantial reductions in income, the threat of brutal confirmation battles has shrunk the talent pool for important appointive positions by discouraging many qualified people from considering government service in the first place.

More distressing than the appointments phenomenon has been the judicialization of politics, which takes into the courtroom differences that traditionally have been resolved through the electoral process. Judicialization has assumed several forms in recent years. First, liberal and then conservative groups began pursuing their policy agendas on issues such as abortion, race, the environment, and land use in court cases rather than in election campaigns. Republican and Democratic officials have used special prosecutors, congressional investigations, and even the impeachment process to attack each other. The ranks of fallen or wounded political leaders include senators, Speakers of the House of Representatives, cabinet members, presidential aides, and presidents. Ginsberg and Shefter point to criminal prosecutions as an index of judicialized political conflict. From the 1970s to the early 1990s, they show, the number of indictments of public officials by presidentially appointed federal prosecutors increased twenty-fold.[5]

In addition to appointment battles and the judicialization of politics, institutional conflict has manifested itself in other ways, according to Ginsberg and Shefter. Filibusters to keep the Senate from considering bills or nominations, which used to be relatively rare, now are used to thwart almost any controversial measure that is opposed by forty-one senators.[6] In contrast to earlier periods of American history, when low voter mobilization correlated directly with weak partisan voting in Congress, the recent era of low turnout has been marked by strongly partisan divisions on congressional roll-call votes.[7] Finally, overt hostility has occasionally erupted between Democrats and the military, especially when Clinton cut defense spending substantially and tried to integrate gays and lesbians into the armed services.[8]

Ginsberg and Shefter are distressed by the displacement of electoral politics by investigations, prosecutions, character assassination, and other forms of politics by other means. They worry that, lacking a firm political base grounded in grass-roots party organizations, "contemporary presidents are much more vulnerable than their predecessors to all manner of political attack."[9] George Bush's drop in public support from 89 percent in early 1991 to 37 percent in the 1992 presidential election and Clinton's impeachment by House Republicans in 1998 are evidence that their concern is warranted. In addition, Ginsberg and Shefter lament the growth of public cynicism and mistrust of politics, which they regard as both cause and consequence of what John Chubb and Paul Peterson call "government that cannot govern."[10] Finally, and most despairingly, Ginsberg and Shefter argue that

> the contemporary pattern of American politics is profoundly undemo-
> cratic. . . . A political process in which only half of those who are
> potentially eligible actually take part, politicians secure power through
> entrenchment in government bureaucracies, and investigatory and
> judicial processes are routinely invoked to limit the effect of, or even
> to reverse, electoral outcomes can hardly be called democratic.[11]

Law, Constitution, and Postelection Politics

The postelection election of 2000 began in the predawn hours of Wednesday, November 8. At about 2:00 A.M. Eastern Standard Time, all of the networks declared that Texas governor George W. Bush, the Republican candidate, had carried Florida, which gave him 271 electoral votes, one more than he needed to become president. Within minutes, Vice President Al Gore, the Democratic challenger, called Bush to concede defeat. Across the country, newspapers went to press with banner headlines reading "Bush!" (*Austin American-Statesman*) and "Bush Wins!" (*New York Post, Boston Herald*).[12] At that point, as in every previous presidential election since 1880, the path from election to inauguration seemed straight and well marked. The electors would be certified by the governors of their states no later than December 12 and then would assemble to vote in their state capitals on December 18. Congress would tally the electoral votes on January 6, and Bush would be sworn in as president at noon on January 20.

Within a short time, however, the situation grew uncertain. The networks decided they had jumped the gun: Florida was actually too close to call. "We don't just have egg on our face," said NBC News anchor Tom Brokaw. "We have an omelet."[13] Gore immediately dispatched a team of lawyers to Florida to investigate charges by local Democrats that they had been cheated out of their votes in various ways. Although a few other states—notably Oregon, Wisconsin, Iowa, and New Mexico—were also too close to call, it became clear that whichever candidate received Florida's twenty-five electoral votes would win the election.[14]

It also became clear that the path from election to inauguration would not be straight after all. Several questions needed to be answered. Would the situation in Florida be resolved in time to meet the deadline for states to choose their electors? Would more than one set of electoral votes from Florida be sent to Congress? What if neither Bush nor Gore received a majority of electoral votes? Above all, who had the authority to make these decisions, and how and when would they do so?

By Wednesday morning, lawyers, historians, political scientists, journalists, and campaign workers were dusting off their law books and poring through the Constitution in hopes of finding answers to these questions. The answers they found were clear in some cases, less so in others.

Presidential Selection in Law and Constitution

Most of what the Constitution has to say about presidential selection can be found in Article II and the Twelfth Amendment. The applicable federal law is Title 3, Section 5, of the *United States Code Annotated,* which was enacted by Congress in 1887 as the Electoral Count Act.[15]

The Constitution provides that "[e]ach state shall appoint, in such Manner as the Legislature thereof may direct, a Number of Electors equal to the whole Number of Senators and Representatives to which the State may be entitled in the Congress." By federal law, each state legislature must determine how its state's electors will be selected in advance of the election. Over the years, every legislature has chosen to empower the voters to make this decision. But if for any reason a state "has failed to make a choice [of electors] on the day prescribed by law," Title 3 stipulates that "the electors may be appointed on a subsequent day in such a manner as the legislature of such State may direct."

After the electors are appointed, the Constitution specifies that they "shall meet in their respective states and vote by ballot for President and Vice President." By law, they must do so "on the first Monday after the second Wednesday in December," which in 2000 fell on December 18. Ordinarily, the voting by electors is so uncontroversial that the media ignore it, and for many years no law provided a means to resolve any disputes that might arise about which slates of electors the voters had chosen. As a result, Congress had to improvise a procedure in 1876 when four states (including Florida) submitted competing sets of electoral votes.[16] It was to avert similar calamities that Congress enacted the Electoral Count Act in 1887.

The Electoral Count Act charges each state, operating under its own laws, to resolve any controversies about which candidate has won the state's electors and to do so no later than "six days prior to said time of meeting of the electors"—in 2000, this meant by December 12. Either on or before that date ("as soon as practicable"), the governor of each state, acting "under and in pursuance of the laws of such State," is enjoined to send the National Archives in Washington, D.C., a "certificate of ascertainment" listing the names of the winning electors. When these electors meet in their state capitals to vote on December 18, the Constitution instructs them to "transmit sealed" the results to the president of the Senate—that is, to the vice president. If a state fails to meet these deadlines, it runs the risk of losing its votes in the election. In that case, the Twelfth Amendment provides that the president and vice president would be chosen by "a majority of the whole number of Electors appointed."

On January 6, the vice president presides over a joint session of Congress to supervise the opening and tallying of all the states' electoral votes and to announce who has been elected president and vice president. By law, if at least one member of the House of Representatives and one senator jointly file a written objection to the legitimacy of any electors, each house of Congress must meet separately to decide whether the objection is valid. Unless both houses agree that it is, the votes of the slate of electors certified by the governor of the state are accepted and counted. Because the Twentieth Amendment provides that the Congress chosen by the voters in November will take office on January 3, it is this Congress, not the old one, that would consider any challenges to electors.

In the event that no candidate for president receives a majority of electoral votes, the Constitution requires the House to "choose immediately" the president from among the top three electoral vote recipients. In doing so, the members vote by state, with each state receiving one vote; a majority of the states are needed for election. Meanwhile, the Senate elects the vice president by a simple majority vote of its members, choosing between the two highest electoral vote recipients for that office.

The Postelection Election of 2000

More through happenstance than by design, the procedures for presidential selection that are grounded in law and Constitution matched up with the facts of the 2000 election in ways that were advantageous to Bush. Institutional combat is the essence of politics by other means, and Bush's supporters occupied more (and more important) institutional vantage points than Gore's did. Florida secretary of state Katherine Harris, who under state law was charged to certify the results of the election and oversee any recounts that took place, was a Republican; indeed, she had cochaired the Bush campaign in Florida. The Florida legislature, which arguably had the power to appoint a slate of electors if all other approaches failed, was heavily Republican. As for the governor of Florida, Jeb Bush was not only a Republican, he was also the candidate's brother. As governor, Jeb Bush was responsible for telling the National Archives which slate of electors had been chosen by his state. If an objection was filed in Congress when the electoral votes were counted on January 6, the votes of the slate he certified would be accepted unless both houses of Congress agreed to reject them. Considering that the House of Representatives had a Republican majority, it was unlikely that both houses would vote to overturn Gov. Jeb Bush's position.

The Bush campaign enjoyed other institutional advantages as well. If somehow the House ended up having to choose the president (never a likely outcome), Bush would benefit from the fact that twenty-eight of its fifty state delegations had Republican majorities. Moreover, any election-related case that might work its way to the summit of the nation's judicial system would be heard by a Supreme Court that consisted of seven justices appointed by Republican presidents and only two justices appointed by Democratic presidents. One of the justices, Sandra Day O'Connor, reportedly said, "This is terrible," at an election night party when she thought Gore was going to win, and Justice Clarence Thomas was charged by a Democratic federal appeals court judge with having a conflict of interest because his wife worked for a conservative research group gathering resumes for a possible Bush administration.[17]

Gore's institutional advantages in the postelection election were fewer and less certain. Because most of the Florida counties in which he was seeking recounts were run by Democrats, Gore's supporters would make most of the judgment calls about whether disputed ballots in those counties should be counted or not. All seven justices of the Florida Supreme Court had been appointed by Democratic governors. At the national level, the 50–50 division in the newly elected Senate was, in effect, a one-seat Democratic majority because, as president of the Senate until January 20, Gore was empowered to break ties on any votes that occurred. But not only were these advantages fewer than Bush's, they also turned out to be less important in some cases than they might have been. For example, the Democratic mayor of Miami-Dade County chose to play a relatively passive role in the recount controversy, and the Senate was not called on to make any election-related decisions.

Public opinion was a more uncertain element in the postelection election. Although the public's direct involvement in the presidential selection process ended on Election Day, winning the battle for public support was an important goal for both Bush and Gore. For one thing, to the extent that elected officials were involved in deciding who would be president—legislators in Florida and Washington, county officials in Florida, local judges, and so on—a strong swing of public opinion to either candidate could affect these officials' behavior. Some Republican electors or legislators, for example, might have defected from Bush if pro-Gore sentiment had become strong enough in their states and districts. Beyond these immediate concerns, whichever candidate became president would not want to be widely perceived by the voters as having stolen the election.

In addition to his institutional advantages, Bush enjoyed certain advantages in the battle for postelection public opinion. The networks' initial declaration that he had been elected president, along with Gore's congratulatory phone call, made Bush appear to be the presumptive winner of the election.[18] So did the fact that he never fell behind during Florida's recount process. Gore, however, was not devoid of political assets. For example, many Americans were upset that several thousand elderly Gore supporters in Palm Beach County were so confused by the butterfly-style design of their county's ballot that they inadvertently voted for Pat Buchanan, the ultraconservative nominee of the Reform Party. Their outrage was somewhat abated, however, when it was reported that the ballot had been sanctioned by a Democratic election official in the county and that the votes of several hundred mostly Republican overseas military personnel also had been invalidated on technical grounds.[19] More important, Gore gave away whatever political advantage he had gained from winning the national popular vote when he announced the day after the election, "Despite the fact that Joe Lieberman and I won the popular vote, under our Constitution it is the winner of the Electoral College who will be the next president."[20]

The Sequence of Events in the Postelection Election

The strategic advantages that Gore and, especially, Bush enjoyed found expression in the sequence of events that took place after Election Day. What follows is a brief chronology of those events.

November 8–9. The initial tally of votes in Florida gave Bush a 1,784 lead, well within the one-half percent margin of victory that, under Florida law, triggers an automatic mechanical recount in all of the state's counties. In addition, Gore's lawyers demanded that the ballots in populous and strongly Democratic Palm Beach, Volusia, Broward, and Miami-Dade Counties, where a punch card system of voting had been used, be recounted by hand. Nearly eighty thousand ballots in these counties had not been included in the mechanical tally, either because they had selection marks for more than one presidential candidate or because they appeared to have no selection marks for president at all. The Gore campaign contended that many of these ballots had been rejected by the tallying machines because the "chad"—that is, the little square of paper that the voter was supposed to punch—had not separated from the card completely but rather had been "dimpled" (dented) or left "hanging" (still partially attached to the card).

Groups of Gore voters in Palm Beach County filed a lawsuit challenging the county's results on the grounds that the butterfly ballot had misled them into voting for the wrong candidate. In addition, civil rights activists charged that minority voters had been turned away at some polling places in Broward County and other locations. Lacking Gore's active legal support, however, the butterfly ballot and civil rights lawsuits went nowhere.

The Bush campaign concentrated its initial efforts on influencing public opinion rather than winning in court. Bush began acting as if he were the president-elect, leaking the names of potential cabinet members and meeting publicly with his leading national security advisers, Colin Powell and Condoleezza Rice. Spokespersons for his campaign argued that Gore's goal was to recount the votes until he got the result he liked. The Gore campaign responded that it only wanted to make sure that every vote was counted.

November 9–13. Local officials in Broward, Volusia, and Palm Beach Counties agreed to Gore's request to conduct manual recounts of their punch card ballots. Bush's lawyers quickly filed suit in federal district court to prevent the manual recounts from proceeding, arguing that to recount votes manually in some counties but not others would violate the equal protection clause of the Fourteenth Amendment to the Constitution. On November 13, Secretary of State Harris, citing a state law that required election results to be certified within seven days of the election, decreed that all counties must submit the results of their recounts by November 14.

November 14–15. Although Gore's lawyers won a ruling from a local Florida judge instructing Harris to exercise discretion in deciding whether to accept late results from the counties that were conducting or considering manual recounts, she refused these counties' petitions for more time. The results of the statewide mechanical recount left Bush with a 300–vote lead, with only overseas absentee ballots, which could be received as late as November 17, left to be added to the state's total vote. Most of these ballots were from military personnel stationed abroad.

November 16–24. The overseas absentee ballots extended Bush's lead to 930 votes. But the Florida Supreme Court ruled unanimously that Harris must extend to November 26 the deadline for counties conducting manual recounts to submit their results. Confronted both with angry Republican demonstrators led by congressional staffers from Washington and with the logistical difficulties of completing a manual recount in such a short time, Mayor Alexander Penelas, previously a strong Gore supporter, and other Miami-Dade officials decided to discontinue their county's manual recount.

Meanwhile, Bush's lawyers appealed to the U.S. Supreme Court to overturn the state supreme court's order extending the recount deadline. They argued that the Florida court's decision, by not acknowledging the seven-day rule for submitting election results that is stipulated in Florida law, violated both the Constitution's provision that the state legislature must determine how a state's electors will be chosen and the 1887 Electoral Count Act's requirement that electors be chosen according to state laws enacted by the legislature before Election Day. Bush's lawyers also appealed the recent rejection of their lawsuit in federal court to stop the manual recounts on equal protection grounds. The Supreme Court quickly agreed to hear the first appeal but not the second.

November 26–27. Accepting the results of Broward County's manual recount, the only one that was completed in time to meet the Florida Supreme Court's November 26 deadline, Harris officially certified that Bush had carried the state by 537 votes. Although pleased with this outcome, Bush supporters were unhappy that more than 600 overseas absentee ballots from military personnel had been rejected for lacking a postmark or on other technical grounds. Gore supporters were equally chagrined that the Republican supervisor of elections in Seminole County had allowed Republican workers to correct incomplete absentee ballot requests by filling in voter identification numbers. For political reasons, Gore declared that he "was not a party" to their suit to have all of the county's absentee ballots thrown out, even though these ballots had gone for Bush by a 4,797-vote majority. To have done so would have undermined Gore's postelection theme that every vote should count.[21]

On the evening of November 26, in a nationally televised address, Bush urged Gore to concede the election and said that he and Cheney "were preparing to serve as America's next president and vice president."[22] Gore responded in an address the following night, asserting that he was seeking "not recount after recount as some have charged, but a single, full and accurate count."[23] Meanwhile, in the Leon County courthouse Gore's lawyers filed a formal contest to Harris's certification that Bush had won the state.[24]

Public opinion polls, which previously had indicated a willingness among most voters to await patiently the outcome of the election, now showed that a majority of Americans wanted Gore to concede.[25] Well in advance of the December 12 deadline for sending the names of his state's electors to the National Archives, Florida governor Jeb Bush signed and mailed a document certifying that the state of Florida had chosen twenty-five electors pledged to George W. Bush for president and Richard B. Cheney for vice president.

December 4. Delivering major blows to Gore's candidacy, Leon County court judge N. Sanders Sauls dismissed the Democrats' challenge to the secretary of state's certified results, and the U.S. Supreme Court, ruling unanimously in *Bush v. Palm Beach County Canvassing Board,*[26] vacated the Florida Supreme Court's earlier decision to extend the deadline for certifying those results in order to include manual recounts. Gore's lawyers quickly filed an appeal with the Florida Supreme Court to overturn Judge Sauls's ruling in the hope that the court would order that the manual recount be resumed.

December 6. Fearing that a successful Gore appeal in the recount case would prevent Florida from submitting any slate of electors that Congress would accept as valid by the December 12 deadline, the Republican-controlled Florida legislature scheduled a special session to consider appointing its own slate of pro-Bush electors. Republicans especially feared that if Florida's electoral votes were not counted, Gore's undisputed electoral votes from the other states, being "a majority of the whole number of Electors appointed," would win him the presidency by a vote of 267–246. A host of uncertainties surrounded this effort, however. The legislature's authority to appoint electors after Election Day was far from undisputed. Conversely, constitutional scholars disagreed about whether a president could be elected with fewer than 270 electoral votes under any circumstances. Thus if Florida was unable to appoint electors acceptable to Congress, the House of Representatives might have to choose the president.

December 8–13. The Florida Supreme Court voted 4–3 on December 8 to overturn Judge Sauls's ruling and, aware of the looming December 12 deadline for the appointment of electors, ordered that the manual recounts resume and be completed by December 10.[27] For a time, it seemed possible that Congress would receive three slates of electors from Florida: the pro-

Bush slate already submitted by Gov. Jeb Bush, a different pro-Bush slate submitted by the Florida legislature, and a pro-Gore slate certified by the Florida Supreme Court.

Bush immediately appealed the Florida court's decision to the U.S. Supreme Court and also asked the justices to grant a stay to halt the recount pending resolution of the case. On December 9, the Supreme Court agreed to hear the appeal and, by a 5–4 majority, granted the stay. All five justices who voted to halt the recount—Chief Justice William Rehnquist and Justices Antonin Scalia, Anthony M. Kennedy, O'Connor, and Thomas—had been appointed to the court by Republican presidents. The only two Democratic appointees—Ruth Bader Ginsburg and Stephen G. Breyer—dissented.[28]

The Court heard arguments in the case of *Bush v. Gore* on December 11 and issued its decision the following night.[29] Overruling the Florida Supreme Court, the same 5–4 majority that had halted the manual recount temporarily now ordered that it be halted permanently. Different groups of justices offered different reasons for the Court's decision, but the rationale on which the majority agreed was that, in the absence of clear standards for discerning voters' intent, any manual recount would be arbitrary in a way that violated the Constitution's equal protection clause. On December 13, in back-to-back nationally televised addresses, Gore conceded defeat and Bush accepted victory.

Conclusion: Politics by Other Means in 2000 and Beyond

Bush won the postelection election of 2000 by successfully pressing all of the advantages that he enjoyed in the institutional combat that constitutes politics by other means. Because the cochair of his Florida presidential campaign was Florida's secretary of state, deadlines for conducting manual recounts that might otherwise have been extended at Gore's request were strictly enforced. Because Bush's brother was the governor of Florida, Bush could expect that, in the absence of clear evidence that Gore had carried the state, the slate of electors that received the governor's official signature would be his. Bush also knew that any disputes about the election that reached Washington would be resolved by a Republican Supreme Court or a Republican House of Representatives. Finally, by conducting himself as if he were president-elect, Bush was able to persuade an increasingly impatient public that Gore, not he, was responsible for prolonging the process of choosing a president.

After winning the election, Bush worked hard to bridge the divide between Republicans and Democrats. He revived the theme of bipartisan cooperation that had marked his tenure as governor of Texas and his campaign for the presidency. He asked the Democratic Speaker of the Texas House of Representatives to introduce him when he gave his victory speech and stressed in his remarks that he "was not elected to serve one party, but to serve one nation."[30] During the transition period, Bush appointed a former Democratic member of Congress and Clinton cabinet member, Norman Mineta, to serve as secretary of transportation. His inaugural address, which he organized around themes of "civility, courage, compassion, and character," was a hymn to national consensus. In contrast to Ronald Reagan's inaugural declaration in 1981 that "government is not the solution to our problems; government is the problem," Bush proclaimed that "government has great responsibilities," including "civil rights and common schools."[31]

During his first weeks in office, Bush conferred with several Democratic groups. But his early words and actions only muted politics by other means, they did not banish it. A court challenge was filed to discredit Cheney's election as vice president on the grounds that he was not from Wyoming, as he claimed, but from Texas, the same state as Bush.[32] Shortly before leaving office, President Clinton charged in a speech that Bush had been illegitimately elected because "our candidate had won the popular vote, and the only way they could win the election was to stop the voting in Florida."[33] Clinton also granted a large number of controversial pardons to financial supporters and political associates who had fallen afoul of federal criminal law. One of them, Marc Rich, was the ex-husband of a major Democratic donor; he had fled the country to avoid prosecution on tax evasion charges and had renounced his American citizenship. On inauguration day, thousands of protesters gathered along the parade route to denounce Bush.

Most important, perhaps, the politics of character assassination was waged against several of Bush's cabinet nominees. Senate Democrats and liberal constituency groups concerned with abortion, civil rights, gay rights, and environmentalism campaigned to defeat or, failing that, to discredit conservative appointees. Linda Chavez, Bush's initial choice for secretary of labor, withdrew in the face of charges that she had employed illegal immigrants. Former Missouri senator John Ashcroft faced a barrage of accusations of racism, homophobia, and religious extremism before being narrowly confirmed by the Senate as attorney general.

The sad irony in these attacks was that they reenacted equally brutal campaigns that had been waged against several of Clinton's nominees by Republicans. Indeed, in 1993 Chavez had publicly criticized Zoë Baird, Clinton's first nominee for attorney general, for employing illegal immigrants.[34] As a senator, Ashcroft had defeated or delayed several of Clinton's nominations. For example, he attacked an African American federal judicial nominee, Ronnie White, as being "pro-criminal" and ambassadorial appointee James Hormel for being openly gay.[35] The awful truth about politics by other means is that what goes around comes around. A nation that historically—and appropriately—has resolved most of its political conflicts through the electoral process has grown accustomed to institutional combat instead, with no end to the era of politics by other means in sight.

Notes

1. Benjamin Ginsberg and Martin Shefter, *Politics by Other Means: The Declining Importance of Elections in America* (New York: Basic Books, 1990).
2. Ibid., x.
3. See, for example, Benjamin Ginsberg, Walter R. Mebane Jr., and Martin Shefter, "The President and the 'Interests': Why the White House Cannot Govern," in *The Presidency and the Political System,* 6th ed., ed. Michael Nelson (Washington, D.C.: CQ Press, 2000), 361–375.
4. Ibid., 371.
5. Ibid.
6. Most controversial measures are brought to a vote in the Senate only after three-fifths, or sixty senators, vote to impose cloture on the debate.
7. Benjamin Ginsberg, Walter R. Mebane Jr., and Martin Shefter, "The Disjunction between Political Conflict and Electoral Mobilization in the Contemporary United States" (paper presented at the annual meeting of the American Political Science Association, September 1993).
8. Initiative campaigns at the state level also could be added to the roster of politics by other means. They too involve efforts to accomplish goals by circumventing the processes of representative democracy. See Chapter 6 in this book.
9. Ginsberg, Mebane, and Shefter, "President and the 'Interests,' " 373.
10. John Chubb and Paul Peterson, *Can the Government Govern?* (Washington, D.C.: Brookings, 1985), chap. 1.
11. Ginsberg, Mebane, and Shefter, "President and the 'Interests,'" 372–373.
12. Mark Hosenhall, "The Night of Bad Calls," *Newsweek,* November 20, 2000, 17.
13. Ibid.
14. Gore narrowly carried each of these states. Bush, concentrating all of his efforts on Florida, did not contest any of them seriously.
15. The relevant law may be found in Walter Berns, ed., *After the People Vote: Steps in Choosing the President* (Washington, D.C.: American Enterprise Institute, 1983), 22–32.
16. Congress created a bipartisan electoral commission consisting of senators, representatives, and Supreme Court justices to determine which slates of electors should be counted.
17. Evan Thomas and Michael Isikoff, "The Truth behind the Pillars," *Newsweek,* December 25, 2000, 46–47; and "Conflict of Interest Seen," online at http://2facts.com/stories/index/2000/195400.as.
18. During the weeks after the election, the networks persisted in portraying Gore as the "challenger" and a "sore loser," according to a study commissioned by CNN. Daniel J. Wakin, "Report Calls Networks' Election Night Coverage a Disaster," *New York Times,* February 3, 2001.
19. The elections supervisor in Palm Beach County, Therese LePorte, had reasoned that because the names of candidates are more widely spread on the butterfly ballot than on traditional ballots, elderly voters with poor eyesight would find it easier to read them. However, the 2000 presidential ballot had ten candidates instead of the traditional three or four, because a 1998 Florida law allowed third-party candidates to get on the ballot more easily than in the past. "A Wild Ride into Uncharted Territory," *Washington Post,* January 27, 2001.
20. Andrew Cain, "Gore Will Accept Electoral Vote," *Washington Times,* November 9, 2000.
21. Gore privately encouraged both their lawsuit and similar ones filed by supporters in Martin County, which had contributed 2,815 votes to Bush's lead, and Bay

County, which had contributed 5,600 votes to Bush's lead. "For Gore, Reasons to Hope Dwindled," *Washington Post,* January 31, 2001.

22. Helen Kennedy, "I Am Ready, Says George," *New York Daily News,* November 27, 2000.

23. Dan Balz, "Gore Asks Nation to Be Patient," *Washington Post,* November 28, 2000.

24. Leon County includes Tallahassee, the state capital.

25. "Polls Show Support for Gore Waning," online at http://www.2facts.com/ stories/index/2000/193780.as.

26. *Bush v. Palm Beach County Canvassing Board,* 69 U.S.L.W. 4020 (2000).

27. While arguing Gore's first case before the Florida Supreme Court, Gore's lawyers had embraced the December 12 deadline, thinking that it would work in their favor. Having done so, they were stuck with their position when the deadline later became helpful to Bush.

28. The other two dissenting justices were David H. Souter and John Paul Stevens, both of them Republican appointees.

29. *Bush v. Gore,* 69 U.S.L.W. 4029 (2000).

30. R. W. Apple, "Now, Lifting the Clouds," *New York Times,* December 14, 2000.

31. "Inaugural Address," *Memphis Commercial Appeal,* January 21, 2001; and "Ronald Reagan's First Inaugural Address," in *The Evolving Presidency: Addresses, Cases, Essays, Letters, Reports, Resolutions, Transcripts, and Other Landmark Documents, 1787–1998,* ed. Michael Nelson (Washington, D.C.: CQ Press, 1999), 218–224.

32. The Constitution states, "The Electors shall . . . vote by ballot for President and Vice-President, one of whom, at least, shall not be an inhabitant of the same state with themselves." Thus if the lawsuit had been successful, Texas electors would have been barred from voting for both Bush and Cheney.

33. "Notebook," *Time,* January 22, 2001, 15.

34. "Feel Her Pain," *New Republic,* January 22, 2001, 7.

35. Nancy Gibbs and Michael Duffy, "The Fight for Justice," *Time,* January 22, 2001, 20–28.